Deconstructing
Service-Learning:
Research Exploring Context,
Participation, and Impacts

A Volume in
Advances in Service-Learning Research

Deconstructing Service-Learning: Research Exploring Context, Participation, and Impacts

Edited by

**Shelley H. Billig
and
Janet Eyler**

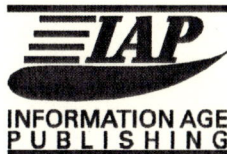

≡IAP

**INFORMATION AGE
PUBLISHING**

80 Mason Street
Greenwich, Connecticut 06830

Library of Congress Cataloging-in-Publication Data

K-12 International Conference on Service-Learning Research (2nd : 2002 :
Vanderbilt University)
  Deconstructing service-learning : research exploring context,
participation, and impacts / edited by Shelley H.
Billig and Janet Eyler.
      p. cm. – (Advances in service-learning research)
"The chapters in this volume were selected from a refereed, blind review
of papers presented in October 2002 at the Second Annual K-12
International Conference on Service-Learning Research, held at
Vanderbilt University in Nashville, TN"–Introd.
Includes bibliographical references and index.
  ISBN 1-59311-070-7 (pbk.) – ISBN 1-59311-071-5 (hardcover)
  1. Student service–Congresses. I. Billig, Shelley. II. Eyler, Janet.
III. Title. IV. Series.
  LC220.5.K14 2003
                                    2003017230

Printed in the United States of America

CONTENTS

Part IV
The Role of Community in Service-Learning

Part V
Impact of Service-Learning on Students

Part VI
International Perspectives

Part VII
The State of the Field

ACKNOWLEDGMENTS

We would like to extend appreciation to Mary Ann Strassner for her incredibly hard work in helping to edit and proofread this volume. Most of the chapters in this volume originated at the 2nd Annual International K–H Service-Learning Conference in Nashville, Tennessee, sponsored by Vanderbilt University. This volume is gratefully printed with the sponsorship of the W. K. Kellogg Foundation Grant Commitment No. P0098720 and AED Sub-Contract No. 3160–RMCRC–01 under contract No. 3160.

INTRODUCTION

Janet Eyler and Shelley H. Billig

The explosion of research on service-learning in higher education, K–12 schools, and teacher education over the past decade has yielded not only a dramatic increase in the quantity of studies, but also in their quality and complexity. While much remains to be done, there is movement away from program evaluation and program description towards better designed research studies. Even though studies of student impact still predominate, there is also an attempt to begin to address important questions about teacher adoption of service-learning pedagogy, institutionalization, community engagement, and impact. There are also attempts to design studies that take into consideration the many interlocking factors that affect implementation and effectiveness of this instructional approach.

This book, the third volume in the *Advances in Service-Learning Research* series, presents service-learning research that focuses on units of analysis ranging from the individual student to the community partnership. Qualitative, quantitative, and mixed methodologies are used to explore a variety of issues, and attention has been paid to the theoretical context for inquiry. The chapters in this volume were selected from a refereed, blind review of papers presented in October 2002 at the Second Annual K–12 International Conference on Service-Learning Research, held at Vanderbilt University in Nashville, TN.

Deconstructing Service-Learning: Research Exploring Context, Participation, and Impacts
A Volume in: Advances in Service-Learning Research, pages ix–xiii.
Copyright © 2003 by Information Age Publishing, Inc.
All rights of reproduction in any form reserved.
ISBN: 1-59311-071-5 (hardcover), 1-59311-070-7 (pbk.)

The first section of the book frames the most critical challenge facing service-learning research; that is, moving from what has been a field largely built on program evaluation or even simply on program description to one that attempts to answer interesting theoretical questions about service-learning practice. The first chapter was written by Bringle based on his keynote address to the Second Annual Research Conference. Bringle makes a clear and detailed case for the power of theory to frame research that improves practice. He gives numerous examples of theoretical perspectives from the disciplines that can help researchers design more powerful studies.

The second section of the book is devoted to studies that focus on complexities of context. Recent strides in our understanding of learning emphasized the importance of the interplay between learner, teacher, characteristics of the material to be learned, and the complexity of the setting in which learning takes place and in which it is expressed. Hecht, in chapter 2, presents an analytic framework in which multiple components of service-learning come into play and influence each other. Each component seems to have key aspects that strengthen or weaken its influence on other variables or effects, and the author deconstructs each of the areas that need to be studies as part of the system. She discusses the power of designs that gather diverse data from many levels (e.g., student, teacher, classroom, school) and suggests ways to incorporate these into a coherent analysis.

The complexity of service-learning implementation is also clear in chapter 3, in which Kapustka carefully examines a school context for service-learning. Through repeated, intensive interviews with teachers, and additional interviews with the principal and a service site director engaged in middle school service-learning programs, she identifies dilemmas posed by conflicting viewpoints. These dilemmas focus on beliefs about teaching and learning, contrasting needs of students and the community, and views of the nature and purpose of service-learning. The study provides a rich description for teachers of the realities of implementing service-learning in a middle school environment and suggests a number of further questions to pursue in understanding how to effectively implement such programs.

The third section continues the emphasis on the complexity of the environments in which service-lekarning is implemented, but moves the focus to the requisites for creating sustainable programs within educational institutions. Two case studies concerned with institutionalization and sustainability interpret attempts to implement service-learning through the lens or organizational change theory. Callahan and Root, in chapter 4, study a program designed to facilitate adoption of service-learning in several teacher preparation programs. They adapt previously developed rubrics for assessing institutionalization of service-learning by incorporating unique challenges for teacher educators, such as accreditation issues. Their subjects were leaders from a project designed to provide technical assistance to teacher education programs and faculty on the campuses involved who were learning to incorporate service-learning into their teacher preparation programs. Through a variety of qualitative techniques, they gather data about the process over the course of a year and identify some of the unique factors associated with implementation and institutionalization of service-learning in a teacher preparation program.

Pontbriand, in chapter 5, examines the factors that have been important in implementing and sustaining service-learning in a high school that has been recognized by the Corporation for National and Community Service as a National Service-Learning Leader School. The case study draws on multiple data sources, including interviews, observations, extant materials, and a faculty survey, to provide an unusually rich picture of the institutionalization of the program over time. Data are organized using a path model linking supports and threats to institutionalization. Implications for others attempting to establish service-learning programs in K–12 education are drawn from this experience.

A continuing criticism of service-learning research literature has been the relative scarcity of studies that focus on the community. Those that do exist have tended to address the issue of whether community members appreciate the work of students; there is relatively little that addresses community impact or the partnership itself.

Section four presents two interesting studies that help to fill this gap. Clarke, in chapter 6, created a process model for understanding role of community in the creation and sustenance of service-learning projects. The three "I" model offers a new approach to community impact evaluation. Based on principles derived from program evaluation, community development, and service-learning, it focuses on the partnership as the unit of analysis and helps in the assessment of the role played by community and campus partners in the initiation of the partnership and program, in the shaping and implementation of the initiative itself and in determining its impact on multiple stakeholders. The model was empirically tested in a community where several service-learning initiatives are underway and provides a useful tool for those seeking to understand the dynamics of creating a partnership with the community.

Schaffer, Paris, and Vogel, in chapter 7, address another aspect of the community campus partnership: the potential ethical conflicts that may arise during service-learning programs. Using semi-structured interviews with faculty members, students, and community partners, they identify ethical problems that arise in service-learning and how these participants resolved them. They classify these ethical problems into six categories and interpret them using alternative perspectives including rule based, virtue oriented, and feminist ethical theories. They discuss implications for reducing ethical conflict in service-learning relationships and relate their findings to the practice literature in service-learning.

The largest number of studies in this field by far has addressed the impact of service-learning on students. These studies, however, generally have not carefully specified and measured the experiences students actually have during service-learning. They rarely clearly measured the independent variable, nor have they carefully assessed the learning that can be expected from service-learning. They have also, like the rest of the field, been largely atheoretical; there are virtually no studies in the literature that test alternative theories. Studies have also rarely built on results of the previous work of others. The three studies in section five begin to address these issues. Steinke and Fitch, in chapter 8, address the lack of well-constructed measures of impact. They developed and validated a tool for measuring two academic outcomes of service-learning in higher education, intellectual development, and cognitive learning. They situated these outcomes in experiential theories commonly used to support service-learning as pedagogy. Building on previous research focused on cognitive outcomes, they designed both a written assessment format that can be integrated into the assignments of a service-learning course and a tool for scoring the resulting work. They also validated this tool with standardized measures to assess epistemelogical and intellectual development. The result provides both a useful reflection and assessment tool and strengthens the theoretical underpinnings for service-learning.

Stenson, Eyler, and Giles in chapter 9 perform a secondary analysis on data from a national study of service-learning in higher education in an attempt to test an important theoretical question in the literature; does providing academic reward for service undermine students' commitment to future service? Using factor analysis, measures of motivation were created; commitment was measured by the students[1] response to post service survey items on future intention to perform service in the community. The model linking service, motivation, and future commitment to service is then tested using structural equation modeling. Results suggest that providing extrinsic rewards for participation in community service by giving classroom credit does not dampen positive attitudes towards and future commitment to service.

In chapter 10, Kraft and Wheeler focus on testing the power of service-learning to increase resilience in disaffected youth. The institution studied was a charter school for high school students considered to be at risk for failing school. Working with a theoretical model of meta-learning, they examine the ways in which service-learning might strengthen the "self-system" (i.e., the students' beliefs about themselves which are thought to be linked to engagement in school tasks). Data to test the model ranged from observations and interviews, to school achievement and attendance records. Measures were also made of student engagement and involvement in service-learning. Powerful relationships were observed between positive

engagement in service-learning and with positive change on student outcome variables.

In chapter 11 in section six, Annette provides an international perspective on the status of service-learning. Using examples from the United
Kingdom and other countries, Annette discusses progress, funding
sources, philosophies, and issues that are associated with the practice of
service-learning. He suggests ideas for comparative research and recom-
mends strategies for the development of a global civic society through
exchange programs and study abroad.

In the final section, chapter 12 by Billig and Eyler addresses the state of
service-learning and service-learning research. Using a field-building
framework, the authors assess whether service-learning is indeed a field
and the factors that contribute to the growth and health of a field, the
progress made toward fulfilling the existing research agendas, and what is
needed to build a strong base of evidence. In concert with Bringle, they
call for both increased emphasis on scientific rigor and on testing theoretically derived research questions.

While the last chapter discusses much that remains to be done, all the
chapters in this volume represent a big step along that path. These chapters add to our understanding of the complexity of service-learning by
identifying and deconstructing context, and in the interrelationships
among participants on campus and in the community. They define particular advantages of service-learning for students in varying circumstances.
They also often anchor these complicated processes in well-articulated theoretical perspectives. Future researchers, attempting to design strong theory based studies, will find much to work with here.

PART I

CHALLENGES FOR SERVICE-LEARNING RESEARCH

CHAPTER 1

ENHANCING THEORY-BASED RESEARCH ON SERVICE-LEARNING

Robert G. Bringle

The relationship between theory and research is critical to improving the knowledge base of service-learning. The nature of theory and how theory enhances the development of research projects are discussed. Psychological theories illustrate how theories from cognate areas can enhance research on service-learning, better inform teaching in general, and contribute to the knowledge base in disciplines.

OVERVIEW

The expansion of service-learning during that past decade is an important development in education for numerous reasons. First, service-learning is consistent with Boyer's call for educators, educational institutions, and students to become more involved in communities in ways that are consistent with their educational goals and in ways that help communities (e.g.,

Deconstructing Service-Learning: Research Exploring Context, Participation, and Impacts
A Volume in: Advances in Service-Learning Research, pages 3–21.
Copyright © 2003 by Information Age Publishing, Inc.
All rights of reproduction in any form reserved.
ISBN: 1-59311-071-5 (hardcover), 1-59311-070-7 (pbk.)

Boyer, 1994, 1996; Bringle, Games, & Malloy, 1999). The call for civic engagement is not only relevant to instruction, but also to the mission, policies, and strategic operations of institutions that command trust, possess huge assets (e.g., physical plants, payrolls, purchasing power), and are permanent members of communities (Bringle et al., 1999; Harkavy, 1996). Second, service-learning provides an example of a pedagogy that consists of elements that are known to enhance depth of understanding in the learning process:

- Active learning;
- Frequent feedback from expert, students, or others (e.g., community practitioners) that is provided in non-threatening ways;
- Collaboration;
- Cognitive apprenticeship (i.e., a mentor with whom students can discuss and learn generalization of principles, transfer of knowledge between theory and practice, how to analyze perplexing circumstances); and
- Practical application in which students are involved in tasks that have real consequences but have a safety net for high stakes mistakes (Marchese, 1997).

Third, service-learning broadens and enriches the educational agenda beyond the discipline-specific focus that is so dominant in higher education (Rice, 1996). Service-learning compels educators and students to analyze issues in interdisciplinary ways and to consider not only the cognitive development of students but also other facets of students' development (e.g., affective, social, communication skills, values, attitudes, philanthropic habits, democratic participation).

Increasing the knowledge base of service-learning is important for practitioners who aspire to becoming reflective practitioners, who seek to enhance their skills and understanding, and who want to ensure that they are offering students well-crafted opportunities for learning. However, with so much promise, it would be unfortunate if knowledge about the virtues of service-learning remains the domain of a few dedicated educators who take the risks and experience the rewards of knowing why service-learning is a good choice and a smart choice. Systematically studying the nature of service-learning, regardless of the means, and codifying that knowledge in accessible ways is important so that all educators can develop an appreciation for and literacy about service-learning.

Conducting research is one means through which these goals can be realized. However, there is more to good research than simply collecting data. This chapter will help establish the case that the collection, analysis, and interpretation of information about service-learning will be more meaningful when all aspects of the research process are guided by and have implications for theory.

THE NATURE AND IMPORTANCE OF THEORY

Theories ask and answer *why* questions. For example, a theory would explain why a particular course quality (e.g., written reflection on alternative problem solving strategies for a community issue) produces a particular outcome (e.g., enhanced self-efficacy on community issues). Theories represent cognitive and linguistic templates that are laid upon phenomena. Yet they are not "merely theories" in the sense that they are inconsequential. McGuire (1980) poignantly stated how indispensable theories are:

> What makes theorizing a tragedy is not that our theories are poor but that, poor as they are, they are essential, for we cannot do without them. The ubiquity of formal and informal theorizing demonstrates its indispensability. To cope with reality we must reduce it to the oversimplified level of complexity that our minds can manage and distort it into the type of representations that we can grasp. We are reduced to groping for theories that are happy instances of brilliant oversimplification whose elected ignorances and distortions happen to be incidental to the matter under consideration, so that within the momentary situation the theory's apt focusing of our creative and critical appraisal yields gains that outweigh the losses caused by its oversights and distortions. (p. 54)

Theories provide conceptual grounding for research when they articulate and detail:

- The nature of constructs (e.g., civic responsibility, motivation to volunteer, racial tolerance, active learning);
- The relationships between a construct and observables (e.g., persons with racial tolerance display the following characteristics . . .); and
- Relationships between constructs (e.g., persons with racial tolerance are motivated to promote social justice).

When research does an adequate job of describing the independent variable (e.g., differences in how courses were conducted) and the dependent variable (e.g., student's self-assessment of civic attitudes), the research findings are nonetheless limited in their ability to suggest implications for other classes. Theories are important because they guide the selection of the independent variables and dependent variables that are manifestations of their respective constructs, provide a rationale for the pairing together a particular independent and dependent variable, and guide the translation of variables into operationalizations (see Bringle & Hatcher, 2000).

There are two dominant research strategies for studying service-learning. First, research has compared service-learning classes to classes taught using traditional methods of pedagogy (Eyler & Giles, 1999; Osborne, Hammerich, & Hensley, 1998). Second, aspects of service-learning (e.g., number of hours of service, types of reflection, types of service activities) have been compared within or across service-learning classes (Eyler & Giles, 1999; Mabry, 1998). Bringle and Hatcher (2000) suggested that the experimental method is one of the best ways in which to study how variations in attributes of service-learning classes are related to particular outcomes. Shumer (2000) identified one glaring problem that is incompatible with an experimental approach to studying service-learning: defining the treatment. Shumer notes that, in the case of studies that have multiple classes, there is tremendous variability in the implementation of service-learning. In addition, even for a single service-learning class, there is variability in how students participate in the course, experience the course, and respond to the characteristics of the course.

Variability in the nature of the intervention is a significant issue in all types of research on service-learning, both quantitative and qualitative. For example, inaccuracies in being able to describe the intervention and variations in individual student's participation with the intervention are issues that undermine the ability to analyze and understand what is occurring in all types of research. Researchers must be able to describe the nature of the intervention in order to extract meaning about the experience from the evidence—if this is not done, then nothing enduring can be learned. However, this variability is a manageable issue when researchers include measures of how service-learning is varying across classes on key dimensions (e.g., nature of reflection, nature of participation in service, differences in student participation and experiences). Furthermore, theories provide coherence across these variations by interpreting the variability in terms of common themes. In this way, theories enhance the understanding of *how* and *why* these variations matter.

When research is derived from theory and evaluates theory-based hypotheses, the work is more systematic, the relationship between the independent and dependent variables is richer, and the findings have broader implications. Thus, one role of theories in research is in the deductive process of generating and testing hypotheses. In addition, theories are important for extracting lessons, principles, and guidelines from research results. Conducting research that is not parochial and limited to a particular setting, combination of circumstances, or period of time is important to building a knowledge base. Research is most informative when the information that is gained through data collection, whether qualitative or quantitative, is relevant to supporting, developing, refining, and revising theoretical propositions that can guide future course and program design and implementation. To provide merely a description of a specific service-learning program or an isolated service-learning class may be severely limited in its implications for practice because of the context-specific and idiosyncratic nature of the case description. To show how the design and implementation of the service-learning program or class was guided by theory and to demonstrate how the experiences and outcomes are consistent or inconsistent with expectations derived from a theory provides a much more productive basis from which conceptual generalizations can be understood and a basis upon which lessons learned from a setting or a set of circumstances can be applied to other settings. Theories also provide a basis for integrating and differentiating disparate observations and findings (e.g., when common elements can be conceptually organized by a theory) and a basis for understanding boundary conditions for phenomena (e.g., when the theory or principle does not apply).

One of the odd paradoxes is that to stress the importance of theory in research seems as if it shifts the emphasis away from practice; however, the opposite is true. When research is testing theory, the combination has the most potential to *contribute to practice* because of the generalizability of the theoretical propositions to other settings, other courses, and other service activities. To quote Lewin (1951), "There is nothing so practical as a good theory" (p. 169).

BALANCE BETWEEN THEORY AND EMPIRICAL DATA

A review of the research literature on service-learning leads to the conclusion that formal theories have not played a prominent enough role in service-learning research. One might ask: Doesn't everyone have theories? The answer at one level is, yes, but not all theories are necessarily in the form that is most useful for increasing the understanding of service-learning. In order to be useful, formal theories need to

- Provide clear hypotheses;
- Provide falsifiable hypotheses;
- Be public; and
- Be systematic and internally coherent.

In some cases, however, there are studies of service-learning in which there is little emphasis on theory (small "t") and strong emphasis on the empirical data (big "D"), yielding a *theory DATA* (t D) pattern.[1] In this case, research principally describes what was done (e.g., in a service-learning class) and what outcomes occurred, without much attention to why there is a connection between the antecedents and consequences. Research of this sort is good program evaluation: "Let's do this and see which of these outcomes occur." Program evaluation *can* test theory, but it typically does not. Any theory about the relationship between outcomes and interventions is often implicit and when theory is implicated, it is only a token statement that is tacked on to the descriptions (e.g., It's reasonable to expect that these outcomes will occur). Quantitative research of this type relies heavily on methods, measurement, and statistics without sufficient explanation as to why certain variables are being studied, why certain outcomes are expected, and how the outcomes have broader implications. Qualitative research of this type has no clear explanation for why certain questions were asked of subjects or of archival material, and the conceptual framework for interpretation is based solely on describing the results through some seat-of-the-pants method of extracting meaning.

One can identify work that fits this t D pattern of heavy emphasis on the primary data and limited attention to theory by comparing the number of citations in the Introduction and the Discussion sections of research reports. Most researchers cite relevant past literature that is both empirical and conceptual in order to set the context for their research; therefore, there will be a rather large number of citations in the Introduction. However, when the number of citations is much greater in the Introduction than in the Discussion, this may indicate that the empirical results have few implications for theory and no theory development is taking place as a result of the empirical work.

The goal of good research is *not* simply to describe a highly idiosyncratic event. The purpose of research is to identify explanations that generalize or to know when they do and do not generalize. Thus, the goal of credible, effective, rigorous, and high quality research, whether it is quantitative or qualitative, is to understand a phenomenon so that something is learned for the future. For example, what is learned might be:

- A principle of good practice—*Service-learning classes that involve structured reflection are . . .* ;
- Something about learning—*Learning is more likely to occur when . . ., Values are more likely to be transformed when . . . .*; or
- Something about community impact—*Greater community impact is obtained when . . . .*

In any case, if the research does not produce knowledge that is relevant to theory that furthers understanding and guides future decisions, policy, or practice, then it is decidedly inferior research.

A second pattern, *THEORY data* (T d), occurs when some data are collected, but the author's thesis is much broader than the information in the data and transcends the data in significant ways. In this type of research, the researcher states the thesis in the Introduction and Discussion sections without heavy reliance on the Methods and Results sections. This type of pattern occurs, for example, when the data are based on a very small, idiosyncratic, and unrepresentative sample or when the discussion section is speculative and goes well beyond the results that are reported. In the case of qualitative research, the T d pattern occurs when the methods of analysis are not explained in sufficient detail to know how the data led to the conclusions or how alternative explanations (i.e., those that deviate from the thesis of the researcher) were eliminated from consideration. Both quantitative and qualitative research fit the T d pattern when assertions are made without sufficient justification from the information that was collected or when theoretical presentations and assertions are not supported by citing past research.

A third pattern, *THEORY DATA* (T D), occurs when there is a discussion of theory in the research and there is extensive data, but theory and data are not well connected. In this case, theory shapes the presentation of the research, but not necessarily the design of the research or the interpretation of the results. For example, past research and possibly theory are presented in the Introduction but the theory plays little role in the development of the hypotheses and the translation of the hypotheses into the research procedures. Furthermore, when theoretical points are made in the Discussion section, they are independent of the results.

Well-designed research has balance and connections between theory and data: *THEORY-DATA* (T-D). This type of research utilizes theory in the conception of the research, the conceptual development of the hypotheses, the rationale for the connection between independent and dependent variable, the selection of methods for investigation, the operationalization of the variables, and the interpretation of the results. When this level of interdependency between theory and research exists, the research has greater potential to contribute to both knowledge and practice.

WHERE THEORIES COME FROM

Giles and Eyler (1994) noted that, "service-learning, as a relatively new social and educational phenomenon, suffers from the lack of a well-articulated conceptual framework" (p. 77). The closest service-learning comes to having a theory of its own is Dewey's educational theory (Dewey, 1916, 1933), and Kolb's (1984) experiential learning theory based upon Dewey's work. Giles and Eyler (1994) and Hatcher (1997) provided excellent examples of how Dewey's educational theory generates testable hypotheses about the design, processes, and outcomes of service-learning classes.

In addition to Dewey's theory, there are two other sources for theories: (1) theories developed specifically for service-learning, and (2) theories borrowed from cognate areas.

Developing Theory

McGuire (1980) identified the following strategies for generating and developing theory.

1. *Intensive Case Study.* Studying a phenomenon in depth is a mechanism for developing conceptual and theoretical insights. The strength of qualitative research can be theory building through analysis of cases. Daloz, Keen, Keen, and Daloz Parks (1996), Coles (1993), and Colby and Damon (1999) explored the nature of community service and service-learning by using case studies.

2. *Paradoxical Incident.* This strategy develops theoretical perspectives through analysis of paradoxes. For example, instructors expect that students in service-learning classes will develop enhanced intrinsic motivation for service. Understanding when this does not happen for all students in a course and studying those cases can lead to new insights about service-learning experiences and generate new theories for understanding the phenomenon.

3. *Metaphor.* Analogies and metaphors are powerful ways for exploring phenomena. Although no metaphor or analogy is complete in its analysis, each has the potential to offer new insights and perspectives and contribute to theory. For example, what insights might result from analyzing service-learning as any of the following: tourism, drive-by service, a laboratory, mission work, therapy, apprenticeship, indoctrination, politics, subversion, oppression. Bringle and Hatcher (2002) assumed that the campus-community partnership was analogous to an interpersonal relationship and used social psychological research, theories, and concepts from close relationships and friendships to study campus-community partnerships.

4. *Rule of Thumb.* This strategy values the wisdom of practitioners to identify lessons and to develop conceptual frameworks. Here is where we can learn from our community colleagues. In addition, several principles of good practice have been proposed for service-learning (see Honnet & Poulson, 1989; Howard, 1993). How do we know if they are correct? Does articulating clear service and learning goals lead to better outcomes? For whom? Under what conditions? With what risks? How can each principle be used as a template for developing more extensive theories about service-learning (e.g., goal setting, communication, educational teams)? Elaborating why a principle does produce desirable results prods the *why* question and identifies mediating variables. A *mediating variable* describes an intervening variable that is assumed to link two variables. Theories are built and developed through an exploration of mediating variables. For example, one might hypothesize that structured reflection activities generate better learning among novice students because the reflection activities produce better conceptual maps of the content domain than do unstructured reflection activities. In this case, the nature of the conceptual map is assumed to mediate or explain the relationship between reflection and learning. If the learning outcomes differ because of the

type of reflection activities for novice students, then it is expected that a measure of conceptual maps will also differ for the two groups.

5. *Conflicting Results.* One way to understand a phenomenon better is to analyze how and why different results are obtained in research. For example, Bringle, Hatcher, Muthiah, and McIntosh (2001) reviewed results from numerous studies, which found that mandatory service, when compared to voluntary service, results in less intrinsic motivation (Bringle, Hatcher, & McIntosh, 1999; Stukas, Snyder, & Clary, 1999), more intrinsic motivation (Bringle et al., 1999), and no difference (Bringle et al., 1999). Why? Similarly, an investigation of principles of good practice would likely yield different, conflicting results—sometimes they matter, sometimes they do not, sometimes the opposite effect is obtained. In these instances, theories are clarified on the basis of moderating variables. A *moderator variable* describes an *it depends* relationship. For example, structured reflection activities might produce better learning for novice service-learning students than do unstructured reflection activities, but the opposite might be the case for experienced service-learning students. Thus, the impact of the type of reflection on learning depends on the background of the learner. Moderator variables help develop theories by clarifying processes, by suggesting boundary conditions, and by identifying exceptions.

Borrowing Theories from Cognate Areas

The American Association for Higher Education's (AAHE) *Series on Service-Learning in the Disciplines* (Zlotkowski, 1999) is a rich resource for examples of how discipline-based theories can enrich and broaden the conceptual analysis of service-learning and guide research. Volumes on psychology, sociology, political science, and education contain conceptual frameworks and perspectives that can be particularly helpful to analyzing students' experiences in service-learning classes. Battistoni (2001) used the disciplines to organize and explore the nuances in conceptual perspectives of civic responsibility and civic behaviors.

The psychological literature is rich in how it applies to the breadth of issues in service-learning. Specific examples of the application of psychological theories are contained in the AAHE psychology monograph (Bringle & Duffy, 1998) and the issue of *Journal of Social Issues* edited by Stukas and Dunlap (2002). A few of these theories are highlighted in the next section.

Functional Theory

Functional theory identifies six motives for volunteering: Values, Career, Social, Protective, Self-Esteem Enhancement, and Understanding (Clary et al., 1998). Bringle et al. (1999) found that a sample of mostly entering students reported that the most salient reason for them to volunteer was Values (mean = 5.44 on a 7-point response scale), followed by Understanding (mean = 4.91), Self-Esteem Enhancement (mean = 4.38), Career (mean = 4.01), Protection (mean = 3.23), and Social (mean = 3.02). These results suggest that students arrived at college with a strong intrinsic interest to help others. Furthermore, these students reported that development, both cognitive and personal, were stronger motives than the more pragmatic motives of furthering their career, reducing personal guilt, and making friends. Also, when motives were examined by intended major (Business vs. Professional vs. Humanities/Arts/Science), there were no differences on the motives of Understanding, Protective, Social, Career, or Self-Esteem Enhancement. Business and other professional students did score lower on Values than other students, but Values was still the strongest motive for volunteering for those two groups of students (Bringle et al., 1999).

Clary et al. (1998) contend that recruitment of volunteers is related to the match between publicity and motives. In addition, persistence of volunteers should be related to the match between motives to volunteer and how well the activity satisfied those motives. They also suggest that persistence of volunteers will be aided by diversity of the motive base rather than the presence of one dominant motive (e.g., only altruistic motive or only selfish motive). The functional theory provides a conceptual framework for studying student motivation and a basis for further understanding the successes and limitations of service-learning as an intervention to develop philanthropic habits.

Attribution Theory

Attribution theory focuses on how individuals answer *why* questions about their social world and the behavior of others. Bringle and Velo (1998) explored how attribution theory can be useful in understanding the answers of students to questions, such as "Why am I helping?" and "Why does the person need help?" How students answer these questions can explain why students might enter service with an attitude that blames the recipient. An additional set of questions focuses on the recipients of help, who ask, "Why do I need help?" and "Why is this person helping me?" Answers to all of these questions can be as simple (e.g., single cause) or complex and the answers can reflect the particular circumstances being analyzed, individual differences in orientation (e.g., political, biases due to role), power and social differences between parties, and social and historical factors (e.g., Augoustinos & Walker, 1995). For example, Heaven (1994) found that poverty was explained in complex chains that possessed both common properties across groups and unique qualities for different groups. Better understanding students' explanations of various social issues could inform educators about approaches to take to reach specific educational goals.

The attributional analysis of questions by helper and recipient provides a basis for understanding why and when recipients are not positive about help received and why helping can undermine the development of self-sufficiency (see Nadler, 2002). For example, for the recipient, receiving help (a) can be affirming because it demonstrates that the person's social environment is sensitive to needs and responsive in appropriate ways; or (b) can be threatening because it implies that the person is incapable of meeting needs and must be dependent on others. In the cases of both the helper and the recipient, having implicit theories that identify causes as fixed entities leads to different motivational and action strategies than viewing them as dynamic and malleable (Dweck, 1996).

Equity Theory

Equity theory posits that, even when the outcomes in an exchange are unequal, when outcomes are perceived as proportionate to inputs for both individuals, a relationship will be satisfying (Walster, Walster, & Berscheid, 1978). Inequitable relationships, in which someone is perceived to be overbenefited or underbenefited, result in distress, and either (a) attempt to restore equity by appropriately adjusting investments or (b) strain toward relationship dissolution (Hatfield, Utne, & Traupmann, 1979; Nadler, 2002). Helping circumstances are inherently inequitable because helpers typically invest more than they gain and recipients typically gain more than they contribute. What are the psychological consequences of injustice and inequities between helper and recipient? According to equity theory, when inequity exists, recipients might resist help because it acknowledges their inferiority and dependence, or they may denigrate the value of the help (and the helper) in order to make the appraisal of the exchange more equitable. Equity theory is, thus, useful for understanding why those receiving help can have unfavorable opinions of the helper and the help. Equity theory also explains how helping can perpetuate power differentials and adversely influence intergroup relations (Nadler, 2002).

Written Reflection

Much reflection in service-learning focuses on written assignments that facilitate connecting the community service and course content (Bringle & Hatcher, 1999; Eyler, Giles, & Schmiede, 1996). Pennebaker's (1990) research suggested that written reflection may provide personal as well as educational benefits for students. Pennebaker, Kiecolt-Glaser, and Glaser (1988), in an experimental study, manipulated whether persons wrote on four consecutive days about either traumatic experiences or superficial topics. Those who wrote about the traumatic event, compared to the other group, had more favorable immune-system responses, less frequent health center visits, and higher subjective well being. Similar effects have been found in many other studies.

> Writing about emotional upheavals has been found to improve the physical and mental health of grade-school children and nursing home residents, arthritis sufferers, medical school students, maximum-security prisoners, new mothers, and rape victims. Not only are there benefits to health, but writing about emotional topics has been found to reduce anxiety and depression, improve grades in college, and . . . aid people in securing new jobs. (Pennebaker, 1990, p. 40)

More relevant to service-learning, Pennebaker (1990) also reported on analyses of the essay's content to determine if characteristics of the narratives were related to the writer's subsequent health and well being. The most important factor that differentiated persons showing health improvements from those who did not was improvement in their constructions of stories that contained causal thinking, insight, and self-reflection. Thus, reflection activities that promote personally meaningful as well as academically meaningful exploration of experiences encountered in service settings have the potential to yield health benefits as well as intellectual ones to the student. Wyer, Adaval and Colcombe (2002) provided an analysis of how narrative representations of events are related to organization of information, judgments, and decisions.

Intergroup Contact

Service-learning typically involves college students in service settings in which they work with disenfranchised populations, including homeless, disadvantaged youth, victims of violence, sick and disabled persons, and elderly persons. Because this service places students in unfamiliar community settings in which they interact with persons with whom they differ on several characteristics (e.g., age, class, race, education) and for whom they may have prejudices and stereotypes, one of the promising educational outcomes is that the service-learning experiences can have positive effects on their understanding and relationships to other groups in society.

One approach to diversity education focuses on changing students' beliefs (cognitive associations) and attitudes (feelings) about other groups. This approach assumes that if attitudes and beliefs change, then behavior toward the other group will subsequently reflect the changes. In contrast to this approach which assumes that changes in attitudes produces changes in behavior, service-learning is based on the alternative causal sequence that changing behavior toward other groups (i.e., getting students to behave in empathetic, compassionate, and helpful ways toward the group) can result in changed attitudes and beliefs.

Does contact with unfamiliar groups reduce or strengthen pre-existing attitudes and stereotypes? According to intergroup contact theory, the answer depends on contextual factors that are present during the interaction. If certain characteristics are present (i.e., pursuit of common goals, provide a basis for friendship, equal status, contact that contradicts stereotype, long-term contact, norms; Hewstone & Brown, 1986), then the contact is more likely to reduce negative stereotypes and result in positive attitudes. If not, then the opposite effects will occur and existing stereotypes will be strengthened. Interestingly, each of these components has the potential to be present in service-learning and to be absent (Erickson & O'Connor, 2000), and therefore, act as a moderating variable for the outcomes of the service-learning experience. Thus, the theory provides a template for organizing analysis of when service-learning is miseducative (con) or educative (pro), and the theory can be a guide for the design of better service-learning classes (see Exhibit 1).

Self-Determination Theory

Self-Determination Theory (SDT) (Deci, Koestner, & Ryan, 1999; Deci & Ryan, 2000) examined the role of extrinsic rewards, such as credit, grades, money, and intrinsic motivation, such as altruistic dispositions, in initiating and sustaining behaviors (e.g., helping). The theory contends that it is appropriate, even necessary, to provide external inducements and controlling conditions in order to involve unmotivated students in community service. The problem with extrinsic and tangible rewards is

EXHIBIT 1
Potential Effects of Intergroup Contact Variables on Service-learning

Pursuit of Common Goals
  Pro: Students and community have aligned interests
  Con: Students and community have different interests
Equal Status
  Pro: Students and community work together as equals, both giving and taking
  Con: Hierarchical relationships with power differences are established
Contact Contradicts Stereotypes
  Pro: Contact results in increased familiarity, which results in perceptions of similarity
  Con: Contact reinforces stereotypes
Long-Term Contact
  Pro: Service-learning provides regular contact and deep involvement
  Con: Service-learning provides short-term contact and shallow involvement
Norms
  Pro: Service-learning promotes interdependency, justice, and empathy
  Con: Service-learning promotes a charity model

not that they increase the target behavior (which they can do), but that they can produce behavioral compliance without internal change. If so, then removing the external controlling conditions, such as requirements and incentives, will lead to a lower likelihood of community service persisting after their withdrawal. Self-determination theory suggests that service-learning classes that require service, a potentially controlling situation, must find ways to promote the following three factors that lead to internalization of motives (Deci, Koestner, & Ryan, 1999; Deci & Ryan, 2000):

1. Relatedness: Developing a sense of belongingness and connectedness to other persons, groups, and society.
2. Competence: Developing an understanding of the activity and goal, and seeing that they have the relevant skills to succeed and sense satisfaction.
3. Autonomy: Controlling environments can promote relatedness and competence, and yield partially internalized motivation. However, grasping the meaning and worth of the goal, according to self-determination theory, only occurs when autonomy is present.

Thus, if a goal of educators is to maintain the motivation of intrinsically motivated students and to produce a transformation of unmotivated students from extrinsic to intrinsic, then service-learning classes must find ways to promote relatedness, competence, and autonomy.

Other Theoretical Perspectives

The importance of theories is not limited to the experiences of students in service-learning classes. Theories can also be employed and developed that have implications for research focused on faculty, institutions, and communities. For example, there are few theories about professional development of faculty, such as motivation, hiring patterns, or career transitions; the function of faculty roles and rewards; and the importance of civic education to faculty involved in service-learning. Bringle and Hatcher (1995) borrowed Kolb's (1984) learning model, which is primarily used as a means for analyzing student learning, and applied it to faculty development.

There are many theories that have been developed on community development from sociology, urban planning, and community psychology. These theories have had limited use in analyzing and researching the community impact of service-learning and broader issues implicated in campus-community relationships. However, service-learning and civic engagement provide an appropriate means for evaluating these theories and for furthering the effectiveness of civic engagement work in higher education.

For an analysis of institutional change, Foos and Bringle (2002) applied principles of dialogue developed by Dewey (1916, 1933) to interventions intended to produce institutional change in higher education. Dewey's work raised a set of issues that focused on particular leverage points that campus leadership, such as service-learning staff or change agents, could use for change (learning) to occur. Based on the work of Giles and Eyler (1994) and Hatcher (1997), the following principles were extracted from Dewey's work that related to identifying leverage points and intervention strategies for institutional change:

1.   Generate interest, awaken curiosity, and appeal to what is intrinsically interesting.
2.   Generate perplexity and dissonance, possibly between what is desired and what is currently happening.
3.   Create a demand for information.
4.   Provide opportunities for face-to-face discourse, as well as other forms of communication, as a means of fostering interest, obtaining information, and reducing dissonance.
5.   Provide time for change and development.

Each of these provides testable hypotheses about how institutional change to support service-learning and civic engagement might be promoted and studied.

CONCLUSION

Persons with interest in conducting research on service-learning have a tremendous opportunity to develop significant programs of research with multiple implications for higher education and communities. First, there is an opportunity to improve the practice and understanding of service-learning. Second, service-learning provides a powerful test bed that is both convenient and appropriate for evaluating hypotheses from theories about human behavior and increasing civic involvement among students. For example, conducting research to test a hypothesis from the intergroup contact theory is typically quite difficult (Hewstone & Brown, 1986) and time consuming research to conduct. Service-learning provides an opportunity that is real, occurs over a relatively long period of time, and has important implications for education. Furthermore, such research is significant not only for better informing practice but also for contributing to the refinement of intergroup contact theory. Thus, studying service-learning within the framework of, for example, social psychology can lead to improvements in instructional practice and can contribute to social psy-chological theory.

Third, research on service-learning, particularly research that contrasts service-learning with other forms of instruction, provides a means for developing the scholarship of teaching. Service-learning research should begin to more comprehensively and more persuasively establish that ser-vice-learning is a pedagogical approach that contains the key factors that produce good learning. Furthermore, this research should also demon-strate to higher education some of the deficiencies of traditional approaches in instruction. Thus, service-learning researchers and practitio-ners are well positioned to teach their institutions how to teach and to improve the quality of all instruction. Practitioners of service-learning can continue to creatively explore additional ways of developing teaching for deeper learning, rather than for the convenience of faculty and the placat-ing of students. In doing so, scholars who study service-learning can be leaders who help other educators better understand student learning, the development of thinking, and the civic purposes of education. Thus, the potential and the promise of theory-based research on service-learning is that it can lead to a better understanding of:

- Scholarly teaching;
- Scholarship on teaching;
- How instruction can contribute to better academic learning and stu-dent development;
- Civic engagement in higher education;
- Campus-community partnerships that have integrity; and
- How higher education can play an even more significant role improv-ing the quality of life in communities.

The best chance for the research to have an impact on the practice of ser-vice-learning, on higher education, and on the disciplines and professions is for the research to be based on theory, to test theory, and to develop the-ory.

NOTE

1.   The author borrows from Sigmon's (1995) typology of different types of patterns for the emphasis on the service and the course content (service LEARN-ING, SERVICE learning, SERVICE LEARNING, and SERVICE-LEARNING) and, by analogy, describe four patterns that can exist between theory and empirical data: (a) t D, (b) T d, (c) T D, and (d) T-D.

REFERENCES

Augoustinos, M., & Walker, I (1995). *Social cognition: An integrated introduction.* Thousand Oaks, CA: Sage.

Battistoni, R. (2001). Civic engagement across the curriculum: A resource book for service-learning faculty in all disciplines. Providence, RI: Campus Compact.

Boyer, E. L. (1994). Creating the new American college. *Chronicle of Public Education,* A48.

Boyer, E. L. (1996). The scholarship of engagement. *Journal of Public Service and Outreach, 1*(1), 11–20.

Bringle, R. G. (2001, October). *Service-learning research as a source of scholarship.* Paper presented at the First Annual International Conference on Service-Learning Research, Berkeley, CA.

Bringle, R. G., & Duffy, D. K. (Eds.). (1998). *With service in mind: Concepts and models for service-learning in psychology.* Washington, DC: American Association for Higher Education.

Bringle, R. G., Games, R., & Malloy, E. A. (Eds.). (1999). *Colleges and universities as citizens.* Needham Heights, MA: Allyn & Bacon.

Bringle, R. G., & Hatcher, J. A. (1995). A service-learning curriculum for faculty. *Michigan Journal of Community Service Learning, 2,* 112–122.

Bringle, R. G., & Hatcher, J. A. (1999). Reflection in service-learning: Making meaning of experience. *Educational Horizons, 77*(4), 179–185.

Bringle, R. G., & Hatcher, J. A. (2000, Fall). Meaningful measurement of theory-based service-learning outcomes: Making the case with quantitative research. *Michigan Journal of Community Service Learning,* 68–75.

Bringle, R. G., & Hatcher, J. A. (2002). Campus community partnerships: The terms of engagement. *Journal of Social Issues, 58,* 503–516.

Bringle, R. G., Hatcher, J. A., & McIntosh, R. (1999, October). *Motives for service among college students.* Paper presented at the Association for Research on Nonprofit Organizations and Voluntary Action, Washington, DC.

Bringle, R. G., Hatcher, J. A., Muthiah, R., & McIntosh, R. (2001, October). *The case for required service in service-learning classes: A multi-campus study of service-learning.* Paper presented at the First Annual International Conference on Service-Learning Research, Berkeley, CA.

Bringle, R. G., & Velo, P. M. (1998). Attributions about misery. In R. G. Bringle & D. K. Duffy (Eds.), *With service in mind: Concepts and models for service-learning in psychology* (pp. 51–67). Washington, DC: American Association for Higher Education.

Clary, E. G., Snyder, M., Ridge, R. D., Copeland, J., Stukas, A. A., Haugen, J., & Miene, P. (1998). Understanding and assessing the motivations of volunteers: A functional approach. *Journal of Personality and Social Psychology, 74,* 1516–1530.

Colby, A. & Damon, W. (1999). *Some do care: Contemporary lives of moral commitment.* New York: The Free Press.

Coles, R. (1993). *The call to service: A witness to idealism.* New York: Houghton Mifflin.

Daloz, L. A., Keen, C. H., Keen, J. P., & Daloz Parks, S. (1996). *Common fire: Lives of commitment in a complex world.* Boston: Beacon Press.

Deci, E. L., Koestner, R., & Ryan, R. M. (1999). A meta-analytic review of experiments examining the effects of extrinsic rewards on intrinsic motivation. *Psychological Bulletin, 125,* 627–668.

Deci, E. L., & Ryan, R. M. (2000). The "what" and "why" of goal pursuits: Human needs and the self-determination of behavior. *Psychological Inquiry, 11,* 227–268.

Dewey, J. (1916). *Democracy and education.* New York: Macmillan.

Dewey, J. (1933). *How we think: A restatement of the relation of reflective thinking to the educative process.* Boston: D.C. Heath.

Dweck, C. S. (1996). Implicit theories as organizers of goals and behavior. In P. M. Gollwitzer & J. A. Bargh (Eds.), *The psychology of action: Linking cognition and motivation to behavior* (pp. 69–90). New York: Guilford.

Erickson, J. A., & O'Connor, S. E. (2000). Service-learning: Does it promote or reduce prejudice? In C. O'Grady (Ed.), *Integrating service-learning and multicultural education in colleges and universities* (pp. 59–70). Mahwah, NJ: Lawrence Erlbaum Associates.

Eyler, J., Giles, D. E., & Schmiede, A. (1996). *A practitioner's guide to reflection in service-learning: Student voices and reflections.* Nashville, TN: Vanderbilt University.

Foos, C. L., & Bringle, R. G. (2002, April). *Consulting and institutional work as experiential education.* Paper presented at the AAHE/Campus Compact Consulting Corps, Washington, DC.

Giles, D. E., & Eyler, J. (1994). The theoretical roots of service-learning in John Dewey: Towards a theory of service-learning. *Michigan Journal of Community Service Learning, 1,* 77–85.

Hewstone, M., & Brown, R. (1986). Contact is not enough: An intergroup perspective on the 'contact hypothesis.' In M. Hewstone and R. Brown (Eds.), *Contact and conflict in intergroup encounters* (pp. 1-44). New York: Basil Blackwell.

Eyler, J., & Giles, D. E., Jr. (1999). *Where's the learning in service-learning?* San Francisco: Jossey-Bass.

Harkavy, I. (1996). Back to the future: From service-learning to strategic, academically-based community service. *Metropolitan Universities, 7*(1), 57–70.

Hatcher, J. A. (1997). The moral dimensions of John Dewey's philosophy: Implications for undergraduate education. *Michigan Journal of Community Service Learning, 4,* 22–29.

Hatfield, E., Utne, M. K., & Traupmann, J. (1979). Equity theory and intimate relationships. In R. L. Burgess & T. L. Huston (Eds.), *Colleges and universities as citizens* (pp. 48–73). Boston: Allyn & Bacon.

Heaven, P. (1994). The perceived causal structure of poverty: A network analysis approach. *British Journal of Social Psychology, 33,* 259-271.

Honnet, E. P., & Poulson, S. J. (1989). *Principles of good practice in combining service and learning.* (Wingspread Special Report). Racine, WI: The Johnson Foundation.

Howard, J. (1993). Community service-learning in the curriculum. In J. Howard (Ed.), *Praxis I: A faculty casebook on community service-learning* (pp. 3–12). Ann Arbor, MI: OCSL Press.

Kolb, D. A. (1984). *Experiential learning: Experience as the source of learning and development.* Englewood Cliffs, NJ: Prentice-Hall.

Lewin, K. (1951). Problems of research in social psychology. In D. Cartwright (Ed.), *Field theory in social science: Selected theoretical papers by Kurt Lewin* (pp. 155–169). New York: Harper & Row.

Mabry , J. B. (1998). Pedagogical variations in service-learning and student outcomes: How time, contact, and reflection matter. *Michigan Journal of Community Service Learning, 5*, 32–47.

Marchese, T. (1997). The new conversations about learning. *Assessing impact: Evidence and Action.* Washington, DC: American Association for Higher Education.

McGuire, W. J. (1980). The development of theory in social psychology. In S. Duck & R. Gilmour (Eds.), *The development of social psychology* (pp. 53–80). London: Academic Press.

Nadler, A. (2002). Inter-group helping relations as power relations: Helping relations as affirming or challenging inter-group hierarchy. *Journal of Social Issues, 58*, 487–502

Osborne, R. E., Hammerich, S., & Hensley, C. (1998). Student effects of service-learning: Tracking change across a semester. *Michigan Journal of Community Service Learning, 5*, 5–13.

Pennebaker, J. W. (1990). *Opening up: The healing power of expressing emotions.* New York: Guilford Press.

Pennebaker, J.W., Kiecolt-Glaser, J., & Glaser, R. (1988). Disclosure of traumas and immune function: Health implications for psychotherapy. *Journal of Consulting and Clinical Psychology, 56*, 239–245.

Rice, R. E. (1996). *Making the place for the new American scholar* (Working paper services: Inquiry #1). Washington, DC: American Association for Higher Education.

Shumer, R. (2000). Science or storytelling: How should we conduct and report service-learning research? *Michigan Journal of Community Service Learning,* Special Issue, 76–83.

Sigmon, R. (1995). A service and learning typology. *L & S Link, 1*(1), 1.

Stukas, A. A., & Dunlap, M. R. (2002). Community involvement: Theoretical approaches and educational initiatives. *Journal of Social Issues, 58*, 411–427.

Stukas, A. A., Snyder, M., & Clary, E. G. (1999). The effects of "mandatory volunteerism" on intentions to volunteer. *Psychological Science, 10*, 59–64.

Walster, E., Walster, G. W. & Berscheid, E. (1978). *Equity: Theory and research.* Boston: Allyn & Bacon.

Wyer, R. S., Jr., Adaval, R., & Colcombe, S.J. (2002) Narrative-based representations of social knowledge: Their construction and use in comprehension, memory, and judgment. In M. P. Zanna (Ed.), *Advances in experimental social psychology, Vol. 34* (pp. 131–197). San Diego, CA: Academic Press.

Zlotkowski, E. (1999). Pedagogy and the environment. In R. G. Bringle, R. Games, & E. A. Malloy (Eds.), *Colleges and universities as citizens* (pp. 96–120). Boston: Allyn & Bacon

PART II

THE INFLUENCE OF CONTEXT

CHAPTER 2

THE MISSING LINK
Exploring the Context of Learning in Service-Learning

Deborah Hecht

Although there is a wealth of anecdotal evidence of the benefits of participating in service-learning, researchers have often struggled to find supporting empirical evidence. Frequently the data have yielded small effect sizes or inconsistent results. However, with increased demands for scientifically-based evidence that demonstrates the impact of programs, service-learning researchers will be increasingly called upon to present empirical evidence of program outcomes. In this chapter an argument is presented for framing service-learning learning research within the context of the service experience. The contextual characteristics of service-learning are defined as those characteristics that make the program and student experiences unique. They are described in this chapter as site context, background context, reflection context, and the planning context. The chapter describes each context and discusses the levels of specificity with which data can be collected and analyzed. Using real data it presents how the findings can be influenced by contextual information. An argument is presented for use of a Hierarchical modeling approach that allows for interactions among different contextual levels and for consideration of these issues during the design phase of a study.

Deconstructing Service-Learning: Research Exploring Context, Participation, and Impacts
A Volume in: Advances in Service-Learning Research, pages 25–49.
ISBN: 1-59311-071-5 (hardcover), 1-59311-070-7 (pbk.)

Over the past 20 years service-learning has gained increased recognition and acceptance within schools, after-school programs, and community-based organizations as a way to engage youth in meaningful community service activities. These activities are linked to academic, social, or other learning goals through facilitated periods of reflection. During reflection, students examine their actions, the consequences of these actions, and consider alternative actions. Along with an increase in the numbers of youth involved in such programs has come a growing demand for research that clearly demonstrates these experiences have a positive impact on the participants.

For years practitioners cited anecdotal evidence of the benefits, including increased engagement in school-related activities, improved peer and adult relationships, and a greater understanding of the community. Researchers tried to demonstrate similar results through studies that range in size and scope from teacher developed classroom-based studies to national studies conducted by educational researchers. While there have been some positive findings, in general the data have yielded small effect sizes and inconsistent results. Additionally, while the studies collectively provide some support for service-learning, it is far from the strong research evidence for which many practitioners have hoped.

As service-learning competes for time and resources with other educational programs, the need for such research evidence becomes even greater. With pressure on schools to meet or exceed rigorous academic standards, educators must often justify their selection of one program over another. Furthermore, the federal government is increasingly calling for scientifically-based evidence that demonstrates the impact of programs using tested, empirical methodologies. With these pressures, service-learning is at a critical juncture for more comprehensive studies to be undertaken.

It is this demand for scientific evidence that must guide current efforts and lead to more rigorous studies. Researchers must build upon what practitioners report is unique and important about service-learning. They must then design strong research studies to capture these qualities and then provide empirical evidence. This is likely to require the use of new and alternative assessment tools as well as complex data analytic approaches.

In this chapter an argument is presented for re-thinking service-learning research; in particular, the context of the service experience. The word context is used to refer to what many call "service-learning components." The decision to use the term context is intentional. Many of the challenges faced by service-learning research are also faced by researchers in other content areas where there is great variability among both the process of the task and student input. Systems theories support this notion that learning and behavior are influenced by innumerable human and environmental factors. Therefore, the term context is used to avoid limiting the discussion to only those topics that directly relate to service-learning.

The contextual characteristics of service-learning are defined as those characteristics that make the program unique. Frequently, the focus of research is on "exemplary programs" with minimal attention to what makes the program unique or exemplary. Here the focus is broadened to a more systemic understanding. A framework is presented that underscores the types of information needed for a more comprehensive study of service-learning. Data from a study of service-learning in middle school are used to highlight parts of the framework and to demonstrate the importance of considering contextual factors when studying service-learning. While this chapter does not focus on sample size or assessment tools, they too are important considerations.

FRAMING OUR THOUGHTS ABOUT SERVICE-LEARNING RESEARCH

Service-learning is about the *experience*, yet research often fails to focus on the experience. A review of the service-learning standards, key elements, and most introductory texts and training manuals points to the importance of *meaningful real-world experiences*. The belief that learning should be meaningful and experiential is not new. Dewey, Piaget, and Vygotsky all stressed the importance of learning by doing. Resnick (1987) discussed the importance of students seeing the connections between what they learn in school and real-life, as well as the importance of students being active learners. For many, this is the heart of service-learning—making real-world connections with academic, personal, or other learning. However, for an experience to be meaningful, one must consider the context in which that experience occurs and how students understand and build upon that experience.

Constructivism is a broad term often used to describe how students learn as they actively "construct" their own understanding of the world and their own learning through interactions with information, concepts, materials, and other people. During service-learning, these interactions occur in multiple settings or contexts, from planning periods to the service site to reflection. Students construct their own understanding of what happens and their role in the events while also making connections with academic, social, or other learning. Hanley (1994) noted, "Meaning is intimately connected with experience. Students come into a classroom with their own experiences and a cognitive structure based on those experiences" (p. 2). Yet, when one looks at the service-learning research, such contextual characteristics are often considered secondary, if at all. This chapter examines why such a model for service-learning research is lacking in most cases.

This chapter builds upon the belief that learning occurs as students construct their own understanding of the world around them. Service-learning enriches a student's world, providing new experiences and challenges. Through planning, service, and reflection, students are encouraged to examine the tasks at hand, to develop plans for dealing with the obvious and unexpected, to take action, and to consider how these actions are understandable given other academic and life knowledge. Service-learning is neither passive nor solitary. Rather, students deal with real-life activities in naturalistic settings. It is these features that make service-learning unique from most other types of learning and these features that need to be considered by researchers.

Designs and Methodologies That Include Context Variables

The context of service-learning is a somewhat amorphous and broad concept. It can refer to where service-learning occurs, who participates, the training received, the reflective activities, and a wide range of other features. It is broad because service-learning can involve so many different activities and occur in so many different places. To create a framework for understanding how the service-learning context can be incorporated into a research study context, it is defined here in four ways. These categories were developed for the purposes of hypothesis testing and data analysis. It is important to recognize they are not mutually exclusive and frequently do not exist on a scaled interval. Some characteristics fall within multiple categories, depending upon the focus of the hypothesis or analyses. The first context discussed is the *site context*. That is, where and how a student performs the community service in which they engage. Four site level contexts are presented. The *background context* includes student background, teacher background, school/program characteristics, and community characteristics. It includes what students and teachers bring to the service-learning experience and the environment in which the experiences occur. A *reflection context* and the *planning context* both bisect the site and background contexts. Both are essential components of service-learning, used by practitioners to support service site activities and both are related to the background context.

Overarching the entire context are the *learning goals* and *service goals* established by the program. It is these goals that should drive all service-learning activities and should be the basis for selection of research outcomes to study. While it may be possible to identify broad learning goals, such as increased engagement in school or broad service goals such as helping others, most learning and service goals are more program specific. They may, to differing degrees, be affected by the various contexts of service-learning. This chapter is not concerned with the specific service or learning outcomes that a researcher chooses to study. It is assumed these outcome areas were carefully selected, theoretically grounded, and appropriate to the program. It is also assumed that the sample size is adequate for the analyses that are performed. The focus here is on the level of specificity with which researchers should seek to understand where and how service-learning occurs.

THE CONTEXT FRAMEWORK

In this section a framework is presented that describes the level of specificity with which the data can be collected. A challenge in presenting this framework is the selection of which variables to include and discuss within each level. As noted above, some characteristics may appear within two levels. Further complicating this is that service-learning is often influenced by and has an influence upon affective and psychological beliefs and attitudes, general dispositions, and behaviors. The characteristics discussed under each level were selected based upon prior research, practical experiences, and the author's beliefs about the nature of service-learning. The names selected to represent each context are similarly based upon experience and beliefs. Different researchers could easily use different terms. The key point is that while studies of service-learning can be presented as a nested design, where students are embedded within sites, sites within schools, and schools within communities, the work is complicated by factors that do not automatically fall into specific levels.

WHAT IS THE *SITE CONTEXT?*

Collecting data about the site context involves understanding and documenting what we mean by *site* and where students engage in service-learning. The site context has four levels of specificity, beginning with the most general and ending with a highly individualized description of a student's experiences.

Level 1a

At Level 1a the focus is on service-learning. That is, a program is broadly defined as service-learning and the question is, do students benefit from participating in this program? When more than one school is sampled, the data are aggregated and simply identified as service-learning. Thus, the *context* is the presence or absence of service-learning. Research at this level might collect and analyze pre-/post-surveys, often contrasting results with data from a comparison group.

Level 1b

At Level 1a, the program is only identified as "service-learning," while at Level 1b a specific program model is selected for study. It is well recognized that a wide variety of programs fall under the umbrella of service-learning. They may have very different goals, use different materials, and support different activities. At Level 1b researchers select a particular model, such as Learn and Serve Programs (e.g., Melchior, 1999, Melchior & Bailis, 2002) or the Helper Model Programs (e.g., Switzer, Simmons, Dew, Regalski, & Wang, 1995). Thus, what differentiates Level 1a and Level 1b is the specificity of the program selected. There is more similarity among programs in the sample at Level 1b. While Level 1b controls more of the variability across programs by including programs that are similar, it somewhat lessens the ability to generalize because the focus is on a specific program type.

Level 2

At Level 2 students are sampled from more than one school or program and the researcher considers possible differences due to school or program. For example, several schools in the same community (e.g., Hecht, 2002) or from across the country (e.g., Melchior, 1999; Scales, Blyth, Berkas, & Kielsmeier 2000) are studied. When the data show that students are similar across different locations, one has greater confidence that any change is due to the program and not other characteristics within the school, such as an individual school that broadly encourages the types of traits being studied. The difference between Level 1 and Level 2 is that the school is included in the design. The concepts of service-learning (as in 1a above) or a specific model (as in 1b above) are also relevant here. Level 2 recognizes that although schools may implement similar programs, these programs are likely to differ *across* schools. When characteristics of the school or program are considered, they provide a background context, as described below.

Level 3a

At Level 3a, the researcher not only considers the service-learning experience, but also further differentiates between types of experiences that a student has as part of service-learning. For example, Learn and Serve America asks grantees to quantify the number of students working at service sites, such as an educational, environmental, public safety, health, government, business, and/or community-based organization. At Level 3a information is collected about the *type of service site* or *service project* in which a student is involved. Researchers may focus on one type of program, such as only studying environmental service-learning projects. Other researchers may decide to contrast students who are engaged in different types of projects, such as comparing students in an environmental service-learning project with students who provide service at a senior center. This is typically the most detailed level at which studies report data.

Level 3b

A more comprehensive design includes information about the "setting within the setting." That is, a study will differentiate not only type of site (e.g., mentoring), but within types of sites (e.g., mentoring in Classroom A or mentoring in Classroom B). At this level of contextual specificity the researcher considers the exact location where the student engaged in service and acknowledges that different opportunities may be provided depending upon where service occurs.

Level 4

The most precise level is not only identification of the specific site (e.g., Ms. A's preschool classroom), but also what occurs within that classroom. Thus, the researcher looks at students' service activities that occur within the site. For example, information about whether students work with peers, with others, read, write, draw, and so forth, might be collected. In this way, students within a single site (e.g., Classroom A) may have very different experiences if they are engaged in different activities.

WHAT ARE THE *BACKGROUND CONTEXTS*?

Service-learning does not only occur at the site and does not only involve the student. The background context includes the general environment in which these activities occur. It involves the student (e.g., experience, demographics), teacher (e.g., training, attitudes), school/program (e.g., mission, resources), and out-of-school community (e.g., type, needs). Other background contexts are possible for individual programs.

Student Level

Students bring a variety of experiences, expectations, and skills to any service-learning experience. Age, gender, grade, ethnicity, and academic achievement are background student level data that are typically collected. With service-learning, information about prior volunteer experience, parental involvement in volunteerism, and community awareness may be important factors. Other variables should be identified by researchers based on knowledge of their student sample, school, and the service-learning program.

Classroom–Teacher Level

As with students, teachers bring a wide range of experiences, expectations, training, pedagogy, attitudes, and beliefs to the service-learning experience. These have an impact upon the opportunities provided to students and most likely on the outcomes that students demonstrate from the experience.

School–Program Level

This category was separated from the site context because it represents characteristics of the school that can impact the service-learning experience. Some characteristics are descriptive of the school (e.g., size, location, number of teachers, mission of school). Other characteristics are more specific to the service-learning program; for example, scheduling of the site experience (e.g., during a content class, as part of service-learning class, after school); frequency of service-learning and site visits; fit with school's mission; number of classes involved; and training.

Out-of-School Community

The out-of-school community context includes both general information about the community, such as whether it is an urban, rural, or suburban area, as well as situationally-specific data that may relate to current events within a community. For example, if a community recently experienced an increase in the crime rate, youth may be reluctant to walk to a service site. Particular types of service-learning projects may be viewed more positively in some communities than in others.

MEDIATING VARIABLES

Two important elements of service-learning are not included in the above framework: planning and reflection. These mediating variables are especially important because, *all service-learning programs are expected to have planning and reflection as part of their program.* However, these two components are rarely included as specific and unique contexts for learning. While their presence may be noted and their characteristics minimally described, they are rarely included as key elements of the research design.

Planning

Perhaps even less frequently discussed than reflection, is the planning that occurs for service-learning. Planning, however, can be a critical time for students to acquire and practice the skills needed for their service site work. For example, if students will be testing water, planning activities may include learning the needed science. The types of training, level of student involvement, resources, research needed, and time spent are critical parts of the planning activities, but these are rarely quantified in a study of service-learning.

Reflection

Although reflection is considered a key component of service-learning, limited work has examined how reflection contributes to student outcomes. Instead, reflection tends to be included as a defining characteristic of the experience, rather than part of the context. Service-learning practitioners often talk about the types of reflective activities, how closely the activities are linked to the service experience, and the frequency of reflection, but these descriptions are rarely included in a study of service-learning.

HOW INFORMATION ABOUT CONTEXT IS USED AND REPORTED

This framework for describing the context of service-learning provides some guidance about the types of information that researchers should consider when designing studies of service-learning. It shows that multiple levels of variability can affect a study's results. Even if there were very small differences across only half the levels listed above, it would most likely min-imize observed differences, whether assessed using a pre-/post-design or service-learning-comparison design. In this section, an overview is pre-sented of the ways that researchers might handle the types of data listed above. Examples using real data are presented later in the chapter to high-light parts of this discussion.

Ignore It—Reporting at Level 1

Although few researchers would choose to completely ignore the vari-ability among and within programs, this is certainly the easiest way to deal with the complexity of the data. Unfortunately, a study that does provide any information about such contextual data will add little to the field in terms of real knowledge. If the findings indicate "service-learning students were more self-efficacious than non-service-learning students," it provides little information to practitioners or researchers who want to know how they can use this information to understand their own program.

Describe the Program—Reporting at Level 2

At the descriptive level, researchers present detailed information about the service-learning program collected from one or more sources. This information is presented to help readers understand the program and determine whether or not the program studied is similar to their own or others. Tables or graphs may be included that *describe* the program, stu-dents, and sites. For example, using a hypothetical program:

> Students visit a senior center once a week for one hour during the spring semester. While there they spend time talking with the seniors and helping them with a variety of projects. The senior center is located within the com-munity and many of the students have grandparents who attend the center. Homeroom teachers accompany students to their sites.

The information provides critical data for understanding the generalizabil-ity of the study. It does not, however, provide information that can be used to understand the service-learning experience.

Use the Data for Post-Hoc Descriptive Interpretation—Reporting at Level 3

Some researchers have used data about service-learning experiences to understand and interpret their results after running the analyses. For example, if differences are found between service-learning and non-service-learning students on acceptance of diversity, but not on academics, researchers may interpret the results using the program descriptions. Using another hypothetical example:

> Examination of program descriptions indicates that five of the six service-learning programs developed projects that were designed to encourage cross-cultural understanding. This was done in response to an observed need in these schools.

Such an interpretation provides more guidance for generating than testing hypotheses.

Include the Data Within the Analyses— Reporting at Level 4

Although more complex, data can be included within the analyses, to do so requires that the data be collected at the start of the program in a way that will allow for their inclusion in the analyses. It is only by including such information that researchers will be able to provide descriptions, such as:

> Students who spent at least 20 hours interacting with senior citizens and preparing an oral history project demonstrated an increased understanding of what life was like during World War II compared with their peers who read about the depression from a first-hand report.

The list presented earlier in this chapter provides a very general overview of how information about context can be used in studies of service-learning. The next section builds upon this discussion by examining differences across the site context levels and the types of results that might be found.

DIFFERENCES ACROSS LEVELS OF SITE

To illustrate the contextual framework presented in this chapter, data from the Service-Learning Impact Study are presented. These data were collected as part of a larger study of service-learning in middle schools.[1] Although the data were collected from numerous sources, the study did not fully assess the context as described here. In fact, the framework was developed based upon analyses of, and reflection about, data collected from this study.

The Example: The Service-Learning Impact Study

The Service-Learning Impact Study spanned three years, examined a wide range of student outcomes, and included data from both service-learning and comparison students. The pre-/post-design relied upon a combination of surveys, interviews, and observations to document student outcomes and service-learning site experiences. The study was designed to include some of the key variables and components in the framework described previously. For the purposes of illustration, this chapter only examines data from service-learning students. That is, the emphasis is on examination across site level, not between service-learning and comparison students.

Sample

The sample consisted of approximately 1,200 middle school students from six schools in the New York City region. Students attended schools with an exemplary service-learning program based on the Helper Model (as in Level 1b). An excerpt from the annual report about this project presents a description of the program and sample (Level 2 Reporting).

> The Helper Model was developed in 1982 specifically for middle school students. It is based on the belief that participation in service-learning benefits the community by helping to meet real community needs and benefits young adolescents by providing opportunities for growth and learning not encountered in the traditional school setting. The criteria for inclusion in the study was that the program was operational for at least two years, service-learning was a required part of the curriculum, and staff of the Helpers Network believed it was a well-organized and well run program. In addition project staff interviewed teachers and administrators at each school and made one site visit before the final selection. The two inner city/urban, two urban fringe, and two suburban schools included ethnically mixed student populations with approximately equal numbers of boys and girls. Each program included a minimum weekly reflection component and at least a 10-week service experience. Students participated in service-learning at over 50 different sites that included preschools, schools for handicapped, elementary school classrooms, special education classes, school-based sites, offices, libraries, senior citizens centers, and parks. Exhibit 1 highlights some of the program and school characteristics.

When presented as a table, the same data provide another overview of the sample as in Exhibit 1.

EXHIBIT 1
School and Program Characteristics

Program	Location	Number of Students	Percent Free or Reduced Lunch	Percent Minority Students	Year Program Began	Grades in Service-Learning	Duration of Program Length	Intensity: Frequency of Site Visits
School 1	Suburban	504	7%	18%	1993	8	10 weeks	Daily
School 2	Inner city	425	85%	98%	1990	8	40 weeks	Once a week
School 3	Urban Fringe	150	33%	41%	1992	5,6,7,8	40 weeks	Once a week
School 4	Suburban	600	8%	22%	1994	6	20 weeks	Twice monthly
School 5	Inner city	1500	99%	99%	1992	6,7,8	40 weeks	Once a week
School 6	Urban Fringe	1500	60%	58%	1989	7	20 weeks	Once a week

Data Collection

For the Service-Learning Impact Study, data were collected at the student, school, and site levels. Since the framework was a result of this study, and was *not* the guiding framework for its design, the study does not follow all or even most of the recommendations presented above.

Student Level Data

A paper and pencil survey booklet was used to collect data from all service-learning students at the start of the school year and again at the end of their service-learning experience. These data were used to assess student outcomes in several areas (e.g., affect toward school and service-learning, academic skills and involvement, interpersonal relations, self-efficacy). The survey booklets included several well-established assessment tools as well as measures constructed for this study.

School Level Data

A school survey was completed by the principal or assistant principal to collect information about the school and service-learning program, including its mission and goal(s) statement and operation. Additional data were obtained from city and state statistics.

Site Level Data

A two-page survey was used to collect data from site coordinators concerning the types of activities in which students were engaged at the site, the learning opportunities for students, and their beliefs about the benefits to the site for participating in service-learning. (It should be noted that although some attempts were made to collect Level 4 data, most of the study is based on Level 3 data collection.)

An Illustration of How Not Considering the Context Can Conceal or Mislead

Since the study did not collect data at all levels, the example is not comprehensive. However, enough data are provided to highlight the importance of considering context when discussing service-learning. The outcome variable examined is students' self-reported perceptions of the academic benefits of service-learning using a 7-item summed scale that could range from 7 (very little perceived benefit) to 28 (very strong perceived benefit).

Site Level 1

At Level 1, the focus is on examining whether participation in service-learning has an impact on students' perceptions of the academic benefits from service-learning. Based upon a matched pairs *t*-test of students' self-reported scale scores, a statistically significant difference was found. The means indicated that on the post-assessment survey students reported *less* or *lower* academic benefits from service-learning then on the pre-assessment. Although both means are relatively close (pre-assessment = 18.48, standard deviation = 5.5; post-assessment = 15.26, standard deviation = 6.3), the difference was great enough to be statistically significant, $t(1130) = 12.251$, $p < .001$.

This result, although somewhat discouraging, highlighted a finding that the author has consistently reported: students often report high expectations for service-learning at the start of a program, and over time, these expectations *decrease*. Based upon student and teacher interviews, it appears that by the end of the service-learning program, students have developed more realistic expectations of what they can learn from a one or two hour service-learning experience, once or twice a week. (This represents a Level 3 Reporting interpretation.) While the mean differences reported above support previous findings of higher initial than end expectations, they provide little information about the service experience or the impact service-learning has upon students.

Site Level 2

At the second level, the focus is on examining whether students view the academic impact of service-learning differently depending upon the school they attend. In other words, is the impact different for different programs? At the simplest level, a one-way analysis of variance (ANOVA) can be performed to explore differences across schools. Because it was found that pre-scores were somewhat inflated, for illustrative purposes, only post-scores were compared. In a more controlled analysis pre-scores would be used as covariates.

EXHIBIT 2
Mean Responses to Post-Service-Learning Ratings of Academic Learning
from the Experience by School

School/program	Number of students	M	SD
School 1	118	10.5	4.7
School 2	79	12.1	4.8
School 3	142	13.3	4.8
School 4	214	14.7	4.9
School 5	211	15.2	6.0
School 6	269	12.2	4.8

Examination of Exhibit 2 suggests that School 5 and School 1 are somewhat different than the other schools. Results from an ANOVA confirms there are differences among the five schools $F(5, 1027) = 19.04$ $p < .001$. Knowledge about School 5 and School 1 provides some assistance in interpreting these results (a post-hoc descriptive interpretation, Level 3 Reporting). School 5 has service-learning infused into a variety of academic courses, unlike the other schools where it is a specific class, such as home and careers (a course similar to home economics). School 1 has a very brief service-learning experience (10 weeks in contrast to the other programs that are at least 20 weeks). While the results make sense, they provide minimum guidance for service-learning practitioners interested in understanding how service-learning impacts students. The data have not tested the hypothesis that curriculum infusion leads to stronger beliefs about the academic benefits of service-learning nor that shorter service-learning experiences lead to weaker beliefs about the academic benefits. Rather, explanations are sought *after* the analyses revealed possible differences.

Site Level 3

At the third site level, the focus is on the type of site experience. Although it would be preferable to also include school level variables, for illustration only, differences according to sites are presented. As the means in Exhibit 3 reveal, the sample included a range of site types and varied number of students within each. Furthermore, although not indicated in the table, there is a strong relationship between site type and school. For example, School 3 provides only site opportunities at regular or handicapped preschools, but this information is not reflected in the table.

EXHIBIT 3

Mean Responses to Post-Service-Learning Ratings of Academic Learning from the Experience by Type of Site

Type of site	Number of students	M	SD
Regular preschool	401	12.0	4.9
Handicapped preschool	145	14.0	5.0
Elementary school	108	12.0	5.2
Elementary special education	61	16.0	4.7
Senior center	11	12.0	7.8
Nursing home	23	13.0	4.6
Special education with peers	48	13.3	5.1
Environmental	93	17.0	6.0
School-based	118	15.6	4.9
Office	17	13.4	3.5
Library	4	12.5	4.4

Ignoring these confounding factors, Exhibit 3 indicates that there are differences across type of service site. For example, responses of students engaged in environmental projects showed the strongest perceived academic benefits after participating in service-learning, followed by students who worked with elementary special education students. An analysis of variance $F(10,1018) = 12.08$, $p < .001$ indicated there were statistically significant differences. However, interpretation of this finding as demonstrating that "students perceive more academic learning when they work at an environmental project" would be very misleading. *All students who were in an environmental project came from School 5!* That is, the same school with the highest mean ratings of perceived academic benefits was also the school with all the environmental programs. The lowest mean was for students who worked at a regular preschool as a site. This represented a composite or average of several different schools. The finding highlights a related issue: researchers must have knowledge of the program in order to interpret the data. The result further suggests that at a minimum of Level 3 Reporting/interpretation is necessary.

Site Level 4

Unfortunately, enough data were not collected as part of the Service-Learning Impact Study at the fourth level of site specificity to allow for analyses. Based upon an examination of the data, student interviews, and observations, it was evident that students within sites were often having very different experiences. However, the data also pointed to the need to collect data from multiple sources.

During the final year of the study, pilot work was completed to examine how information about site activities could be quantified. Data were collected from up to four sources: students, site-director, site-representative (person directly working with the student), and service-learning teachers. Observations were also conducted at a few sites. Responses varied widely across sources. It was unclear whether these differences reflected different knowledge about what students actually did at a site or different perceptions about these activities. Although attempts were made to make the response options concrete (e.g., reads to others) even these appeared to be open to interpretation. The few observations that were conducted indicated a further problem. Not only did student activities within *the same* site differ, but also, activities differed from week to week. The issue appeared to become both the amount and quality of the various opportunities that are provided at the site.

MOVING TOWARD LEVEL 4: DATA COLLECTION AND INTERPRETATION

What the above results clearly reveal is that researchers *must* be knowledgeable about and understand the multiple contexts in which service-learning occurs. The findings also reveal the complexity and inter-relationships among these levels and contexts. When students are nested within sites, and sites are nested within schools, it is reasonable to assume that the site contexts, background contexts, and mediating variables will all affect the students' performance on the outcome measures. This becomes even more likely when one considers the wide range of site experiences likely with service-learning.

Since traditional ANOVAs and regression analyses fail to adequately separate individual variation and site variation from school variation, additional analytic methods are needed to fully interpret the data. Hierarchical Linear Modeling (HLM) is one approach that could be used (e.g., Bryk & Raudenbush, 1992). However, these programs are often cumbersome to use and difficult to interpret. The results are often far removed from the original data, and practitioners often find it difficult to see how the results are meaningful within the context of the real service-learning experience. Furthermore, it is often difficult to decide which variables to include and which to eliminate when applying these methods. As this chapter illustrates, there are a multitude of variables that might be reasonably included in a multi-level design analysis such as HLM. Selection of those variables to include or exclude should be driven by both theory and the data.

One solution to variable selection is to use something like the Approximation Model developed by Schmidt (2000). This approach uses a series of traditional regression analyses to explore the data and select salient variables for a full HLM Analysis. Schmidt described this method as a "first pass" that allows researchers to intelligently select variables and gain important insights into the data. The Approximation Model is also more easily interpreted without a sophisticated understanding of multi-level modeling. Although HLM programs continue to be made more user friendly, interpretation still relies upon either the researchers' faith in the program or a fairly high level of understanding of the approach. For these reasons, a full HLM analysis is not presented here. Instead the following section briefly describes the Approximation Model and the result when applied to these data. More detailed results can be found in Hecht and Schmidt (2000). HLM would allow for the entire model to be simultaneously fitted and should be considered the final step in the process of exploring service-learning data within context.

An Example Using the Approximation Model

The Approximation Model involves the calculation of two sets of regression coefficients. First a general linear regression analysis is examined to help establish the context for later analyses. Then regression slopes and intercepts are calculated for each individual site using individual student level predictors to predict student outcomes on the impact variables. These slopes and intercepts become two new dependent variables. Each is then regressed onto the site level and school level characteristics, producing two new sets of regression coefficients.

To illustrate use of the Approximation Model, one outcome variable was selected: *perceived academic benefits of service-learning*. Students were asked how much service-learning helped them learn in seven academic areas, and a summed score was calculated (alpha reliability = .843.) Seven student-level variables were included:

- Academic Expectations for Service-Learning: a summed score about expectations in seven academic areas (alpha reliability = .848.);
- Developmental Opportunities for School Classes (Newmann & Rutter, 1983), an 18-item summed score;
- Affect Toward School: a summed score of ratings of school (e.g., feel trusted, grown-up, with alpha reliability of .79);
- Grade;
- Gender;
- Whether or not parents volunteer in community; and

- Whether nor not students were previously involved in service-learning.

Site level variables included:

- Site type (dummy coded): regular school (preschool and elementary), special education school (preschool and elementary), senior center/nursing home, office/library, and environmental;
- Average rating of site as excellent, good, fair or poor;
- Whether or not site coordinators had received training;
- Time at site: ranging from 10 to 40 weeks;
- Student opportunities to take responsibility (reported by site coordinator);
- Student opportunities to learn and work with others (reported by site coordinator);
- Student opportunities to problem solve (reported by site coordinator); and
- Beliefs that service-learning had benefited the site (site coordinator rating).

Step 1

The first regression analysis examined the outcome variable *academic benefits of service-learning*, ignoring site type. Academic benefits were regressed onto the seven student level variables (gender, parental volunteer involvement, grade, whether or not new to service-learning, expectations for service-learning, perceived developmental opportunities in school, and affect toward school). These variables accounted for only 9 percent of the variance in academic benefits. The significant predictors were grade level, whether or not the student was new to service-learning, and whether a student's parent was involved in volunteer work. This overall analysis, however, did not take into account differences across sites. For example, even though the various individual-level predictors explained only 9 percent of the variance in perceived academic benefits, it is unknown if certain sites do a better job of influencing perceived academic benefits than others.

Step 2

Separate regression analyses were performed for each site. The results (see Exhibit 4) showed a wide variability by site. The amount of variance

EXHIBIT 4

Variation in Intercept and Slope Coefficients by Site: Predicting Perceived
Academic Benefits of Service-Learning Post-Service-Learning

	N	*Minimum*	*Maximum*	*M*	*SD*
Constant	74	-163.33	82.58	6.32	46.57
Gender	49	-12.47	71.45	1.14	11.15
Parents volunteer	45	-167.27	49.82	-1.49	27.74
Grade	6	-4.59	17.48	4.28	9.93
New to service-learning?	5	-1.07	28.95	5.72	13.03
Expectation service-learning helps academics	59	-22.36	2.00	-.55	3.03
Developmental opportunities in school	53	-1.24	12.27	.20	1.78
Affect toward school	73	-11.18	8.49	.15	2.17

explained ranged from practically zero to as much as 54 percent ($R = .734$; site was a preschool at School 1). There was similar variability in the strength of the various other predictors. In particular, for the variable that measures parental involvement in volunteer activities, the slope coefficients ranged from -167.27 to 49.82, with a mean of -1.43 (significance levels ranged from .03 to .98, with a mean of .51). This finding suggests that, in general, a parent's involvement in volunteerism seems to negatively affect a student's beliefs in the academic benefits of service-learning. Thus, parental involvement is a significant predictor at some sites, but not at all important at others. This may partly be a function of school differences (i.e., parents of students at some schools volunteer more than parents of students at other schools). Grade-level expectations for academic benefits from service-learning and perceived developmental opportunities in school also appear to be important. In summary, across the different sites, students' beliefs that service-learning provided academic benefits was best predicted by *different* site variables.

Step 3

The next step was to predict the intercept and slope terms using the site level data. These regressions were conducted to explain the variability in the slopes and intercepts resulting from the first level regressions. The site level variables explained a significant amount of variability in the intercepts across sites ($R = .654$). Variability in the intercepts, which can be interpreted as the expected academic benefits post-test score for students with a value of zero on all the predictors, ranged from -163.33 to 82.58

(mean = 6.32). Because these variables were not centered, their interpretation is somewhat unclear. However, the findings indicate that different sites have different impacts on student beliefs concerning the academic benefits of service-learning. The best predictor at the site level was the time at the site (ß = 2.008, p = .052), which would indicate that the longer a child stays at a site, the higher the perceived academic benefit, independent of individual level predictors. Next the author explored the interpretation of the prediction of the variability in the slope coefficient for a variable that in the overall regression looked important (i.e., whether a student's parent is involved in volunteerism). For this second level model, the site level predictors account for 69 percent of the variance in the variability in the slopes for this predictor (R = .829). The significant predictors of this variability were the amount of time a student spent at the site (ß = 3.458, p = .014) and whether a student worked in a regular education classroom (ß = 89.287, p = .024). So, for students in a regular education setting and with more time at that setting, parental experience with volunteerism is a stronger, more positive predictor of whether parents believe service-learning provides academic benefits. Since the data were not centered, further fine interpretations are impossible. However, these results clearly indicate that both site characteristics and student characteristics affect student outcomes. By only focusing on individual student level predictors or only on site differences one fails to understand how service-learning impacts students. Furthermore, if the ultimate goal of service-learning research is to help practitioners develop and support high quality service-learning programs we need to understand under what conditions service-learning is most effective.

WHAT DOES IT ALL MEAN?

Researchers interested in studying service-learning need to consider the multiple levels of the experience in both the design and analyses phases. Selection of salient contextual variables can be difficult and at times overwhelming. When the service-learning impact study began, the focus was on site type only. Based upon work with the schools and students and based upon an examination of the data, it became clear that there was a need to look much further and deeper. Studies need to be designed that incorporate the various levels of specificity into the assessment tools and sampling procedures. Service-learning programs need to be selected that are representative of the major contexts being studied and to include adequate sample sizes to allow for the needed statistical analyses. Using existing data sets and applying a wide range of analyses, from simple t tests to HLM, can provide some guidance for selection for variables of study. Exhibit 5 was developed based upon such analyses and presents a summary of variables that

EXHIBIT 5
Preliminary List of Key Context Variables

Context	*Key characteristics related to outcome*	*Characteristics that appear less strongly related to student outcomes*
Site	• Characteristics of the site (e.g., student responsibilities, level of activity) • Close relationship between school and site • Types of student activities (e.g., reading, writing, problem solving, etc.) • Type of site (e.g., preschool, senior center)	• Location of site
Program	• Frequency and duration of site visits • Adequate time for planning & implementation • Structured time for reflection • Involvement of teacher in both site and reflection • Clearly defined learning goals	• How implemented (e.g., gradewide, course) • Years program is operational
School	• Administrative support for program • School climate (and level of child-centered approach to education) • Year when study is conducted • Changes in staff, structure, and so on.	• Socioeconomic status • Location (e.g., urban, suburban, rural) • Size of school • Ethnic makeup of students • Number of years engaged in service-learning
Student	• Parental involvement in volunteer activities • Gender • Age • Expectations for service-learning • Prior experience with service	• Academic ability
Teacher	• Teacher buy-in to program • Level of training about service-learning • Attitudes about service-learning	• Experience of teacher in classroom • Age • Gender
Reflection	• Structured time provided • Facilitated by adult who is knowledgeable about the site • Diversity of experiences • Links with curriculum	• Where it occurs (at site or school)
Planning	• Training related to service-activities • Links with curriculum	• Who provides the training

may be important to more fully understand service-learning and its impact on students. These are variables that might be included in a multi-level analysis, whether the full HLM or using the Approximation Model, to further refine the variable selection process. As noted throughout this chapter, selection of variables is critical and must be guided by theory and data. It is also important that each of the levels be considered, or if not included, a rationale for their exclusion or collapse be presented.

It is likely that some of the contexts will prove to be more important than others. However, the framework presented here provides a starting point for modeling solutions that may eventually lead to a more comprehensive understanding of service-learning and impact on students. Specifically, the focus needs to shift, not from whether service- learning is a benefit to students, but rather, under what conditions is service-learning a benefit in which areas to which students.

There are additional ways to use this framework. A researcher could compare programs that differ on key features. This is neither just a sampling issue (selection of specific programs based on key features) nor a data analysis issue (testing for differences based on the presence or absence of the key feature). Rather it requires such questions be incorporated into the initial design. The right programs need to be studied. Adequate data need to be collected. Complex analyses need to be completed.

NOTE

1.   Details concerning the full sample can be obtained from the author.

REFERENCES

Bryk, A. S., & Raudenbush, S. W. (1992). *Hierarchical linear models: Applications and data analysis methods.* Thousand Oaks, CA: Sage.

Hanley, S. (1994). On constructivism. Retrieved June 1, 2003, from http://www.towson.edu/csme/mctp/Essays/Constructivism.txt

Hecht, D. (2002). *A study of the effects of participation in the helper model of service-learning in early adolescence.* Unpublished report, Center for Advanced Study in Education, City University of New York.

Hecht, D., & Schmidt, A. E. (2000, April). *Service-learning: Relating student outcomes with service experiences.* Presentation at the American Educational Research Association Annual Meeting, New Orleans, LA.

Melchior, A. (1999). *Summary Report: National Evaluation of Learn and Serve America.* Waltham, MA: Brandeis University, Center for Human Resources.

Melchior, A., & Bailis, L. N. (2002). Impact of service-learning on civic attitudes and behaviors of middle and high school youth: Findings from three national evaluations. In A. Furco & S. H. Billig (Eds.), *Advances in service-learning research: Vol. 1. Service-learning: The essence of the pedagogy* (pp. 201–222). Greenwich, CT: Information Age Publishing.

Resnick, L. B. (1987). Learning in school and out. *Educational Researcher, 16*, 13–20.

Scales, P., & Blyth, D. (1997, Winter). Effects of service-learning on youth: What we know and what we need to know. *The Generator,* 6–9.

Scales, P. C., Blyth, D. A., Berkas, T. H., & Kielsmeier J. C. (2000). The effects of service-learning on middle school students' social responsibility and academic success. *Journal of Early Adolescence, 20,* 332–358.

Schmidt, A. E. (2000). An approximation of a hierarchical logistic regression model used to establish the predictive validity of scores on an exam with a dichotomous criterion. *Educational and Psychological Measurement, 60(3),* 463–478.

Switzer, G., Simmons, R., Dew, M., Regalski, J., & Wang, C. (1995). The effect of a school-based helper program on adolescent self-image, attitudes, and behavior. *Journal of Early Adolescence, 15,* 429–455.

CHAPTER 3

DILEMMAS OF SERVICE-LEARNING TEACHERS

Katherine M. Kapustka

The goal of this qualitative case study of one urban middle school was to investigate and portray teachers' beliefs about the dilemmas they faced as they implemented service-learning in their classrooms and how they managed these dilemmas within their specific school context. Through an analysis of interview, observation, and document data gathered over a five-month period, three broad dilemmas emerged: needs of the server vs. needs of the served, traditional vs. experiential education, and teacher control vs. student independence. These dilemmas arose as teachers at the middle school attempted to reconcile the expectations of a variety of educational stakeholders, including parents, administrators, and state and local school boards, the needs of those at the service sites, and their own beliefs about teachers, teaching, and students. Using the language of dilemmas which allows for a consideration of "the macro in the micro" it became clear that the dilemmas identified existed partially because of a pervasive teacher culture that hinders work among teachers at a school and between teachers and individuals at service sites. Also, issues of school reform sustainability are inextricably linked to service-learning, both because service-learning is a reform itself, and because service-learning is impacted by other reforms, such as the move toward standardization of curriculum and assessment.

Deconstructing Service-Learning: Research Exploring Context, Participation, and Impacts
A Volume in: Advances in Service-Learning Research, pages 51–74.
ISBN: 1-59311-071-5 (hardcover), 1-59311-070-7 (pbk.)

INTRODUCTION

A middle school teacher identified this dilemma: at a local elementary school where his 7th-grade students provided service once a week, a pair of students was asked to assist the elementary teacher with clerical tasks, including stapling and cutting papers. While this teacher understood that his students were there to provide a service to the school, and should perform tasks that meet the needs of the school and its teachers, his goal, and the goal of the middle school in general, was to have the students interacting with and assisting the younger children. The middle school teacher was unsure whether to discuss his concerns with the teacher at the service site, at the risk of alienating her and appearing to be unconcerned about providing a needed service, or to accept the current situation, even though it did not fulfill his expectations or the program's goals. This dilemma, identified by a participant in this study, was just one example of the challenges faced by a service-learning teacher.

The Language of Dilemmas

This study is grounded in the belief that teachers are actively engaged in dealing with the dilemmas that occur as a result of conflicting belief systems and demands from within and outside the institution of the school. Berlak and Berlak (1981) provided the theoretical base for this assertion through their specific critique of the distinction between the "macro," that which relates to broad concerns of society as they relate to education, and the "micro," that which concerns individual components of schooling. Instead of accepting this chasm, the authors identified the language of dilemmas as a way to bridge the gap:

> Our effort is to cast these two concerns as one—to provide a language for examining the macro in the micro, the larger issues that are embedded in the particulars of the everyday schooling experience. (p. 4)

This characterization provided for an understanding of dilemmas of schooling grounded in the assumption that the work of educators in the classroom cannot be separated from the school, institutional, and bureaucratic contexts in which schooling occurs.

METHOD

This study was grounded in constructivist theory within the postpositivist paradigm of inquiry. In studying the nature of the dilemmas faced by teachers involved in service-learning, the goal of this research was to portray a "local and specific constructed reality" (Guba & Lincoln, 1998, p. 203). Although not specifically arguing for research guided by constructivist theories, Conrad and Hedin (1991) made a case for this type of research when they commented on the unique challenges of research on service-learning. They stated: "The fundamental difficulty is that service is not a single easily definable activity like taking notes in a lecture" (p. 746). The variety of meanings and manifestations of service-learning therefore necessitated a paradigmatic orientation and resulting methodology that allowed the researcher to consider the meanings and realities of individuals within a specific situation.

This study used an embedded case study approach (Yin, 1994). One middle school served as the case, and four service-learning teachers were specifically considered as important actors within the larger context of the school. Peshkin (1993) stated: "The assumption behind the story of any particular life is that there's something worth learning" (p. 25). For the purposes of this study, it was assumed that both the stories of the teachers and the school as a whole contained "something worth learning." The goal, therefore, was to construct, through interviews, observations, and document analysis, one interpretation of teachers' beliefs about the dilemmas they faced as they implemented service-learning within their specific school context.

Setting

Community Middle School for Service (CMSS)[1] opened in 1992 with the goal of providing a non-traditional education to students in Grades 5 through 8. During the semester this study was completed, there were 13 full-time teachers and approximately 160 students. This school was housed in the same building with a community high school and many facilities were shared. The students were organized into eight classes. Fifth- and sixth-grade students were taught in cross-graded classes, and 7th and 8th graders were taught separately. All students were involved in service activities for 60 minutes each week at local public and private preschools and elementary schools under the supervision of their advisory teachers.

Sample

The sample for this study included four of the eight advisory teachers who were directly involved in the preparation for, supervision of, and reflection after the service activities. The principal and a service site director were also interviewed, because each provided additional data toward understanding the contextual underpinnings of the dilemmas identified by the service-learning teachers. As integral facilitators of service-learning implementation, their insights were essential to understanding the larger context of service-learning at CMSS and the specifics on how the service-learning teachers negotiated the dilemmas they experienced.

Of the four primary participants, two teachers, Anne, with five years experience, and Lynn, with 30 years experience, taught all subjects to their cross-graded 5th/6th classes. Lynn was also the informal service-learning coordinator at the school. Chloe, a first-year English teacher, taught 7th and 8th grade and accompanied her 8th-grade homeroom to their service site. Al, an 11-year veteran, taught social studies to 7th and 8th graders and accompanied his 7th-grade homeroom to their service site.

Methods of Data Collection

Each of the four teachers participated in four 45-minute interviews during a five-month period. Each teacher was also observed three times during this period for between 8 and 12 hours. The principal and a service-site coordinator were each interviewed once for approximately 45 minutes. The researcher completed additional informal observations during lunch with the teachers, at a service-learning recognition dinner, and while spending time in the hallways and library between interviews. In order to provide context, relevant documents, including newspaper articles, service site and school brochures, school and district annual reports, and a school video, were also reviewed. Upon completion of the individual interviews and observations and the preliminary document analysis, one focus group was held with three of the four primary participants in order to discuss emerging themes.

DILEMMAS AT COMMUNITY
MIDDLE SCHOOL FOR SERVICE

On a daily basis, the teachers at CMSS considered the expectations of a variety of educational stakeholders as they engaged in the planning, implementation, and evaluation of their service-learning program. The principal, with the assistance of the 5th-/6th-grade teacher and informal service-learning coordinator, decided the logistical and programmatic details. He told the teachers the service sites where they should bring their students, which day they were scheduled to serve, and the duration of the service. At the service sites, the teachers who received the student volunteers exercised their rights to determine what the students would do while they were there and the roles the middle school teachers would play in their classrooms. As they engaged their students in service-learning, the middle school teachers had to consider their own beliefs about teachers, teaching, and students while remaining mindful of the expectations of parents and the mandates of state and local school boards. The confluence of these expectations resulted in three fundamental dilemmas that needed to be negotiated by these middle school teachers:

1. Needs of the server vs. needs of the served;
2. Standardized vs. experiential education; and
3. Teacher control vs. student independence.

Teachers' Views on Dilemmas

One of the goals of this study was to construct a portrayal of teachers' experiences with service-learning that previously has been missing from the body of empirical literature on this topic. For this reason, it was important to consider how the teachers felt about the concept of dilemmas as a way to represent their experiences. To accomplish this goal, teachers were provided with a brief explanation of the term (dilemma), and a non service-learning example was used to illustrate a possible educational application. They were then asked for their comments on whether they felt the term dilemma was appropriate for describing their experiences as service-learning teachers. In their responses, the teachers focused on, and seemed most satisfied with, the components of the conception of dilemmas that conveyed that there were many possible options for managing these challenges but not one option that could clearly be defined as the best or *right* alternative. They quickly agreed that in education in general, and with much of their service-learning work, they faced many challenges that could not be easily solved, because each possible solution created additional difficulties.

Needs of the Server vs. Needs of the Served

Within the field of service-learning, it is generally accepted that in the process of serving, students should meet a genuine need of the school or community while also furthering their own academic growth (Duits & Dorman, 1998; Luce, 1988; Schukar, Johnson, & Singleton, 1996; Waterman, 1997). Buchanan, Baldwin, & Rudisill (2002) furthered this assertion when they stated: "Community partners reap benefits from the program while student participants gain valuable knowledge and skills" (p. 28). While the work of Buchanan, Baldwin, & Rudisill focused on service-learning within teacher education, the belief that both students and the recipients of service should receive benefits from service-learning partnerships is central to the implementation of service-learning at all levels of schooling. In considering the implementation of service-learning at CMSS, however, it became clear that this desire for mutual benefit is easier stated in theory than achieved in practice.

The dilemma of "needs of the server vs. needs of the served" is grounded in the unique interplay between participants that characterizes service-learning. Because service-learning usually originates from a school, one emphasis is on providing educative experiences to further the academic and social development of the students. As the teachers and students leave the school to perform a service, they encounter individuals at the service sites who have the expectation that their needs will be met. While these two sets of expectations can often be addressed when students perform a service that is closely integrated with their academic curriculum, sometimes the goals of the teachers and the needs of those at the service sites are not closely aligned, and tensions may result.

Service Site Selection

In order to understand how the teachers at CMSS experienced and managed the dilemma of the needs of the server vs. the needs of the served, it is important to consider the nature of service-learning implementation at the school. One of the issues that each of the participating teachers mentioned was the difficulty in finding sites that met the needs of the middle school and that were willing to accept the service that a group of approximately 20 middle school students could provide once a week.

Historically at CMSS, the teachers and administration attempted to provide a variety of types of service. Several years ago, the goal was to have half of the students serve at local senior citizens' homes and half of the students serve at elementary and preschools, but parents resisted the idea of their children serving the senior population in the community. The 8th-grade students also had the opportunity to serve as junior docents at a local science museum, but this service was discontinued, because although the program worked reasonably well the first year, the second year a new volunteer coordinator at the site and the culture of the students led to insurmountable obstacles.

The teachers were aware of the school's difficulties placing students in service locations that were appropriate and acceptable, did not place undue burdens on the school, or cause conflict with the parents. However, each of the teachers who participated in this study expressed the concern that having the students serve at elementary and preschools for four years did not provide enough variety to keep the students motivated and engaged. Many teachers expressed a desire to expand the sphere of service, but explained that their ideas had been squelched for a variety of reasons. Anne described her experience when she suggested alternatives to the current service activities.

> We tried to do it in the past and usually there's something that we can't do. We've suggested the parks and we were told: 'Well, you know, they're just not picking up paper and things like that. You never know what's on the ground, especially . . . in [this] city.' You know, so you have things like that they can't do. We had talked about possibly cleaning off graffiti, and we were told we couldn't do that because of the chemicals that are used. We talked about doing work here, and they said: 'Well it's hard because, you know, we are a small school, so there wouldn't be enough placements for each child to do something.'

She explained that there were always reasons why the new ideas for service sites were unacceptable for every possibility she or other teachers suggested.

The difficulty finding suitable service sites influenced how the teachers dealt with the dilemma of meeting the needs of those at the site while still providing their students with educative experiences. An outsider might question why the teachers did not simply leave these sites and find ones where this dilemma did not exist, or was not so prevalent. As illustrated above, these teachers felt there were limited opportunities for their students to perform service, and since they were dedicated to the service-learning program at their school, they may have chosen to remain in less than ideal situations rather than risk leaving a site and not finding an acceptable replacement.

Needs of the Service Sites

One of the primary tenets of service-learning is that students provide a service to meet a genuine need of the school or community. A consideration of the teachers' thoughts on their experiences at the service sites, however, illustrated that this characteristic was not as unambiguous as it might originally appear. Throughout the interviews, three of the four teachers expressed concerns that the presence of their middle school students was met with ambivalence by some of the teachers the students ostensibly serve.

> Some of the teachers are very enthusiastic about getting the kids; others you kind of sense they've been coerced so they just sort of said, 'Ok, I'll take them.'

> [The service site coordinator] needs at least 10 teachers from her building that are willing to do this and unfortunately there will be those one or two teachers that will say: 'Ok, I'll do it, but I don't want any of the extras.'

Some of [the teachers] might appreciate the fact that these students come to teach, come to help them out. Some of them might not.

In contrast to the teachers' concerns that the services provided by their students were not valued by the teachers at the service sites, each teacher also commented that many teachers at the service sites appreciated the roles the students played in their classrooms, and were reaping the benefits of the assistance.

Some of them are pretty enthusiastic and want some help.

The teachers in general who participate in the program love it. They look forward to us coming.

I heard from some of the teachers that they are so happy that these kids were there. That makes you feel good, that they are that helpful.

Some of the teachers are extremely warm and they make sure that every time they see me they tell me how great their kid is doing: 'This kid is so great, the best I ever had. I wish I could keep him or her.'

Part of this dilemma, therefore, is embedded in the juxtaposition of attitudes displayed in these two sets of responses. The teachers negotiated situations in which the assistance of their students was met with attitudes that were at times contradictory. They continued to question whether they were providing a worthwhile service at the site, and by extension, they also questioned the overall value of their service-learning program.

Service Site and Teacher Expectations

Each teacher and the principal mentioned situations where the needs of the teachers at the service site conflicted with what they felt were the best interests of the middle school children, or the existing structures at the service site did not allow for the most educative experiences for the middle school students. While these conflicts were not so severe as to cause reconsideration of the program, the unanimity of the responses indicates that these occurrences were indeed significant. The teachers' responses exemplify the dilemma of the needs of the server vs. the needs of the served because they illustrate how easily the needs of those at the service site can come into conflict with the middle school educators' beliefs about what is best for their students.

The others are doing stuff like monitor work. They're shuffling papers, or stapling . . . I think some of them spend a lot of their time really just observing.

There was a teacher a few years ago I had a disagreement with. She had my students doing what I felt were inappropriate things, such as taking the smaller kids to the bathroom . . . but I explained to her, for health and safety reasons this was not something 5th- and 6th-graders should be doing.

I thought that some of the teachers would help them out, basically let them teach also . . . but they're not really in charge of the class. I thought that was going to happen, but [they're] basically just helping the teachers.

[The students] don't want to see the same thing every week. They want unpredictable things. . . They don't want to have circle time, snack time, computer time, go home. They want activities switched for them, which usually cannot be because they have a schedule.

[Sometimes] they'll give my kids clerical work to do in class. I prefer if they didn't do that. I mean, they're helping, but I would prefer that they are working with an individual child or small groups. I had one group that for the time that they were there all they did was snack. You know, they walked in at snack time and they helped them with the snack, and that wasn't terribly productive.

Beginning with the premise that a goal of service-learning is to provide assistance to meet a genuine need of the community, those at the service site might say activities such as helping with snacks, assisting with clerical tasks, or even taking children to the restroom meet the needs of the teachers at the service site. Al spoke specifically on this issue:

It may be that that's what the teacher needs done, and that may free up the teacher to do work with kids which she wouldn't normally be able to do. So they are . . . helping in an important job even though what they may be doing is menial.

The middle school teachers and principal, however, had other ideas of how their students could best make use of the experience while still being of service. Chloe, for example, wanted her students to have an opportunity to teach lessons, and Mike the principal, made it clear that he saw value in the interaction of the middle school students with the younger children.

Just as the middle school teachers and the teachers at the service sites had different views on what the students should be doing at the sites, some of the middle school teachers also experienced conflicts with regard to their roles at the service sites. Anne, for example, explained that while some teachers at the service site welcomed her into their classrooms, others told her directly that they found her presence disruptive.

There are some teachers who've been part of the program since the beginning because they love it; our goals are somewhat similar. They're very open about sharing what's happening in their classroom with me and I do the same. Whereas there are other teachers that look at it as: 'We don't mind having [the students] in the classroom, but we want nothing to do with you. We don't want you in here. We don't want to be bothered.'

While the other three teachers had not been told this so bluntly, they understood that the teachers at the service sites might be uncomfortable with their presence. Al explained:

> No teacher has even said ['Stay out of my classroom'] to me, but I know what it is to be a teacher with a class, and you really don't want to be interrupted . . . . It's really my choice based on my perception that a teacher doesn't really want to be interrupted.

Again these experiences speak to the dilemma of the needs of the server vs. the needs of the served because if the teachers' primary emphasis is on meeting the needs of those at the service sites, then they may choose to remain outside of the classrooms because this is what is best for those being served. However, if their main goal is to provide the middle school students with experiences that support their academic and social development, then the teachers might need to play a larger role in what goes on at the service site so that they can monitor and encourage their students, and evaluate the effectiveness of each service-learning placement.

In dealing with the issues of needs, goals, and expectations as they relate to this dilemma all teachers' behaviors must be viewed within the context of their beliefs that the continued acceptance of the middle school students at the service sites is somewhat precarious. Because they realized their service was not welcomed enthusiastically by some of the teachers who accepted the students in their classrooms, for the most part, when conflicts occurred, the middle school teachers remained silent. They avoided entering the classroom if they felt their presence would inconvenience the teachers and only approached the teachers when they felt their students were at risk.

Lynn was the most vocal in saying that the needs and expectations of the service site must come before the needs of her students, and she was the only one who couched explanation of her behaviors at the site in terms of meeting the needs of those being served. The rest of the teachers spoke of not wanting to impose on the teachers, who may or may not have wanted the middle school students in their classrooms in the first place. Lynn, however, focused on meeting the needs of the site and on helping her students get a positive experience within the guidelines set by the site.

> I would always put what the site wants first and then adapt my program around that . . . I've had teachers say: 'Please don't send them with projects. I have no time to do them.' Then I wouldn't . . . I think the important part is that the site gets what they want and what they need and that our children find a way to provide that service and still not lose academically.

For example, Lynn explained that when her students found themselves in classrooms where they were given very little responsibility, she advised the students to "make up for it by really getting involved with the children, and helping the children directly . . . so they get their fulfillment there. They may not get it as a teacher's assistant, but they get it in another way."

It is also important to note, however, that of the four teachers, Lynn had the strongest relationship with her site. Since the middle school opened in 1992, she had accompanied students to serve at this preschool, and she routinely commented on the positive relationships she had with the director and the teachers at the site. In striving to understand why Lynn might resolve the dilemma of the needs of the server vs. the needs of the served differently, or by using a different mindset from the other teachers, it is important to consider the context in which her students served. Unlike her colleagues, she felt that her students were wanted at the site, and she had a positive network to draw upon when there were difficulties. The rest of the teachers interviewed, however, made decisions based on the knowledge that the service site teachers did not necessarily welcome the middle school students.

STANDARDIZED VS. EXPERIENTIAL EDUCATION

Just as the teachers at CMSS struggled to meet their students' needs at the service site while also remaining mindful of the needs and expectations of the teachers there, these teachers also balanced the conflicts that inevitably arose when engaged in a traditionally unfamiliar educational activity; that is, service-learning in school and societal environments that focused on quantifiable evidence of student progress toward uniform goals as measured by standardized tests. The foundation of this dilemma exists in the tensions between the desire for quantitative measures of students' academic progress toward city and state educational goals, and the realization that the educators' experiences sometimes speak to a different type of student progress. Similarly, the teachers also endured an internal struggle because they realized the value of the service experiences, but wondered if it was acceptable to take so much time away from "academics."

Testing

The principal at CMSS said that when grant money was provided to the school by service-learning organizations, they often wanted proof of students' academic growth, usually in the form of quantitative analyses of test scores. Mike explained that this can be problematic not only because improvement in test scores might be related to factors other than service-learning, but also because the growth that occurs might not be academic, and most likely will not be measured easily by a pre-/post-test design. He said:

> [The grantmaking body] of course wanted quantifiable results, and I guess we could sit down and take test scores, and compare them point A and point B. I'm not quite sure service-learning is the reason why the test scores increased. I think we give the kids a lot of responsibility . . . I said if they come out of it with higher self-esteem and a good heart and a good understanding of the human condition . . . I think that's been a greater plus.

As a principal in a large urban district where academic performance, as measured on yearly standardized tests, is an ever-present concern, Mike was not downplaying the importance of academic success for his students. Instead, he was emphasizing that the benefits of service-learning might go beyond additional points on a standardized test.

While Mike's comments about service-learning made it clear that he was proud of the resulting student outcomes, teachers at the school seemed conflicted about spending time away from academics. Al, for example, expressed concern about the amount of teaching time lost when students were at the service-learning site.

> It does take time away from academic subjects. Presumably the time we spend at a service site, they would be in class. It's losing two periods of teaching time, whatever those classes might be, and over the course of the eight months we are there, it's a lot of time.

Al was not alone in expressing these concerns. All of the teachers expressed some reservations about the time spent away from the classroom, and in each case, their qualms were embedded in concerns about meeting the required standards and having the students perform well on the standardized tests. For example, Lynn said:

> Because service-learning is such a huge time commitment . . . that takes away from other subject time . . . So I feel obligated to find ways to make up for time that I'm taking away from other subjects, and that's a tremendous pressure on me. I feel that I'm not giving them everything they need.

Lynn's comments mirrored the attitudes of the other teachers interviewed at this school. They felt that they needed to prepare the students academically to meet the standards and pass the standardized tests. Service-learning, while beneficial, was not a "need" and for that reason the teachers felt conflicted about the time spent in service related activities.

Student Progress

The issue of students' academic progress was particularly exigent at CMSS, because many of the students who applied to attend there did so because they had not been successful at their previous schools. In many cases, these were students whose academic potential was high, but for whatever reason they were not meeting that potential. The small classes and small school atmosphere were designed to meet the needs of these struggling students. A local newspaper article[2], published in December 1992, several months after the school opened, explained:

> The gifted and talented students seemed to get plenty of attention. So did the students with clearly identifiable problems. But the ones who fell somewhere in the middle were drifting away, and educators in [this district] wanted to change all that. So they created a brand new school, aimed at that child in the middle, the one for whom parents and teachers had high hopes—along with some anxiety. The student most likely to be labeled, 'not working up to his or her potential.'

In this environment, teachers were charged with the task of helping students, who had not previously been successful in school, to achieve the uniform standards set forth by the city and state. This often led to the concern among teachers that while service-learning might be beneficial, some students might be better served by spending additional time at school. Anne, for example, explained that she and other teachers sometimes struggled with the decision of whether to have all students attend the service-learning activities or, because it takes away from academic time, whether to limit service opportunities to certain students.

> The state outlines what we have to do . . . There are times when I feel guilty saying, 'Well there are maybe five children who really, really would be better off staying here, working on their reading or working on their writing, rather than going to service-learning . . . . There's always a struggle, because I'm very pro service-learning but then on the other hand, if these kids aren't meeting exactly what the standards say they're supposed to meet, then there's that struggle. Ok, what do I do? Do I leave them here to do that extra work? Do I leave the class back entirely to do that extra lesson with them academically? Or do we say, 'Ok, we can give that up for now and go on to service-learning?'

This dilemma that teachers experienced was exacerbated by the context in which they worked. These teachers taught struggling students, yet district, city, and state education authorities judged student achievement, and thus teacher performance, based on results of uniform standardized tests that did not consider issues, such as students' previous educational experiences, their social or emotional growth, or whether or not they have learned to be active participants in their community.

Benefits Accrued by Students

The middle school teachers clearly were concerned about whether the time spent in service-learning detracted from students' academic learning, and they understood that parents, education authorities, and grantmaking agencies look for concrete indications of students' academic progress while placing less emphasis on their social and emotional development. When asked about vivid experiences with service-learning, however, the teachers were quick to discuss their students' success stories, especially the achievements of students who struggled either academically or socially in their middle school classes.

> We have success stories for students who are not succeeding here in any way, but they are succeeding over there, and every year I'll hear something like that from a teacher. I've heard that this year, and it was a kid who is failing practically everything, and last year it was the same thing–the teachers going out of their way to compliment some kid who really can't do much here as really doing a good job there for whatever reason.

> I had one student, a little boy, [who] was very, very, very shy [and] very, very afraid of making friends or actually doing anything . . . It wasn't until maybe March or April. . . I happened just to be passing . . . and he was actually sitting in a chair, with maybe six or seven students around him, and he happened to be sharing a project that he happened to do on his own that I didn't ask him to do. What he did was he brought a book in, and he was reading the story . . . it had to do with colors and shapes, and he had actually made a poster with all the different colors and shapes. He was asking the children as he came to that particular point in the book to point to it and they were very excited.

> I have this kid, I guess you can call him a problem kid in my class. He seems to behave really well at the service-learning site, and that's the interesting part about it.

> Some of them come to us and the only positive part of the week that they own is service-learning and they get a lot of recognition there . . . So that's an oasis for them, and it's a chance to really be peaceful and happy, and to produce what they can produce on their terms . . . So those children might benefit in a totally different way.

It is examples like these that contributed to the dilemma of standardized vs. experiential education experienced by these teachers. The first inclination seemed to be to consider the academic aspects of students' development, to view service-learning with suspicion because it takes time away from the academic subjects, and to question the logic behind removing academically struggling students from classrooms for 90 minutes each week. Still, the teachers also saw the benefit of putting students in situations where they could be successful despite the pressure to demonstrate students' academic growth on annual standardized tests.

TEACHER CONTROL VS. STUDENT INDEPENDENCE

One of the common themes found in service-learning literature is that students should play a major role in making decisions about service-learning activities. Pritchard (2002) stated that one characteristic of service-learning programs is "student involvement in selecting or designing the service activity" (p. 7) and Zeldin and Tarlov (1997) asserted that one benefit of service-learning is that students have the opportunity to "make decisions and contributions" and "take on new and progressively more complex roles and responsibilities" (p. 177). In discussing teachers' experiences, and observing teachers as they interacted with their students at service sites, it was clear that this objective is not easily attained, and that the middle school teachers struggled with how much responsibility to give their students.

Students' Motivations to Serve

The teachers at CMSS clearly understood that the middle school years presented them with a unique opportunity to impact students' development. However, just as the teachers saw service as an important part of the maturation process, inherent in this belief was the realization that their students were really just children, who, in many cases, were self-centered and primarily interested in having an enjoyable time. Many of the teachers voiced the concern that their students were only interested in going on a trip on a school bus or playing at the service sites. Anne, for example, explained: "They think at this point it's a time to be out of the school building. They look at it as a free trip once a week. They look at it almost as if it is a time for them to play." Lynn made a very similar comment when she discussed the struggles she faced each year in trying to help her students understand the importance of their service.

> Well, every year I have a few children who consider going to service-learning on a par with going to the playground–no responsibility and no school . . . So

that's a disappointment because I want to feel in September that I'm going to be able to reach every child, and I'm still hearing [in April], 'Oh goody, we're going on the bus,' and 'Oh goody, I don't have to do anything for an hour and a half.'

Al expressed a concern common to all of the teachers when he explained that although his students were focused on "How can I have fun? What am I going to enjoy?" he felt a responsibility to teach the children the value of service. He stated: "I think my place is dealing with my kids, so I try to convince them to accept their role, or if possible to change it, to change their attitude, or whatever it may be." These teachers wanted their students to acquire a proclivity toward service, or at least an understanding of the value of service, and saw it as their responsibility to ensure that this occurred.

Student Independence

In addition to dealing with attitudes that may not be conducive to educative service-learning experiences, the teachers also dealt with the difficulties that occurred when students were given significant responsibility or freedom at the service sites, or they were allowed to work with minimal teacher oversight, either in preparation for service or at the service sites. For example, one common theme in Lynn's responses was that she felt that her students often took advantage of the freedom they were allowed at the service site. She explained that she had to deal with a student who caused a minor panic at the service site and at the middle school when she decided to go to another classroom without notifying Lynn, or the teacher she usually served. She also mentioned two of her students who took advantage of the freedom they were given at the service site and used the time to meet with one another to socialize. She said: "There are children who are going to make their own rules."

Similarly, the teachers also struggled when they allowed students options and freedom with service-related assignments. Often the students were not able to follow through with a task or did not make choices that provided them with the most educative experiences. Anne explained her frustration when, at the end of the year, she allowed her students to design a project that they would bring to the service site. She felt that she had provided her students with enough assistance over the course of the year that they could complete this assignment successfully. She was disappointed when it did not happen and struggled with issues related to maintaining control. She wanted her students to be successful, but found that this required her to limit the amount of responsibility her students were given.

Chloe also explained her concerns after she asked her students their preferences regarding where to serve at their service site, a local elementary school. She said: "I had one student who wanted to help in a 6th-grade math class and I knew that he was not able to do it . . . and I had to basically coax him into a lower grade." Chloe allowed her students to make significant choices with regard to their placements at the service-learning site, but then faced a dilemma when a student's choice conflicted with what she thought would be the best environment for him, and the best way for the site to have its needs met.

Just as with the other dilemmas the teachers experienced, teachers managed this dilemma in different ways. Lynn and Anne, working with the younger children, focused on using reflective journals as a way to help their students think about the greater issues related to service. They believed that this was one way for the students to realize some of the broader goals associated with service. Al, who worked with a seventh-grade homeroom, focused on getting his students to understand the importance of service through conversations with them during their advisory periods. In observing Chloe, it became clear that while she did not address issues related to service with the class as a whole, she used her time on the bus, and immediately before and after service, to speak with students individually. She attempted to help them understand the value of what they did.

DISCUSSION AND IMPLICATIONS

Teachers at Community Middle School for Service were confronted by three dilemmas:

1. Needs of the server vs. needs of the served;
2. Standardized vs. experiential education; and
3. Teacher control vs. student independence.

It is not enough, however, to name and describe these dilemmas, or even to explain how the teachers dealt with them as they negotiated the expectations of the principal, state and local school boards, those at the service sites, and parents, while simultaneously considering their own beliefs about teaching and learning. It is essential to advance this idea one step further: to describe how these dilemmas are inextricably connected to the specific characteristics of Community Middle School for Service as well as the broader themes of teacher culture and educational reform.

The conclusions that follow are derived from the interplay of the findings previously discussed with the theoretical and methodological frameworks on which this study was based including Berlak and Berlak's (1981) emphasis on "examining the macro in the micro" (p. 4) and Guba and Lincoln's (1998) focus on identifying a "local and specific constructed reality" (p. 203). The conclusions, therefore, are a result of considering the larger issues that are embedded in the everyday lives of the teachers in this study, and are a result of the reality constructed by the researcher and participants during the research process and are specific to their local context. However, just as the dilemmas described previously may reflect the lived experiences of teachers at other schools who attempt to utilize service-learning in their classrooms, these conclusions and implications should be considered for their possible relevance to all involved with service-learning.

SOURCES OF DILEMMAS

Berlak and Berlak's (1981) goal was to provide a means to describe the lived experiences of teachers within the institutional and bureaucratic contexts in which they work. Similarly, in identifying the sources of dilemmas, the goal is to illustrate how the confluence of a variety of educational expectations and structures leads to the dilemmas faced by teachers.

Characteristics of Community Middle School for Service

The dilemmas experienced by the teachers at CMSS cannot be separated from the contexts in which they occurred. In considering the needs of the server vs. the needs of the served, for example, it is important to realize that part of the difficulty in finding appropriate service sites might be a direct result of several characteristics of CMSS, including scheduling and staffing.

Service-learning at CMSS had a clearly defined and generally non-negotiable "place" in the school schedule, and this schedule stemmed from some of the school's unique characteristics as well as state directives. CMSS shared its building with a high school, thus time in shared areas, such as the gymnasium and cafeteria, needed to be carefully negotiated. The school also conformed to state mandates for the amount of time students spent learning each subject. This resulted in service-learning being relegated to a 90-minute block on the schedule. Allowing for transportation time, students had approximately one hour to spend at the service sites each week. A more flexible schedule that allowed teachers to plan service activities around the schedules of the service recipients instead of the middle school's schedule might have made it easier for the educators at CMSS to find quality service sites where both students and service recipients benefited from the partnership, but the school's organization did not allow for this flexibility.

The opportunity to identify additional options for service was also somewhat hindered by one of the school's most attractive characteristics, its "small school" status. Although the school had only 13 full-time faculty and 160 students, the teachers at the school attempted to provide the students with many of the experiences and opportunities students would have had at a larger middle school. These experiences included sports and cheerleading teams, a school newspaper, and a yearbook. Faculty members must oversee these extracurricular activities leaving little time for anyone to making contact with and identify new service sites. The difficulty in finding time to search for new service sites, therefore, was not a result of the teachers' lack of dedication to the school or its service-learning focus. Rather, it was a practical matter; the teachers did not have the time to make these additional contacts while still meeting their other responsibilities.

In addition, service and academic learning at CMSS were often isolated from one another, with the teachers seeing little connection between the service activities and their students' academic growth. This context is important in understanding the second dilemma, standardized vs. experiential education. In another situation, where a school has endeavored to define what it means by service-learning, set reasonable goals based on this definition, and connect service with state and city mandates, this dilemma might not occur, or it might be less pervasive.

The third dilemma, teacher vs. student control, is also inextricably linked to the characteristics of Community Middle School for Service. This school was designed specifically to meet the needs of 10- to 14-year olds as they transition from elementary to secondary education. One of the schools' foundational beliefs was that in a small school, with a small student-to-teacher ratio, the unique needs of young adolescents could be met. However, it is important to note that this group of young adolescents included 10- and 11-year-old students, who were, in many school districts, still considered elementary students. They were often given responsibilities, but struggled to meet those responsibilities. Similarly, at their service sites, advisory teachers did not supervise their students closely because the middle school students were working individually or in pairs to serve the service site teachers. The irony of this situation is that CMSS was designed to meet the specific needs of young adolescents, yet it is these specific needs that led to the dilemma of teacher control vs. student independence.

These characteristics, while specific to this school, might also be a reality for other service-learning schools, and thus should be considered for their implications for service-learning researchers and practitioners. For example, those involved in supporting service-learning implementation need to understand the intricacies of school schedules and help schools work within these schedules to identify a variety of service sites that have a genuine need that can be met by the students. Similarly, teachers must also be assisted in developing strong connections between the service the students provide and the academic curriculum they are expected to master. Finally, both practitioners and researchers need to continue to consider the age-specific needs of students involved in service-learning and analyze how these needs impact service-learning programs.

In considering the dilemmas outlined previously, and in reviewing the conclusions and implications discussed here, it is important, as Berlak & Berlak (1981) asserted, to consider the macro in the micro. Specifically, in this embedded case study, the micro was the teachers, their classroom environments, and the school in which they worked. When these influences were reviewed, it was clear that the dilemmas experienced by the teachers exist, at least partially, because of a lack of defined goals and expectations, an inflexible schedule, a student population with specific age-appropriate needs, and service sites that prohibit close supervision. The macro, on the other hand, was the larger educational and societal contexts in which the teachers in this study worked, and as described below, these contexts included issues of teacher culture and school reform.

Teacher Culture

Lortie's (1975) seminal sociological study of teachers provided significant insight into the collegial norms within the profession. For example he stated: "The etiquette rule seems to be 'live and let live, and help when asked'" (p. 195). Similarly, he asserted:

> Teachers attach great meaning to the boundaries which separate their classrooms from the rest of the school, and of course, the community. Teachers deprecate transactions which cut across those boundaries. Walls are perceived as beneficial; they protect and enhance the course of instruction. All but teacher and students are outsiders. (p. 169)

While Community Middle School for Service was not in existence when Lortie (1975) collected his data in the 1960s and 1970s, these commentaries on teachers' culture could very well have been written to describe the teachers at CMSS and the service sites. For example, like many teachers, teachers at CMSS were isolated from one another in what Lortie called a "cellular" (p. 14) organization, and by a desire to remain autonomous in their classrooms. The teachers were physically separated from one another, isolated into classrooms on three different floors of the school. Even Lynn and Anne, who share the same open classroom, used bookshelves and bulletin boards as "walls" in order to maintain the boundaries between their classrooms.

Service-learning as it existed at CMSS begins to disrupt these bound-aries and norms by asking the middle school teachers to leave their cellular spaces and for the teachers at the service sites to accept outsiders into their space. This disruption of boundaries combined with the teachers' desire to cling to the remaining vestiges of their cellular existence was one of the sources of dilemmas teachers at this school faced. In considering the first dilemma, needs of the server vs. needs of the served, the last part of the "help when asked" etiquette rule Lortie (1975) used to explain teachers' relationships with one another is challenged. While the goal was for the middle school students to provide a needed service, it is obvious from the quotes of the teachers that this did not always happen. Even if the service site teachers originally asked for assistance, 60 minutes once a week might not be the kind of assistance that is most helpful, and it is not within the norms of teacher culture for assistance to be received positively if it is not specifically requested. Similarly, these teachers were being asked to wel-come "outsiders," both teachers and students, into their classrooms. This may have led them to be less willing to accept students, or unwilling to work with the middle school teachers to provide the best experiences for both the served and the servers. Complicating this situation is the fact that the middle school teachers, because they were teachers, were aware of the same norms, and were thus hesitant to enter the classroom or to encroach on the "boundaries" any more than necessary for the basic function of the service program.

While the other two dilemmas, standardized vs. experiential education and teacher control vs. student independence, are not as directly related to these teacher culture norms, the cellular nature of schooling described by Lortie (1975) played a role in the creation and maintenance of these dilemmas because since the teachers were isolated from one another, both physically and by cultural norm, they did not have the opportunity to observe their colleagues managing dilemmas or to discuss this manage-ment with them. For example, a teacher struggling with how to integrate service-learning with the academic curriculum and meet the needs of stu-dents who are not performing well enough to pass the mandated standard-ized tests, or a teacher wondering how to balance allowing his or her students independence at the service sites while still maintaining the con-trol necessary for students to remain welcome guests in a preschool or ele-mentary school, would not have witnessed other teachers managing these situations nor would he or she have the opportunity or the inclination to discuss these situations with the other teachers.

School Reform

Service-learning can be seen as both a school reform effort, and as a teaching innovation impacted by other attempts at school reform. In viewing service-learning as a school reform, issues of sustainability come to the forefront. For example, Billig (2002) explained:

> Despite its growth over the past decade, service-learning continues to remain a fragile reform that is highly dependent on individuals to be sustained. Like other K-12 innovations, service-learning runs the risk of becoming the 'fad of the day' unless certain factors are in place to sustain and institutionalize practice over time. (pp. 245–246)

Billig (2002) also identified five factors that lead to the sustainability of service-learning: strong leadership, cultural norms and organizational expectations, incentives, visibility, and availability of financial resources. Community Middle School for Service, as is evidenced by the dilemmas described previously, had few of these characteristics, and it struggled to sustain its service-learning program, despite a school and district commitment to its existence. For example, over time, funding, staffing, and training had slowly been eliminated, thus leaving the faculty with varying levels of knowledge about service-learning and its implementation, and no way to address concerns as they occurred. It is this lack of attention to issues of sustainability and the absence of many factors that promote sustainability that exacerbated the dilemmas experienced by the teachers at CMSS. It also points to the implication that support for service-learning in schools that comes from outside agencies must be ongoing, not just limited to the adoption and implementation phases of program development.

Service-learning can also be viewed as an education innovation impacted by other school reforms. Teachers at a school such as CMSS are clearly impacted by school, district, city, and state decisions that mandate how children should be taught and how their learning should be assessed. In an ideal world, the decisions and reforms at each of these levels would be compatible. Pearson (2002), for example, noted: "Implementation and sustainability of quality service-learning is better facilitated when a school or district aligns it with educational goals" (p. 114). While she only commented on the alignment of school and district goals, it is not difficult to extrapolate this to city and state standards. At CMSS, city and state mandates led to dilemmas when teachers felt torn between meeting mandated standards, as assessed on standardized tests, and providing students with opportunities to perform service within their communities. Attempts at educational reform, therefore, when not aligned with teachers' views on service-learning, can contribute to the dilemmas teachers experience.

Acknowledgments: This project was supported in part by the Corporation for National and Community Service, through the National Service Fellows Program.

NOTES

1.   In order to protect the confidentiality of the participants, all proper names have been replaced by pseudonyms, and care was taken to disguise any identifying characteristics. Participants were notified in informed consent documents; however despite these precautions, there was a risk of identification by fellow educators and those within the educational community knowledgeable about the school.

2.   To maintain the confidentiality of the school and the participants, a full reference is not included for this article. Additional information about the source of the quotation can be obtained by contacting the author.

REFERENCES

Berlak, A., & Berlak, H. (1981). *Dilemmas of schooling: Teaching and social change.* New York: Methuen.

Billig, S. H. (2002). Adoption, implementation, and sustainability of K-12 service-learning. In A. Furco & S. H. Billig (Eds.), *Advances in service-learning research: Vol. 1. Service-Learning: The essence of the pedagogy* (pp. 245-267). Greenwich, CT: Information Age Publishing.

Buchanan, A. M., Baldwin, S. C., & Rudisill, M. E. (2002). Service-learning as scholarship in teacher education. *Educational Researcher, 31*(5), 28–34.

Conrad, D., & Hedin, D. (1991). School-based community service: What we know from research and theory. *Phi Delta Kappan, 72,* 743–749.

Duits, C. S., & Dorman, A. K. (1998). *Reaching out through reading: Service-learning and adventures with literature.* Englewood, CO: Teacher Ideas Press.

Guba, E. G., & Lincoln, Y. S. (1998). Competing paradigms in qualitative research. In N. K. Denzin & Y. S. Lincoln (Eds.), *The landscape of qualitative research: Theories and issues* (pp. 195–220). Thousand Oaks, CA: Sage.

Lortie, D. C. (1975). *Schoolteacher: A sociological study.* Chicago: University of Chicago Press.

Luce, J. (Ed.). (1988). *Service-learning: An annotated bibliography for linking public service with the curriculum.* Raleigh, NC: National Society for Internships and Experiential Education.

Pearson, S. S. (2002). *Finding common ground: Service-learning and education reform—A survey of 28 leading school reform models.* Washington DC: American Youth Policy Forum.

Peshkin, A. (1993). The goodness of qualitative research. *Educational Researcher, 22*(2), 23–29.

Pritchard, I. A. (2002). Community service and service-learning in America: The state of the art. In A. Furco & S. H. Billig (Eds.), *Advances in service-learning research: Vol. 1. Service-learning: The essence of the pedagogy* (pp. 3–21). Greenwich, CT: Information Age Publishing.

Schukar, R., Johnson, J., & Singleton, L. K. (1996). *Service-learning in the middle school curriculum: A resource book.* Boulder, CO: Social Science Education Consortium.

Waterman, A. S. (1997). Preface. In A. S. Waterman (Ed.), *Service-learning: Applications from the research* (pp. xi-xii). Mahwah, NJ: Lawrence Erlbaum Associates.

Yin, R. K. (1994). *Case study research: Design and methods* (2nd ed.). Thousand Oaks, CA: Sage.

Zeldin, S., & Tarlov, S. (1997). Service-learning as a vehicle for youth development. In K. J. Rehage (Series Ed.) & J. Schine (Vol. Ed.), *Ninety-sixth yearbook of the National Society for the Study of Education: Vol. 1. Service-learning* (pp. 173–185). Chicago: National Society for the Study of Education.

PART III

INSTITUTIONALIZATION OF SERVICE-LEARNING

CHAPTER 4

THE DIFFUSION OF ACADEMIC SERVICE-LEARNING IN TEACHER EDUCATION
A Case Study Approach

Jane Callahan and Susan Root

In the past decade, there has been a growing movement to integrate academic service-learning into teacher education. However, the competing demands of teacher preparation, coupled with issues related to not only using, but also teaching the pedagogy of academic service-learning, may make the diffusion in teacher education more complex than in other disciplines. This chapter presents the results of a study that investigated the effectiveness of a particular model of training and technical assistance on the diffusion of academic service-learning in four teacher education programs. Case studies of the programs are presented and results are related to those in the literature on educational change and other disciplines in higher education.

Deconstructing Service-Learning: Research Exploring Context, Participation, and Impacts
A Volume in: Advances in Service-Learning Research, pages 77–101.
Copyright © 2003 by Information Age Publishing, Inc.
All rights of reproduction in any form reserved.
ISBN: 1-59311-071-5 (hardcover), 1-59311-070-7 (pbk.)

INTRODUCTION

In the past decade, there has been a growing movement to integrate academic service-learning into teacher education in order to improve the quality of teacher candidates and to prepare them to use academic service-learning in their own classrooms. In a study reported at the First Annual International Conference on Service-Learning Research, Anderson and Erickson (2001) found that 301 teacher education programs nationwide included academic service-learning and 63 percent of those prepared teacher candidates to use academic service-learning as a teaching strategy. This trend was consistent with Myers and Pickeral's (1997) recommendation that "academic service-learning should be a . . . central process within teacher preparation programs . . . to increase the ability of students to be successful teachers and leaders of the reform of public education" (p. 13).

While the growing adoption of academic service-learning in teacher preparation is a significant accomplishment, little is known about the process through which it occurs. Investigators have examined the institutionalization of academic service-learning in higher education and K–12 institutions (Billig, 2002; Holland, 1997); however, the barriers and challenges encountered there may differ from those faced by teacher-educators. In addition to preparing the internal organizational context and potential users, teacher educators seeking to integrate academic service-learning into their programs must consider external demands, such as the requirements of national and state accrediting bodies and partnerships with schools where teacher candidates can practice knowledge and skills. These demands coupled with issues related to not only using, but also teaching the pedagogy of academic service-learning, suggest that the diffusion of academic service-learning in teacher education is more complex than in other disciplines. The purpose of this study was to investigate the effectiveness of a particular model for faculty training on the diffusion of academic service-learning in four teacher education programs.

The project, "University Consortium to Advance Academic Service-Learning Throughout Michigan" was funded by a grant from the Corporation for National and Community Service awarded to Eastern Michigan University (EMU) Office of Academic Service-Learning. Its purpose was to utilize EMU's Faculty Fellow Development Model (Rice & Stacey, 1997) to promote the diffusion of academic service-learning in teacher education programs at four regional universities within Michigan, and for these universities, in turn, to become regional training and technical assistance centers for area K–12 systems, institutions of higher education, and community partners.

The EMU Faculty Fellow Development Model of training faculty is designed in light of recommendations (e.g., Shumer, 1997) that "rather than emphasizing short-term workshops and training, we need to concentrate more on long term efforts to engage teachers in the context of their work . . . " (p. 121). In the model, faculty meet in weekly seminar of two hours duration over a semester with an experienced academic service-learning faculty facilitator. Faculty Fellows discuss a common set of readings on the key elements of academic service-learning including the definition, rationales for adoption, forming community partnerships, assessment, and reflection. Throughout the semester, faculty also develop and receive feedback on course syllabi that include an academic service-learning component. The goal of the University Consortium project was to implement Faculty Fellow seminars at each of the four participating institutions for five semesters over the course of the three-year grant.

Rogers (1995) defined diffusion as "the process by which an innovation is communicated through certain channels over time among members of a social system" (p. 10). Elaborating on this definition, Ellsworth (2000) proposed a "change communication model" which includes a change agent, the innovation, the change process, the change environment, and intended adopter(s). Ellsworth's model portrays the change agent as seeking to communicate an innovation to an intended adopter through a process and within an environment, which may include forces of resistance.

Researchers have examined different components of the diffusion process and their influence on the success and rate of innovation adoption. For example, Rogers (1995) identified several features of innovations that influence the rate of adoption:

- Relative advantage (whether the innovation is superior to what it replaces);
- Compatibility (whether the innovation is a good fit with the beliefs, needs, and past practices of potential users);
- Complexity (whether the innovation is difficult to understand or use);
- Trialability (whether the user has the opportunity to try out the innovation prior to adoption); and
- Observability (whether the user has the opportunity to observe others using the innovation).

Fullan and Stiegelbauer (1991) focused on the role of stakeholders in K–12 education with (potential) change agent roles, including teachers, principals, students, district administrators, and consultants, discussing the advantages and obstacles faced by each.

Hall and Hord (2001) described aspects of adopters' experiences with innovations that can mediate the success of diffusion. They delineated seven stages of concern through which teachers progress in attempting to come to terms with a novel instructional approach, ranging from awareness and a desire to learn more about the innovation, to concerns about the impact of the innovation on the self and managing the new practice. At the most advanced levels, teachers shift to concerns about the impact of the innovation on students, integrating their practice with that of others, and refining and improving the new practice. The authors noted, however, that it is possible for individuals to express concerns at more than one level. In addition to analyzing individual faculty members' level of concern, Hall and Hord (2001) identified various levels of use. As they implement an innovation, teachers' practice evolves from nonuse, to preparation for use, to mechanical application. With enough experience, practice becomes routine and, at the highest levels, undergoes refinement and renewal.

Several authors have examined the institutionalization of academic service-learning in educational institutions. For example, Billig (2002) conducted case studies of the adoption, implementation, and sustainability of academic service-learning in K–12 schools that had received funding to integrate academic service-learning. She found that the adoption of academic service-learning was influenced primarily by teachers' belief in authentic, contextualized learning and the availability of funding. Other variables that influenced adoption included word-of-mouth and research support for academic service-learning, the visibility of these activities, and support from a state academic service-learning coordinator. Factors which facilitated implementation of academic service-learning included inclusion of all participants in the planning process, administrative support, technical assistance, regular opportunities to exchange ideas and sufficient financial and human resources. Billig found that sustainability was most likely to occur in sites that had adopted academic service-learning on a schoolwide basis.

Holland (1997) and her colleagues conducted case studies of the institutionalization of academic service-learning in higher education. One of their projects involved case studies of four institutions which had identified academic service-learning and community-based scholarship as central to their missions. In a second study, Holland (2000) and colleagues examined the institutionalization of academic service-learning at 19 institutions that had received grants to support its adoption. Using data from both studies, the authors developed a matrix for coding the degree to which service and academic service-learning were accepted as a priority at the institutions. The vertical axis of their matrix lists potential institutional loci for the expression of institutional commitment to academic service-learning, such as mission, promotion, tenure and hiring policies, and faculty involvement. The horizontal axis is a continuum of levels of commitment ranging from low relevance to full integration. For example, if no mention of service or academic service-learning were made in an institution's mission statement, the assumption would be that these activities were of low relevance. In contrast, full integration would be evident if service were a central and defining characteristic of the institution.

The purpose of this study was to examine the impact of the implementation of the Faculty Fellow model under the University Consortium project on the diffusion of academic service-learning in the participating teacher education programs. The study sought to explore and describe the change process at two levels: in the programs themselves and in the potential adopters. The specific research questions for the study included:

- How did the diffusion of academic service-learning in the participating teacher preparation programs occur?
- What factors, both unique to and common across the institutions, appeared to facilitate or impede the diffusion process?
- What levels of concern and use characterized faculty progress in implementing academic service-learning and how did these differ across programs?

METHODS

A case study method was used to examine the diffusion of academic service-learning within the participating teacher preparation programs. Zeichner (1999) noted that the use of case studies reflects "the recognition that the reality of every teacher education program is so complex that it is virtually impossible to communicate that complexity to outside audiences short of the . . . systematic and detailed analyses that case studies provide" (p. 9). Root and Swick (2000) recommended the use of case studies of academic service-learning in teacher education in order to inform other teacher educators about the lived experience of those seeking to implement academic service-learning.

Subjects

Subjects for the study included three liaison faculty members from Eastern Michigan University who provided training and technical assistance to contact faculty in the teacher education programs at each of the four universities. The four contact faculty were responsible for administrating the grant on their campuses and conducting the Faculty Fellow seminars. Subjects also included the 42 faculty members who participated in the Faculty Fellow seminars on those campuses.

Data Collection

Data collected in the study include individual and focus group interviews with liaison, contact, and participating faculty. In addition, periodically throughout each year of the grant, responses to e-mail prompts about progress toward implementation were collected from the participants and analyzed.

Data Analysis

Qualitative data analysis was employed to analyze the change process with respect to academic service-learning at both the level of the participating faculty member and the level of the teacher education program. To analyze diffusion at the institutional level, a Systemic Change Matrix (Exhibit 1) was created for this project. The matrix includes several of the loci of institutional commitment to service identified by Holland (1997) and others. In addition, it incorporates dimensions that may be unique to the diffusion of academic service-learning in teacher education, including alignment with state and national teacher education accreditation standards and efforts to teach the pedagogy of to future teachers. Together, these elements seem to create an environment for diffusion that differs significantly from other contexts in higher education.

Five dimensions comprise the vertical axis of the Systemic Change Matrix:

1. Program Visions/Beliefs;
2. Communication;
3. Teaching and Learning Changes;
4. Administrative Roles and Responsibilities; and
5. Alignment With Standards.

The dimension of *Program Vision and Beliefs* concerns the degree to which academic service-learning is referenced in key expressions of program beliefs, such as the conceptual framework, course syllabi, assessment plan, and course catalogue descriptions. The dimension of *Communication* relates to how much, and through what means, information about the innovation is shared. Examples of communication strategies include discussion of academic service-learning in Faculty Fellow seminars, personal conversations, and formal presentations in department meetings.

The dimension of *Teaching and Learning Changes* refers to faculty members' integration of academic service-learning in their teaching. Modifying or creating new courses to include academic service-learning, and efforts to prepare candidates to use academic service-learning in their future teaching are evidence of integration. The area of *Administrative Roles and Responsibilities* concerns key administrators' knowledge and endorsement of academic service-learning, as well their willingness to allocate resources to support its implementation. Studies have raised questions about the role

Exhibit
Systemic Change Matrix

	Maintenance	Awareness	Exploration	Transition	Emergence of new infrastructure	Full adoption
Vision/Beliefs	Satisfaction with old structure, possible resistance to academic service-learning.	Faculty realize need for change and/or advantages of academic service-learning.	Stakeholders promote ideas for change; discussion of strategies and models for change; growing numbers of faculty realize advantages of academic service-learning.	Emerging consensus about need for change. Under-standing of need for linkages between academic service-learning and other components of program.	Expanding influence of academic service-learning to include all aspects of program (student outcomes, underlying beliefs). Refinement of vision.	Academic service-learning an integral part of program. Use characterized by acceptable to best practice.
Communication	No or minimal communication about the academic service-learning.	Announcements of initiatives associated with the academic service-learning. Individual faculty sharing.	Dissemination and discussion of supporting literature (related to start-up).	Faculty share ideas and strategies of implementing academic service-learning. Communication networks expand.	Use of established communication channels to share information about academic service-learning and discuss impacts on program.	Academic service-learning no longer discussed in isolation, but in context of routine department business.
Teaching and learning changes	Investment in existing program and courses.	Faculty recognize the instructional benefits of the academic service-learning. A few faculty are implementing academic service-learning.	Faculty and program invest resources to understand academic service-learning, seek common definitions, expand understanding.	Faculty implement and evaluate effects of academic service-learning. Recognition of the impacts of the academic service-learning (changes needed and resources required).	Assessments encourage improvements and plans for all students to have experience. Ongoing faculty development and support for research.	Academic service-learning is fully integrated. All students participate in academic service-learning.

(continued)

EXHIBIT 1
(Continued)

	Maintenance	Awareness	Exploration	Transition	Emergence of new infrastructure	Full adoption
Administrative roles and responsibilities	Adherence to status quo; focus on technical aspects of manage-mint.	Administrators recognize need for change.	Administrator developing knowledge of academic service-learning. Some resources allocated for exploring academic service-learning.	Administrators provide resources for implementation and ongoing faculty development (e.g., time, stipends).	Knowledge of academic service-learning considered in hiring, priorities shift based on academic service-learning. Establishment of permanent staff position(s) and budget line to support academic service-learning.	Administrator takes lead in effort to infuse academic service-learning, advocates for academic service-learning internally and externally.
Alignment with standards	No understanding of connection between academic service-learning and standards.	Faculty recognize that academic service-learning may enhance compliance with standards.	Faculty explore the potential of academic service-learning to enhance compliance with standards.	Consensus about connections between academic service-learning and standards is reached. Faculty articulate and provide examples of connections.	Important program documents identify standards that are met through academic service-learning.	Mission and conceptual frameworks articulate connections and reflect reciprocal influence of academic service-learning.

of leadership in implementing academic service-learning (Bringle & Hatcher, 2000; Driscoll, Holland, Gelmon, & Kerrigan, 1996) so understanding the level and kind of leadership could provide a critical piece of information about the institutionalization process.

The fifth dimension of the matrix is *Alignment With Standards*. As previously stated, teacher education programs are required to meet state and national accreditation standards for teacher preparation, and in Michigan, to provide evidence that they are preparing candidates to help their own students master state content standards. Programs' efforts to integrate academic service-learning with their attempts to align program components and accreditation standards should demonstrate that the strategy was achieving a central place in the teacher education program.

There are six levels of diffusion on the horizontal axis of the Systemic Change Matrix. *Maintenance*, the first level, implies adherence to and satisfaction with the status quo. The second level is *Awareness*, the level at which faculty and administrators become aware of a need for change and develop some knowledge of academic service-learning and how it might contribute positively to course or program outcomes. At the *Exploration* stage, there is discussion of the pedagogy among faculty, and administrators may allocate some resources to its development and use by faculty members. Faculty may attend conferences to deepen their understanding of how academic service-learning can be implemented, and may experiment with it in individual courses.

At the fourth level, *Transition*, there is emerging consensus on the need for change and an understanding of how academic service-learning can support program goals and outcomes. Faculty share ideas and strategies for use of academic service-learning and implement and evaluate its effects. Administrators provide support for ongoing faculty development, and there is consensus about connections between academic service-learning and accreditation standards. At the *Emergence of New Infrastructure* level, discussion of academic service-learning occurs through established communication channels, such as department meetings; knowledge of academic service-learning is considered in hiring procedures; and administrators consider the needs generated by academic service-learning in establishing budget priorities.

At the final level, *Full Adoption*, academic service-learning is an integral part of the teacher education program. Its use is characterized by acceptable best practice. Academic service-learning is fully integrated into the mission statement and program assessment plan, discussed in the context of routine department business, and aligned with accreditation standards.

To assess change among individual faculty members, e-mail prompt responses and other data were analyzed using the Stages of Concern and Levels of Use developed by Hall and Hord (2001), shown in Exhibits 2 and 3.

EXHIBIT 2
Stages of Concern

- Unrelated
- Self
  - No Awareness
  - Informational
  - Personal
- Task
  - Impact
  - Collaboration
  - Refocusing

Hall & Hord, 2001

EXHIBIT 3
Levels of Use

- Non-use
- Orientation
- Preparation
- Mechanical
- Routine
- Refinement
- Integration
- Renewal

Hall & Hord, 2001

RESULTS

The following narratives describe the results of the analysis of faculty and organizational change in the participating programs.

University One

Originally a teacher's college, University One has evolved into a doctoral/research public university. Thirty-six hundred students are enrolled in five teacher education programs offering Elementary, Secondary, and Special Education certification and taught by 29 faculty.

The contact faculty member at University One is a full professor in the Department of Elementary Education/Secondary Education and Special Education. For several years prior to this grant project, Dr. Martin (a pseudonym) had been integrating academic service-learning into his student teaching course by teaching its pedagogy and offering students the option of creating and implementing projects in their placement classrooms. He had also led several academic service-learning workshops for K–12 educators.

At the beginning of the grant project, Dr. Martin estimated that 20 to 25 percent of faculty in the elementary, secondary, and special education programs understood academic service-learning and believed it had value as a curricular approach. Nevertheless, despite teaching with methods consistent with service-learning's philosophy, such as cooperative and inquiry learning, few faculty members had integrated academic service-learning in their courses.

By the end of the first year of the grant, Dr. Martin had trained one Faculty Fellow group of six, and they had developed plans to integrate academic service-learning into their 2001-2002 courses. However, except for conversations with individual faculty members, there had been little communication about academic service-learning among faculty members or in department meetings.

Analysis of Dr. Martin's liaison and participating faculty responses to e-mail prompts led to the following conclusions about the diffusion of academic service-learning at University One in Year Two of the project. With respect to the dimension of Vision/Beliefs, the department seemed to be between the Exploration and Transition stages. During the fall 2001 semester, the first group of Faculty Fellows integrated academic service-learning into four courses in the Department of Elementary Education/Secondary Education and Special Education. As a result of two more Faculty Fellows seminars that year, new cohorts of six faculty each began planning courses. By the end of the second year of the grant, Dr. Martin estimated that 50 percent of undergraduates in the department and 15 percent of graduate students were participating in academic service-learning, that almost all department faculty understood it, and that a majority viewed it as valuable. However, academic service-learning was neither a regular agenda item at meetings, nor was it integrated into formal department documents or procedures, such as its conceptual framework or evaluation activities.

With respect to the dimension of Communication, the program seemed to be between the Transition and Emergence of New Infrastructure stages. The contact faculty member was very active in encouraging the adoption of academic service-learning through personal conversations and e-mail. At a department meeting, he gave certificates to first-year Faculty Fellows and announced the names of those second-year members. In addition, he organized gatherings to help Faculty Fellows write presentation proposals on their academic service-learning activities, which led to a number being accepted for conferences, two articles being written, and one article being published. He also observed that more communication about academic service-learning was being initiated by other faculty members, and that "young faculty" were "really excited" about it. However, there were few established communication

EXHIBIT 4
University One Year Two Systemic Matrix

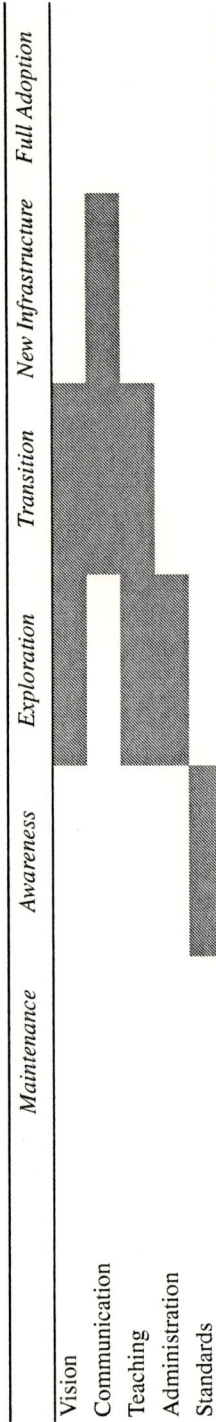

channels being used consistently to share information about academic service-learning, and it was not regularly discussed in department or program meetings.

Progress in the second year on Teaching and Learning Changes could be categorized between the Exploration and Transition levels. Faculty invested time in order to understand academic service-learning and several began implementing it in their courses. For example, after the terrorist attacks on September 11, 2001, the reading methods class and instructor created curriculum packs for children in a 5th-grade class on Staten Island whose classroom windows had looked out on the World Trade Center towers and began a correspondence with them. However, evaluation of the effects of academic service-learning was not yet informing subsequent waves of practice, and there was no systematic plan to ensure that all students would be introduced to academic service-learning.

Administrative support remained at the level of Exploration in the second year of the grant. There appeared to be broad institutional support for academic service-learning and some support from the chair (e.g., a director of service-learning was hired and the university was circulating a grant proposal for a Rural Academic Service-learning Center with connections to several community colleges and P–12 districts).

University One appeared to be at the Awareness level with regard to the fifth dimension, Alignment with Standards. Faculty users were beginning to discuss linkages between academic service-learning and National Council for Accreditation of Teacher Education (NCATE) standards. However, no formal discussion or consensus had occurred within the department, and there was no systematic effort to link academic service-learning to standards-adherence efforts.

At the end of Year Two, most participating faculty seemed to be at the Personal or Task Impact stages of concern and at the Preparation or Mechanical levels of use. Dr. Martin noted that all faculty members who had been Faculty Fellows and who were implementing academic service-learning were "just starting out." His perception was that their concerns centered around how to find a service-learning project "that makes sense and isn't going to take untold hours to set up and establish." Responses from Faculty Fellows to e-mail prompts in the second year confirmed these impressions. For example, one commented early in training, "This fits right into what good teachers should be doing." However, she was concerned about "the time and money needed for implementation of a project." A second Faculty Fellow from Year Two noted that academic service-learning "has great potential to impact the K–12 educational system" and "creates the type of win-win situation we are looking for in our partnerships and field experiences," but was concerned about "the time demands" involved in academic service-learning.

University Two

University Two is an institution of 8,000 students. Originally a normal college, the university now offers associate, bachelors, graduate degrees, and several profes-

sional studies programs. Sixteen faculty members staff an education department with approximately 500 undergraduate candidates and provide courses leading to certification in elementary, secondary, and special education.

The contact faculty member for the project at University Two is the director of field experiences and a tenured professor. Dr. Franklin (a pseudonym) was interested in academic service-learning, but, at the beginning of the project, felt that his knowledge was limited. His belief that "service can effect social change" was the strongest influence on his decision to become involved in the grant.

According to Dr. Franklin, although education faculty introduced candidates to student-centered pedagogies such as problem-based learning, none were using academic service- learning at the beginning of the grant. He anticipated that time demands, negative responses from colleagues, and the University's already overloaded teacher education curriculum would be major barriers to the adoption of academic service-learning.

Although Dr. Franklin identified eight potential Faculty Fellows in fall 2000 for a seminar in winter 2001, he decided to integrate discussion of academic service-learning into meetings of the Elementary Methods Block Program Planning Committee, rather than follow the Faculty Fellow model of regular seminars. In January 2001, Dr. Franklin introduced academic service-learning as part of a discussion about the program's need to "redefine and conceptualize our field experiences in terms of academic service-learning." The committee initially discussed ways to integrate academic service-learning in the Methods Block, but cancelled meetings at the end of the semester and decided to continue discussions in the fall of 2001.

During the second year of the project, Dr. Franklin again decided against trying to convene a Faculty Fellow seminar and instead offered small grants to individual faculty seeking to develop academic service-learning courses. Applicants were required to write a proposal that served as an incentive to contact Dr. Franklin for individual technical assistance. Although he provided assistance to some faculty members, Dr. Franklin felt that academic service-learning integration had not been successful at University Two.

Analysis of interview responses of liaison faculty and Dr. Franklin, and e-mail prompt responses of individual faculty, led to the following conclusions about the diffusion of the Eastern Michigan Faculty Fellow Development Model of academic service-learning at University Two in Year Two. With respect to the dimension of Vision/Beliefs, the department seemed to be in the Maintenance stage. Efforts to engage both elementary and secondary faculty in integrating academic service-learning had met with little success. When Dr. Franklin sought to initiate meetings for planning with the secondary faculty he "found very limited interest." In addition, academic service-learning had not been integrated into key statements or activities of the department.

The teacher education program seemed to be between the Maintenance and Awareness stages with respect to the dimension of Communication. Dr. Franklin engaged in a number of strategies to communicate about the project in Year Two:

- Presentations at two department meetings, one by the liaison faculty member;

EXHIBIT 5
University Two Year Two Systemic Matrix

	Maintenance	Awareness	Exploration	Transition	New Infrastructure	Full Adoption
Vision						
Communication						
Teaching						
Administration						
Standards						

- *Informal discussions with faculty; and*
- *Introduction of the project at meetings of both local supervising teachers and the department's teacher education Advisory Council.*

In addition, Dr. Franklin contributed an article about academic service-learning to TEACH, the Advisory Council's newsletter. Nonetheless, individual faculty members did not initiate spontaneous discussions about their use of academic service-learning and academic service-learning activities were not a topic of discussion at department meetings.

Regarding the third dimension of the matrix, Teaching and Learning Changes, University Two's status appeared to be between the Maintenance and Awareness levels. Some faculty members valued academic service-learning and had begun implementing it. By spring 2002, three elementary courses and one secondary methods course included academic service-learning, and the total of student participants across the year was estimated at 38 percent. However, most faculty appeared to be indifferent.

Administrative support remained at the level of Exploration in the second year of the grant, although the chair of the Education Department allocated a graduate student to the project. With respect to the fifth dimension, Alignment with Standards, diffusion was categorized in the Maintenance stage. Faculty had not discussed connections between academic service-learning and accreditation standards, either informally or at committee or department meetings.

In relation to faculty concerns and use, only one faculty member responded to e-mail prompts during the second year. Her responses suggested that she was at the Task Impact stage of concern, and the Mechanical level of use, trying to find the best way to integrate academic service-learning with existing course content. She reported that her students had developed service projects for their field experience schools and felt that the project contributed to students' understanding of the course material, "as the students used the knowledge." This faculty member planned to use academic service-learning in future courses. She expressed concern primarily about the time available during class for discussion of projects commenting, "I would like to use the experience more in class." In addition, Dr. Franklin noted that most faculty who were using academic service-learning were primarily concerned about technique—"how to use it."

University Three

University Three is a student-centered research institution with an enrollment of nearly 30,000. The College of Education offers teacher certification in six areas and enrolls 2,000 undergraduates. The contact faculty at University Three, Dr. Bradley (a pseudonym), is a tenured faculty member in the Department of Educational Studies and a former Faculty Fellow. She is committed to academic service-learning and feels that "with its focus on both service and academic goals, it fits well with the nature and purpose of teacher education."

During the first year of the grant, Dr. Bradley recruited Faculty Fellows through verbal communication and flyers about academic service-learning. In the winter semester, nine College of Education faculty and two sociology faculty participated in seminars. All participating faculty intended to make course changes and their comments were positive. Most felt that "the potential for service was huge."

However, even with the enthusiasm of a number of faculty at the end of Year 1, Dr. Bradley stated that given the size of the College of Education, "the majority of faculty don't know about academic service-learning." She also noted that administrators "pay lip-service to academic service-learning, but are not willing to provide any concrete resources" beyond those provided by the grant.

During Year Two, Dr. Bradley took a year-long sabbatical and her responsibilities were assumed by an elementary education faculty member. At the end of the second year, University Three was in the Exploration stage in the dimension of Vision/ Beliefs. According to the contact faculty, many faculty were aware of and seemed to value academic service-learning, but few had an accurate understanding of it. In addition, academic service-learning had not yet penetrated general program statements, policies, or procedures.

With respect to the dimension of Communication, University Three seemed to be in the Transition stage. Various communication strategies were used in the first year, but in Year Two, recruitment efforts were primarily interpersonal. First year faculty participants engaged in informal conversations about individual courses and student action research projects. However there was little discussion of academic service-learning among faculty outside of this group, and academic service-learning has not yet been mentioned in formal departmental communications.

University Three appeared to be between the Transition and Emergence of New Infrastructure stages regarding the third dimension of the matrix, Teaching and Learning Changes. Academic service-learning had been integrated in 10 courses, including elementary, secondary, special education, leadership, and sociology of education. Faculty Fellows were enthusiastic about the use of academic service-learning. One noted that "student reflections indicated that their own understanding of history and teaching history and social studies in the elementary setting was greatly enhanced;" while another commented, "students seem to be inspired about academic service-learning and the potentially powerful role that it can play in their future teaching." According to Dr. Bradley, an estimated 5 to 6 percent of education undergraduates were participating in academic service-learning courses, but high program enrollment and numerous course sections meant that the majority of students might never have this opportunity.

Administrative support at University Three seemed to be between the Awareness and Exploration stages of the matrix. Although administrators in the College of Education demonstrated knowledge of academic service-learning, they allocated no resources to its inclusion beyond those provided by the grant. Although some administrators of smaller units met with contact faculty to discuss including academic service-learning in program courses and one Faculty Fellow organized a university-wide

EXHIBIT 6
University Three Year Two Systemic Matrix

	Maintenance	Awareness	Exploration	Transition	New Infrastructure	Full Adoption
Vision						
Communication			▓	▓		
Teaching				▓	▓	
Administration			▓	▓		
Standards		▓	▓			

meeting to discuss the possibility of a campus academic service-learning office, no administrative support or direction was provided for academic service-learning. With respect to Alignment with Standards, University Three appeared to be at the Awareness level. Some faculty seemed to recognize the power of academic service-learning in advancing candidates' understanding of diverse students and social justice issues. However, there was little movement toward connecting academic service-learning outcomes to particular NCATE accreditation or beginning teacher standards.

According to Dr. Bradley, University Three's status as a research university causes academic service-learning to "take a back seat" to other professional expectations. She noted, "unless administrators and tenure and promotion committee members can be educated about academic service-learning and young faculty can be encouraged to find ways to connect academic service-learning to research that promotes presentations and publications, it will remain on the margins in the College of Education."

Participating faculty concerns and use appeared to be between the Task Impact and Collaboration stages of concern and at the Mechanical level of use. Three faculty members responded to e-mail prompts during Year Two. Their primary concerns centered on being able to talk together about their experiences with integrating academic service-learning. One participating faculty member expressed her apprehension about "the impact this design will have on my . . . students' learning in Social Studies" due to "the amount of contact time spent on service-learning." However, other faculty could see gains in student involvement. One faculty member observed, "Even though we are studying the same content, those who are involved in doing service-learning are engaged in content; those who are not doing service-learning, but are just studying about it, are much less engaged and enthusiastic."

University Four

University Four is a large urban university with over 23,000 students. Its College of Education is the largest in the state with over 100 full- and part-time faculty. Academic service-learning has had a significant, long-term presence on campus. An Office of Academic Service-Learning provided training and technical assistance both to faculty in the university and to others in the state.

Because of difficulties establishing leadership of the Faculty Fellow grant at University Four, the role of contact faculty was assigned at the end of the first year to Dr. Dunn (a pseudonym), a relatively new faculty member. Little was accomplished during the initial period of the grant while Dr. Dunn familiarized herself with the training model and recruited participants or Faculty Fellow seminars.

During Year Two, Dr. Dunn reported difficulty making academic service-learning a priority among the faculty of the College of Education because of a current "directive to increase enrollment without increasing faculty numbers," that made the integration of academic service-learning appear to faculty as an additional burden. In addition, because of previous promotion of the Faculty Fellow model and academic

EXHIBIT 7
University Four Year Two Systemic Matrix

	Maintenance	Awareness	Exploration	Transition	New Infrastructure	Full Adoption
Vision						
Communication		▓				
Teaching		▓				
Administration			▓			
Standards			▓			

service-learning through the University Office of Academic Service-Learning, recruiting new participants for the University Consortium grant was more difficult because many faculty either knew about academic service-learning and were not interested in learning more or had already been trained using the model.

In the second year of the grant, eight faculty participated in Faculty Fellow seminars, and approximately 140 students took a course that included academic service-learning. During the fall semester, four undergraduate courses included academic service-learning, and three more were offered by the same faculty in the winter term. Most students in academic service-learning courses worked in schools, for example, creating learning centers, planning recess activities, facilitating clubs, and developing new student welcome packets.

During the second year of the grant, the College of Education at University Four was between the Awareness and the Exploration stage on most dimensions of the Change Matrix. With respect to Vision/Beliefs, University Four was classified at the Awareness Stage. Some faculty were very positive about academic service-learning and recognized connections to course outcomes for students, particularly in relation to development of teaching skills. However, there did not seem to be discussion about the value of academic service-learning to any particular program or department, nor any links seen to program missions or assessments.

Communication about academic service-learning at University Four also seemed to be at the Awareness Stage. The only formal communication occurred in the initial phase of the grant as part of efforts to recruit the first wave of Fellows. In the second year, communication between the contact faculty member and potential recruits was by word-of-mouth. Faculty who took the first academic service-learning seminar were continuing to talk about it among themselves, but there seemed to be little or no discussion of academic service-learning among non-participating faculty or through formal department or program communication channels.

With respect to the Teaching and Learning dimension of the matrix, University Four was also in the Awareness Stage. Only a small number of faculty were using academic service-learning, and although those that were appeared to be aware of its value as a teaching strategy, there was no discussion of linking academic service-learning to program goals and outcomes and no evidence that faculty were examining ways in which it could be used to enhance candidate learning across the program.

In terms of Administrative Roles and Responsibilities, diffusion was at the Maintenance Stage. Although academic service-learning was familiar to and supported by some high ranking university administrators in the College of Education and its various departments, academic service-learning was a low priority.

University Four was at the Maintenance Stage concerning the fifth dimension of the matrix, Alignment with Standards. Although some individual faculty members valued academic service-learning, no discussion seemed to have occurred about connecting it to particular NCATE or beginning teacher standards.

Regarding stages of concern and use, faculty seemed to be at the Task Impact stage of concern and the Mechanical level of use. Four faculty members replied to the e-mail prompts. All used academic service-learning in the same course at two differ-

ent times. Individually they developed activities, reflections, and assessments of stu-dents that included academic service-learning, and modified and adapted these in conjunction with reflections on their teaching and feedback from students. There was little evidence of collaboration about academic service-learning use as faculty were focused on strengthening their own use of the strategy and using it to facilitate course outcomes for students.

DISCUSSION

Researchers have studied the institutionalization of academic service-learn-ing in various educational settings; however, there has been little examina-tion of the process in teacher education. For teacher education programs, the requirements of external accrediting bodies, relationships with schools and teachers, and the need to teach the pedagogy of academic ser-vice-learning would seem to present unique challenges to the diffusion of academic service-learning. The purpose of this project was to use case study methodology to examine the impacts of the Eastern Michigan Uni-versity Faculty Fellow Development Model of training and technical assis-tance on the diffusion of academic service-learning within the teacher education programs of four large regional institutions in Michigan.

The diffusion processes at the four institutions differed markedly, a find-ing attributable to the quality of implementation of the training model, features of the change process and change environment at each institu-tion, and the interaction between these forces. Diffusion appeared to be most advanced in the programs (i.e., Universities One and Three) that most closely followed the EMU Faculty Fellow Development Model. These two sites witnessed the most frequent, regular seminars and the highest fidelity to the curriculum materials and sequence recommended under the model.

In addition to fidelity to the model, other variables suggested by the lit-erature on diffusion also clearly influenced the rate and success of the spread of academic service-learning (e.g., contact faculty members/change agents with more extensive knowledge of and commitment to aca-demic service-learning clearly effected greater change than others). At University One, the contact faculty member was involved with academic service-learning for many years. He both used the strategy and promoted it through his university and the state. At University Three, the contact fac-ulty member was a former Faculty Fellow in her university. She understood the model and believed in the potency of academic service-learning in teacher preparation. She was able to speak to and recruit colleagues with conviction and enthusiasm.

In contrast, in the programs demonstrating more limited diffusion, the change agents had less experience with and expertise in academic service-learning. For example, the contact faculty member at University Two, though committed to service, had minimal knowledge of the pedagogy and was apprehensive about how his department would receive it. Although Dr. Dunn, at University Four, was enthusiastic and had some prior knowledge of academic service-learning, her position as a relatively new faculty member meant she brought little status or authority to the recruitment of Faculty Fellows.

The findings also confirm the importance of the perceived compatibility of an innovation with individual and organizational goals, responsibilities, and histories. For example, Dr. Franklin at University Two believed that a majority of his colleagues felt the curriculum was "already too full" and would be reluctant to add a new strategy to teach to teacher candidates. The curriculum and faculty members' full schedules led him to attempt to embed training in the activities of existing departmental committees. However, although he may have been accurate in anticipating difficulty in recruiting participants in the project, Dr. Franklin's approach probably limited University Two faculty members' exposure to and understanding of academic service-learning and circumscribed the change process.

Additionally, the results support the significance of the relative advantage of an innovation and perceived complexity as predictors of the success of diffusion. Both Dr. Martin and the contact faculty members at University Three took specific steps to enhance academic service-learning's perceived advantages to potential users. Career pressures related to tenure and promotion mean that faculty must constantly consider demands for scholarship and service in determining how to allocate their time. In response to these pressures, not only did Dr. Martin introduce the pedagogy of academic service-learning, but he also supported participant writing and presentation by, for instance, holding sessions for Fellows to co-author conference proposals. Similarly at University Three, both contact faculty members collaborated with Fellows on research projects and conference proposals. At University Three, the contact faculty also assisted Fellows in locating funding for service projects, thus enhancing ease of implementation.

While these findings are consistent with the literature of diffusion, some of the results of the study were unexpected. Although contact faculty members cited specific types of support received, none viewed administrator support as a determining factor in their ability to promote academic service-learning. Many models of change cite the importance of administrative backing (e.g., Holland, 1997), yet it appears to have had marginal influence in these programs. It may be that the role of administrative support is less critical early in the diffusion process when the need is for adoption by individual faculty members rather than later when program change is the goal. Faculty autonomy and the complex organizational structure within the teacher preparation programs studied may also explain the limited influence of administrator backing.

Although it was hypothesized that accreditation standards would influence the diffusion of academic service-learning in teacher education, there was no indication of this in any of the programs. In fact, no spontaneous mention of accreditation occurred in any e-mail responses, and interviews with contact faculty revealed it to be a low priority. Faculty Fellows seemed to concentrate mainly on integrating the strategy into their courses and its effect on teaching and student learning, rather than on connecting academic service-learning to standards. This finding may indicate the peripheral importance of accreditation for participating faculty at the institutions studied or the fact that most participating faculty were at the "preparation to use" or the "mechanical" levels of use of academic service-learning and had little time or attention available for reflecting on larger program goals. As more faculty members in these programs become familiar with and skilled in using academic service-learning, greater consideration of how it connects to program mission and goals and to accreditation standards may be seen.

CONCLUSIONS

In conclusion, the teacher education programs in the University Consortium project, which made more rapid progress toward the adoption of academic service-learning, were those that more closely adhered to the Faculty Fellow model. Additional determinants of the success of diffusion were similar to those identified in the literature on educational change: a knowledgeable and committed change agent and efforts which might be expected to enhance potential users' perceptions of the compatibility, and relative advantage and manageability of academic service-learning appeared to be critical to the speed of adoption. Neither administrative support, nor a program's ability to reconcile academic service-learning with accreditation standards exerted the expected effects on the rate of diffusion. As more faculty members in these programs become familiar with and skilled in using academic service-learning, we hope to see greater consideration of how it connects to program mission and goals and to accreditation standards.

Acknowledgments: Contents of this chapter were developed under a grant from the Corporation for National and Community Service, Grant No. 00LHEM1062. However, these contents do not necessarily represent the policy of the Corporation for National and Community Service, and you should not assume endorsement by the federal government.

REFERENCES

Anderson, J., & Erickson, J. (2001, October). *Service-learning in teacher education: State of the field 2001.* Paper presented at the First Annual International Conference on Service-Learning Research, Berkley, CA.

Billig, S. H. (2002). Adoption, implementation, and sustainability of K–12 service-learning. In A. Furco & S. H. Billig (Eds.), *Advances in service-learning research: Vol. 1. Service-learning: The essence of the pedagogy* (pp. 245–270). Greenwich, CT: Information Age Publishing.

Bringle, R., & Hatcher, J. (2000). Institutionalization of service-learning in higher education. *Journal of Higher Education, 71*(3), 273–290.

Driscoll, A., Holland, B., Gelmon, S., & Kerrigan, S. (1996). An assessment model for service-learning: Comprehensive case studies of impact on faculty, students, community, and institution. *Michigan Journal of Community Service Learning, 3*, 66–71.

Ellsworth, J. (2000). *Surviving change: A survey of educational change models.* Syracuse, NY: Clearinghouse on Information and Technology.

Fullan, M. G., & Stiegelbauer, S. (1991). *The new meaning of educational change.* (2nd Ed.). Ontario, CAN: Oise Press.

Hall, G., & Hord, S. (2001). *Implementing change: Patterns, principles, and potholes.* Boston: Allyn & Bacon.

Holland, B. (1997). Analyzing institutional commitment to service: A model of key organizational factors. *Michigan Journal of Community Service Learning, 4*, 30–41.

Holland, B. (2000). Institutional impacts and organizational issues related to service-learning. *Michigan Journal of Community Service Learning* Special Issue, 52–60.

Myers, C., & Pickeral, T. (1997). Service-learning: An essential process for preparing teachers as transformational leaders in the reform of public education. In J. Erickson & J. Anderson (Eds.), *Learning with the community: Concepts and models for service-learning in teacher education* (pp. 13–41). Washington, DC: American Association for Higher Education.

Rice, D., & Stacey, K. (1997, Fall). Small group dynamics as catalyst for change: A faculty development model for academic service-learning. *Michigan Journal of Community Service learning,* 57-64.

Rogers, E. (1995). *Diffusion of innovation.* New York: The Free Press.

Root, S., & Swick, K. (2000). A framework for conceptualizing and doing research on service-learning. In J. Anderson, K. Swick & J. Yff (Eds.), *Service-learning in teacher education: Enhancing the growth of new teachers, their students and communities.* (pp. 141–152). New York: American Association of Colleges of Teacher Education.

Shumer, R. (1997, October). What research tells us about designing service-learning programs. *NASSP Bulletin, 81*(591), 18–24.

Zeichner, K. (1999). The new scholarship in teacher education. *Educational Researcher, 8*(4), 4–15.

CHAPTER 5

THE SUSTAINING FACTORS OF SERVICE-LEARNING AT A NATIONAL LEADER SCHOOL
A Case Study

Bruce J. Pontbriand

This chapter examines the factors related to sustaining a fully implemented and nationally recognized high school service-learning program. It reveals why community service-learning has been sustained for the past nine years at a suburban high school recognized as a National Service-Learning Leader School by the Corporation for National and Community Service. The study exposed the broad narrative of the case from the perspective of four data sources: observations, documents and artifacts, interviews, and a faculty survey. The findings indicate that a variety of constituencies became vested in the innovation because of the shared value of "community development" that the project added to the academic curriculum.

Deconstructing Service-Learning: Research Exploring Context, Participation, and Impacts
A Volume in: Advances in Service-Learning Research, pages 103–121.
Copyright © 2003 by Information Age Publishing, Inc.
All rights of reproduction in any form reserved.
ISBN: 1-59311-071-5 (hardcover), 1-59311-070-7 (pbk.)

INTRODUCTION

Between 1994 and 1997, the Center for Human Resources at Brandeis University studied service-learning programs at 7 middle schools and 10 high schools around the country as part of a national evaluation of Learn and Serve America program grant recipients. Few of the sites had success initiating formal, organized efforts to expand the use of service-learning into the overall curriculum. A significant number of programs also showed "limited success" as vehicles for institutional change and were weakly institutionalized (Melchior, 1999, p. 26).

The implementation of Community Service-Learning (CSL) at one school sparked a significant restructuring of curriculum and instruction through interdisciplinary projects and co-teaching. Since its fourth year of implementation, the superintendent reported that the program was funded out of the operating budget, and the school committee did not question continuation of funding for service-learning. In 1999, the program's successful and effective implementation resulted in the school being recognized as a Leader School, the Corporation for National and Community Service's highest honor for K–12 schools.

A review of the research involving implementation and institutionalization of an organizational innovation points to the depth, supports, and breadth needed to sustain service-learning. Rogers (1962) viewed successful innovation as a "diffusion" process where each stage needs to be well managed in order to maximize the probability of success. Light (1998) highlighted a service model of leadership that creates the conditions for others to succeed as a condition for sustainability in the innovation process. Definitions of institutionalization in the literature call for understanding the entire innovation process as a whole rather than treating institutionalization as a separate stage of development. Miles (1983) suggested that programs become institutionalized when they become "built-in" to the life of the school and its organizational routine. Louis and Miles (1990) suggested further that an innovation should be embedded within a variety of leadership levels in the implementation process in order to be institutionalized.

Service-learning is at a critical juncture. According to Kendall (1990), waves of interest only have a few years to be institutionalized or "they will recede with the tide to the next idea wave that comes along" (p. 12). Kendall noted that the current interest in service-learning is similar to "a wave of interest in community and public service in the late 1960s and early 1970s" (p. 7). By the time programs enter into their fifth year, they encounter similar problems that programs in the 1960s and 1970s confronted, such as balancing differing goals of agencies, students, and schools; assessing learning; and gaining institutional support.

RESEARCH QUESTIONS AND THEORETICAL RATIONALE

The study explored the factors and processes that sustained service-learning at this Leader School. The following research questions guided the inquiry:

1. What were the key events, decisions, and basic features of the process during the periods of planning, initiation, and implementation?
2. What were the supports and obstacles during the periods of planning, initiation, and implementation?
3. What supports and coping strategies were associated with overall implementation?
4. How well institutionalized is the program into the ordinary structures and procedures of the school and the district?

Supports and Obstacles to Sustainability

In order to understand the organizational conditions, supports, and coping strategies that were related to overall institutionalization of service-learning, this study examined the process of implementation and the supports for and obstacles to sustainability using the research-based descriptors of Melchior (1999) and Louis and Miles (1990). The study also looked for evidence and degree of institutionalization using indicators based on the research of Berman (2000) and Huberman and Miles (1984). Using these theoretical frameworks, the goal was to conceptualize the paths to institutionalization and highlight the corresponding supports and conditions necessary for this process.

Billig (2000a, 2000b, 2000c) believed that service-learning needs many of the same supports to sustain it as are needed for other educational innovations. These supports may include active leadership, quality professional development, a vision and action plan of how service is to be implemented, alignment with standards, assessment systems that are aligned with activities and curriculum, a person to help coordinate activities with community agencies as well as sufficient funding and other resources. Melchior (1999) also noted that the lack of a broader impact and integration does not appear to be the result of active minor and major opposition to service-learning, but is more likely the result of a host of major and minor barriers to institutional change in schools. These barriers may include lack of funds and available time for professional development, competing professional development priorities, concerns about meeting new standards and graduation requirements, lack of planning time for teachers, logistical problems, inflexible school schedules, and continued emphasis on community service over service-learning (Melchior, p. 23).

According to Toole (2000), service-learning implementation is an example of multi-tasking. He found that practitioners face a wide and divergent set of issues related to educational change. Similarly, Bolman and Deal's (1991) approach to managing such change emphasized multiple frame analysis to generate perspectives on a single organizational phenomenon, as well as studying the interrelationships between frames. These frames are the structural, symbolic, human resource, and the political dimensions of an organization.

In their study of urban high schools, Louis and Miles (1990) identified evolutionary planning, vision building, resource management, and coping skills as key action motifs related to sustainability in the context of school improvement. This study built on prior research showing that large-scale education innovations are sustained by the amount and quality of assistance that their users receive once the changes are under way (Hargreaves & Fink, 2000). Louis and Miles explained further that changes needed both implementation support and pressure.

Indicators and Qualities of Institutionalization

Berman (2000) detailed the following systemic indicators of institutionalization: presence in all curricular areas and grades, faculty participation in professional development activities; user consistency in service-learning standards (e.g., participation and reflection); connection to curriculum frameworks; percentage of student and teacher participation; endorsement in district policies; public recognition; sustained funding; and a stated value of service-learning in hiring, mission statements, and the school committee's goals for the district.

Huberman and Miles (1984) determined that the degree of institutionalization of an innovation was reflected in supporting organizational conditions. They found that about half their sites succeeded in institutionalizing innovative programs. Innovations moved through the "passages" and "cycles" of routinization to stable continuation. Sites with strong institutionalization made clear organizational changes—mandating the innovation, building it into the curriculum, and changing working procedures or structures—that were relatively irreversible (p. 221).

CONTEXT OF THIS STUDY

The site for this study was chosen because of the longevity of its program, its accessibility, and its recognition as a Leader School for its full integration of service-learning into the school's academic curriculum. It was also selected because of the willingness of the school superintendent, the principal, the CSL director, and the district's CSL consultant to share data about the program. The researcher's connection to the site was developed through a three-year learning relationship with the program as an interested observer and fellow practitioner.

School and Community

The school, a suburban, public high school (Grades 9–12), is located in a metropolitan area in the Northeast. It is located in a growing suburban town of 16,000. In 2001, there were 1,030 students enrolled with a staff of 98. The faculty at this Leader School changed dramatically from 1995–2001, with 75 of 95 teaching staff members hired since 1995. The school also had five different principals since 1992. The superintendent, curriculum coordinators, and elementary school principals, however, remained a stable force during this time period. There have been two CSL directors from 1992 until the present.

Chronology of Implementation

In 1992, the superintendent wrote a foundation grant to create a system-wide, service-learning initiative. A $500,000, three-year grant was awarded from a private philanthropist and the formal implementation of CSL began in September of that year. The goal was to build on earlier efforts at the school to instill in students the values of public service, compassion, initiative, and leadership, while at the same time making learning more meaningful. The superintendent reported that school funding for this initiative remained at approximately 2 percent ($170,000 in 2000) of the overall operating budget since 1998.

Program Structure

The high school has a full-time CSL director and a support staff of three people based in the building. The director oversees four other schools in this systemwide initiative. The three elementary schools and one middle school have CSL liaisons based in their buildings.

There are five main components to the present CSL program:

1. Connecting service to the academic curriculum;
2. An internship program;
3. Promoting co-curricular service opportunities;
4. Facilitating traditional community service activities (i.e., collections, fundraising); and
5. The demonstration and dissemination of service-learning methods to the outside community and other practitioners.

The school system provides funds in the form of mini-grants to pay for teacher planning time, supplies, and speakers to promote the use of service-learning as an instructional pedagogy.

RESEARCH DESIGN

The study relied heavily on qualitative research methods to help focus the research on complexities and dynamics at work at this site. The approach consisted of structured and semi-structured interviews, onsite observations, and analyzing objective data sources (documents, program artifacts, district/state reports). A structured survey of the high school faculty was also used. As a result, a broad case narrative was developed using the perspectives of these data sources. There were no formal student interviews in this study.

Lincoln and Guba (1985) suggested four criteria to establish rigor, or trustworthiness, in the collection of qualitative data. Credibility is assured by prolonged engagement, triangulation, peer debriefing, and member checking. This study satisfied prolonged engagement and persistent observation through 10 formal site visits over a year's time. Onsite observations of CSL meetings and workshops, individual interviews with teachers and community stakeholders, a structured survey, and program documents and artifacts revealed ideas that satisfied the criteria for triangulation. To ensure member checking (Creswell, 1994; Lincoln & Guba, 1985), data collection and review were collaborative efforts between the CSL director, the CSL consultant, and the researcher. The emerging findings were the focus of ongoing personal and electronic conversations during the study. These conversations were also a source of peer debriefing.

Population and Sampling

The primary population for the study included the 100 professional staff members of the school system. Ninety-eight members of the population were load or non-load bearing teachers, counselors, curriculum coordinators, administrators, and service-learning staff at the high school. The other two members were central office administrators. The samples chosen for the interviews were purposive. They included those adults who had either participated in a service-learning activity, had demonstrated public support, or those who had the longest institutional memory of the program. Exhibit 1 is an overview of the study's interviews.

EXHIBIT 1
Structured and Semi-Structured Interviews

School Site Interviews	Other Interviews
Building principal (1)	Superintendent (1)
Assistant principal (1)	Assistant superintendent (1)
Curriculum coordinator (2)	School committee/parent (1)
CSL director (1)	Council on Aging director (1)
CSL district consultant (1)	
CSL staff assistant (1)	
High school teacher (6)	
CSL internship coordinator (1)	
Former community service advisor (1)	
Total number of interviews = 19	

In addition to the interviews, the study also involved a structured survey given to 93 teaching and non-load bearing support staff in order to provide data about the level of participation and motivational factors and additional data about the perceived supports and obstacles to the innovation. There were 33 (35.5%) responses out of the population of professional staff, not including CSL personnel. The results of the survey, triangulated with other data sources, helped highlight meaningful variables related to institutionalization and narrowed down integral factors that contributed to sustainability.

Data Analysis

Observations and interviews were transcribed and read, and descriptive codes were developed. The qualitative analysis software HyperRE-SEARCH™ was then used to code or assign more categorical units of meaning to the qualitative data compiled during the study. Categories were collapsed into overall patterns or themes related to the research questions. Document and artifact data were coded by hand rather than electronically, but followed a similar analytical process. The researcher's thematic interpretations were shared and tested with the CSL director and district consultant before integrating data into explanatory frameworks.

Results

The data revealed that CSL was more of a learning process or pedagogy rather than a distinct program. Observational and interview data provided deeper insight into the cultural readiness and commitment towards a service approach to learning that enabled a strong fit with the philosophy of the school system. High system-level support was also consistently mentioned in the data sets as a factor that led to implementation and sustainability of CSL. This appeared to offset the lack of strong, administrative endorsement for CSL at the high school as reported in the survey results.

A theme that ran through the findings was that program leadership for CSL has been adept at using multiple approaches to implement and sustain CSL. Overall findings pointed to a strong integration of CSL with curriculum standards and frameworks as well as the implementation of a market-based approach to meeting the individual needs of students, local businesses, and the community at large. Both CSL champions and non-users were in agreement that a primary CSL outcome was community development.

There was also some disagreement among the data sets about certain supports in the development of CSL. Interview findings stressed teacher collaboration as a mediating factor to CSL growth. Interviews also revealed the school reform goals of professional collegiality and school climate were outcomes. However, there was high variance in the survey data (Exhibit 2) with respect to teacher collegiality and collaboration between users and non-users. Both groups in the survey were also in disagreement about school climate as a recognized outcome. The wide range of user latitude, coupled with survey comments, made a sense of shared ownership for CSL at the high school difficult to discern.

Paths to Institutionalization

In an effort to explain institutionalization, key variables from the findings were displayed in a sequenced network. This general model (Exhibit 3) describes the course of events leading to high, moderate, and low outcomes and is arranged according to the supports provided and threats encountered during the process.

The story begins with *cultural readiness* for service-learning and the award of the *foundation grant*. The grant galvanized fragmented commitment and practice to CSL. Community service initiatives were already present at the site, resulting in a *good program fit of CSL* with the system's characteristics and the *central administrative commitment* to service. Aggressive grant writing became a funding strategy that helped alleviate concern about shifting funds from other programs and thus engendered system support.

EXHIBIT 2

Mean Scores, Standard Deviations, and Standard Error of Means for Both Groups on Perceived Usefulness of Service-Learning

	Participates in CSL project	N	M	SD	SEM
Teacher collaboration **	User	20	3.7000	1.4179	.3171
	Non-User	13	5.0769	.9541	.2646
Effect on student learning	User	20	2.2000	1.3219	.2956
	Non-User	13	3.0769	1.4412	.3997
Effect on student behavior	User	20	2.8500	1.6944	.3789
	Non-User	13	2.7692	1.5892	.4408
Service impact on the community	User	20	3.1000	1.3727	.3069
	Non-User	13	2.6923	1.8879	.5236
School climate***	User	20	3.6000	1.8750	.4193
	Non-User	13	3.9231	1.3821	.3833
Teacher effectiveness/ renewal**	User	20	3.9500	1.7006	.3803
	Non-User	13	4.6923	1.1821	.3279

Notes: 5-point scale: 1 = strongly disagree, 2 = somewhat disagree, 3 = neutral, 4 = somewhat agree, 5 = strongly agree

Significance based on F statistic model for each group: $*p < .05$, $**p < .10$, $***p < .25$

Strong central administrative commitment led to the hiring of a full-time program coordinator located at the high school. Central administrative pressure on building principals, directors, and coordinators to implement CSL also contributed to system-level support and pressure. Support and pressure for CSL amongst the elementary principals and curriculum coordinators was nurtured through the stability of central office personnel. Program leadership stressed user assistance and promoted teacher empowerment and collaboration. This resulted in increased user effort and commitment as well as a variety of projects with both curriculum and community connections. The findings showed that external network collaboration resulted in greater commitment for users through more resources for assistance, as well as outside recognition for the program that

EXHIBIT 3

Data Grounded Path to Institutionalization of CSL at a Leader School

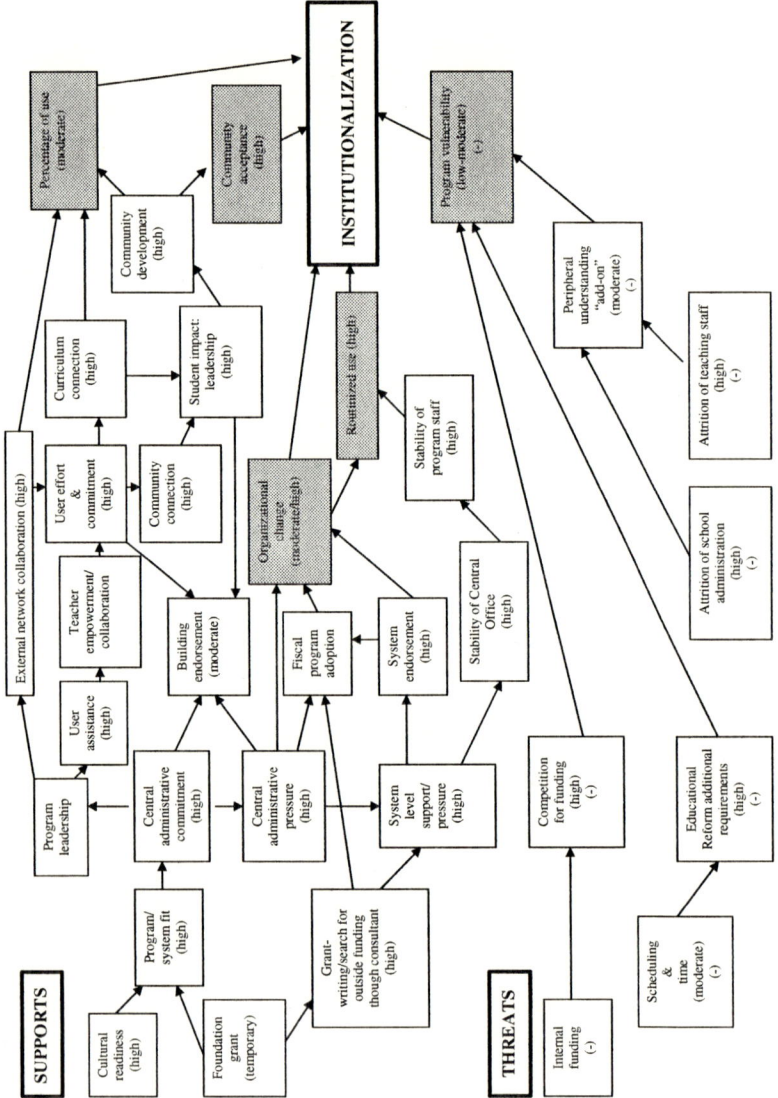

INSTITUTIONALIZATION

Percentage of use (moderate)

Community acceptance (high)

Program vulnerability (low–moderate) (-)

Community development (high)

Curriculum connection (high)

Student impact: leadership (high)

External network collaboration (high)

User effort & commitment (high)

Community connection (high)

Routinized use (high)

Peripheral understanding "add-on" (moderate) (-)

Attrition of teaching staff (high) (-)

Teacher empowerment/ collaboration

Building endorsement (moderate)

Organizational change (moderate/high)

Stability of program staff (high)

Program leadership

User assistance (high)

Fiscal program adoption

System endorsement (high)

Stability of Central Office (high)

Attrition of school administration (high) (-)

Central administrative commitment (high)

Central administrative pressure (high)

System level support/ pressure (high)

Competition for funding (high) (-)

Educational Reform additional requirements (high) (-)

SUPPORTS

Program/ system fit (high)

Grant-writing/search for outside funding through consultant (high)

THREATS

Internal funding (-)

Scheduling & time (moderate) (-)

Cultural readiness (high)

Foundation grant (temporary)

contributed to building endorsement. Students and teachers took great pride in sharing their projects with other systems. Key examples of the project sharing were the annual showcase, workshop, and celebration during which CSL projects were presented to community members and service practitioners from across the region. Observations of the "showcase day" revealed strong evidence of student leadership in the CSL program.

CSL activities were highly publicized resulting in more student and teacher interest, an increased percentage of use, and community acceptance of the program. System-level support and administrative pressure led to system endorsement through a reworked mission statement and fiscal program adoption once the foundation grant expired.

When the program was fiscally adopted, central administrative pressure took more direct action to bring about organizational change. Combined with a stable program staff, all of these supports made up for a lack of overt leadership from the high school administration and contributed to high, routinized use in that building.

It was necessary for CSL to ward off threats to sustainability during this process. First, there was the question of continued internal funding after the foundation grant ended. Although the program was supported fiscally, there still continued to be strong competition for funding within the town's annual budget cycle. Structural issues like time and scheduling continue to be ongoing threats to institutionalization. Procedural changes that support the program have gone through cycles at the high school, but have not had consistent building leadership to sustain these changes. Additional requirements from educational reform legislation made scheduling and time reoccurring obstacles to participation. Strong central administrative and system-level support counteracted the negative effect of high attrition of the high school's administration and teaching staff to program understanding. Moreover, the peripheral understanding of community service as a less serious learning experience is a problem in parts of the high school's culture that was fueled by the addition of many new staff members. High user assistance through professional development was used as a remedy to make the program less vulnerable to this environmental turbulence. The general message of the model was that a combination of high central administrative pressure, consequent system-level support, and skillful program leadership centering on high user assistance were necessary factors for institutionalization.

SUMMARY

This case study focused on the factors and processes that sustained service-learning at a Leader School. The results are interpreted with respect to the research questions posed earlier in this chapter.

1. *What were the key events, decisions, and basic features of the process during the periods of planning, initiation, and implementation?*

   Although community service initiatives were present at this site since the 1970s, the award of a foundation grant blended these fragmented activities into a systemwide initiative. A programmatic focus on community development engendered system endorsement, community acceptance, and led to fiscal adoption by the town. Fiscal adoption in the fourth year enabled the central administration and CSL director to establish the organizational supports needed for wider CSL participation throughout the system.

2. *What were the supports and obstacles during the periods of planning, initiation, and implementation?*

   Two general streams of support were present during the stages of CSL development. A combination of strong user assistance and administrative pressure created a web of support that enabled CSL to ward off threats to its sustainability. User effort and commitment to CSL were enhanced through assistance provided by a full-time director and building liaisons. Ongoing structural support was provided through a mini-grant process that not only provided resources, but also fostered curriculum connections and teacher collaborations, especially through cross-school partnerships. Other structural concerns such as transportation and making connections with community partners were supported through coordination from the director and a part-time staff assistant.

3. *What supports and coping strategies led to overall implementation?*

   A series of active leadership strategies supported the program's development from the initiation and adoption stages to overall implementation and institutionalization. Much thinking about K–12 service-learning implementation was directed at structural concerns. In this case, six organizational areas were supportive to the implementation process: the political, symbolic, structural, human resource, cultural, and the ethical. Organizational frame analysis of school change draws from the work of Bolman and Deal (1991) and has been explicitly connected to service-learning implementation by Toole (2000).

   Under the original director, the CSL program started with a political and symbolic approach to implementation. In its first year, the director built coalitions with intellectually respected staff members at the high school. The director approached teachers and curriculum coordinators who were identified as the school's instructional leaders. This political approach was highly instrumental in connecting with people who had the capacity to understand and talk to others about this new innovation.

   The CSL retreat in the program's third year was important to building cultural willingness to implement a new innovation. The following year saw system leaders rework the high school mission statement to include service-learning goals as a way to deepen the impact of learning and enhance teaching. Thus, the political and symbolic approaches to implementation combined to raise the level of professional discussion around CSL, enhance its credibility, and create an influential base of support. All of these factors were contributing factors to fiscal adoption in the fourth year.

In the seventh year, the second director began with a wide-based, structural approach to implementation. An attention to human resources was combined with a different cultural approach to support CSL. Whereas the last director built a supportive culture within the school organization, this director focused more on agencies and town organizations to build support within their own respective groups. In fact, the director became a member on a number of advisory boards in the community. A consistent emphasis throughout implementation has been on the ethical purposes of service-learning. Although projects varied in length and scope, durable projects supported opportunities for youth, family, and community leadership. Exhibit 4 summarizes the types of supportive leadership approaches for institutionalization.

4. *How well institutionalized is the program into the ordinary structures and procedures of the school and the district?*

EXHIBIT 4
Supportive Leadership Approaches to Implementation and Institutionalization

Phase I: Initiation to Fiscal Adoption	
Political	Coalitions built with key, instructional leaders of the school. Users selected and identified based on high capacity for support and demonstration.
Symbolic	CSL linked to school/system mission and shared learning goals.
Cultural	Focus on building collaboration and support in school organization.
Ethical	Activities promote community leadership opportunities.
Phase II: Implementation to Institutionalization	
Structural	Wide-based in system through school liaisons, direct participation in administrative routine, and frequent mini-grants.
Human Resource	Resources and assistance matched to a variety of user capacities and interests.
Cultural	Focus on building collaborative relationships forged in larger community.
Ethical	Activities promote community leadership opportunities.

Using the indicators and a conceptualization suggested by Miles (1983), the CSL initiative exhibited the conditions and completed the necessary passages necessary for program institutionalization at both the school and system-level (see Exhibit 5). Stronger institutionalization at the system-level and a curriculum-based sequencing of activities were contributing factors to the routinized use of CSL at this Leader School.

DISCUSSION OF INSTITUTIONALIZATION AND SUSTAINABILITY

Indicators at this site matched the qualities of program institutionalization as identified by Huberman and Miles (1984).These qualities were present to a moderate or high degree at the site and included community acceptance, organizational change and routinization. Key points in the passage were the survival of CSL through six annual budget cycles and its durability through the arrival and departure of five principals and 75 teachers. Clear organizational changes built into the routines in the high school and school system, such as CSL staffing, the mini-grant process, mission statements, and professional development goals reflected Huberman and Miles' indicators of institutionalization. Their research defines strong institutionalization as organizational transformation, accompanied by a reasonable amount of assistance, to bring about stabilized use by a large percentage of users. At this site, stabilized use by users was promoted by system-level support and external stakeholder expectations of continued service. Considering the large turnover of high school personnel during this process, the site demonstrated Huberman and Miles' indicators for strong institutionalization.

The following list presents those factors that appeared to influence CSL institutionalization at Leader School.

1. *Good program and system fit.* There was already cultural readiness and philosophical commitment to service present at this site. The program was designed to advance this service commitment through linkage to the curriculum for more wide-based participation and educational centrality.

2. *Program leadership.* A full-time director with a staff assistant provided the coordination and assistance necessary to advance a wide range of user participation. The administrative structure allowed the director the flexibility to promote linkages to many different constituencies in the system and town by reporting directly to the superintendent. Using a variety of organizational approaches, the director's leadership has been central during all periods of implementation.

3. *Administrative commitment and pressure.* The superintendent's articulated commitment to service-learning and a connection to the system's core values advanced both system and building endorsement of CSL. This commitment was balanced by pressure to implement CSL exerted through an administrative network of curriculum coordinators and building principals. Pressure to implement and integrate CSL into professional development efforts was coupled with a high level of user assistance from the CSL office.

4. *Pedagogical embeddedness.* Service-learning was not implemented as merely an adjunct program, but rather it was institutionalized as way of learning. As a comprehensive pedagogy, CSL included its own educational anthropology and world view.

5. *Clear place in institutional objectives.* In the path to institutionalization, CSL goals were written into mission statements (high school, system, school committee) and school improvement plans. The central place of service-learning as an educational value was made clear to students, parents, and community members through school literature and even by signs at the entry points to town.

6. *Support of multiple constituencies.* With its unique ability to act as a link to many environments, service-learning can impact many constituencies both inside and outside the school. System, building, and community endorsements were due in a large part to motivated students acting as ambassadors of the program. In addition, a political approach by both the first director and superintendent to build fiscal support and external program recognition advanced it through the important passage of "soft-to-hard money."

The findings of this study confirmed key supports to service-learning implementation and institutionalization revealed by Berman (2000) and Billig (2002) in their research. Evidence of active leadership by the superintendent, director, and building principals that integrated a high level of professional development, coordination, and a connection to curriculum standards was found in all the data sets. This finding supports the Louis and Miles (1990) theory that programs must be embedded in a variety of leadership levels in order to be institutionalized.

A person to coordinate activities was not only an important factor in implementation, but the CSL director's clear accountability to the superintendent rather than other middle managers also gave political, cultural, symbolic, human resource, and structural leverage to the position. Billig (2002) also highlighted sufficient funding and other resources as a key supports. This was seen in the consistent employment and aggressive grant-writing of the CSL consultant since the program's inception.

Although CSL did not take the approach of a long-term school improvement strategy as suggested by Berman (2000), a broad-based path to institutionalization was confirmed by the findings. Wide participation of faculty in professional development activities, user consistency in service-learning standards (e.g., reflection, reciprocal relationships, demonstration of impacts); connection to curriculum frameworks; endorsement in system policies; external recognition; sustained funding; and as a stated value in hiring and mission statements were all evident in the path to institutionalization gleaned from the findings. However, specific involvement of both directors in various agencies and town groups also helped institutionalize CSL, through particular activities, into the lives of these organizations. This community development strategy engendered the family and community ownership that has supported the routinization of CSL.

The action motifs for sustainable change, suggested by Louis and Miles (1990), were evident in the design and implementation process. Evolutionary planning took place before the award of the foundation grant. Obstacles to implementation such as transportation, teacher resistance, and coordination were considered in the grant proposal and dealt with at a very early stage. The support staff also acted as a consistent monitoring system that addressed emerging problems before circles of doubt about the innovation began to grow.

The path of high user assistance to institutionalization supports research findings (Hargreaves & Fink, 2000; Louis & Miles, 1990) that emphasize the amount and quality of user assistance as important for sustainability once change is underway. User assistance promoted quality standards such as critical reflection, student voice, academic connections, and rigor, as well as celebration/demonstration components that engendered a web of support needed for widespread acceptance.

Theoretical Implications

Literature on K–12 service-learning institutionalization stressed integration models containing such influencing factors as mission, philosophical fit, curriculum, administrative commitment, and sustained funding (Berman, 2000; Melchior, 1999). An integration of contributing school-based factors also featured heavily in the path to institutionalization at this site and supported this research. However, the "market model" identified by Levison (1994) in his cross-case study on traditional community service, which focused on meeting tangible needs and wants of both students and community members, was also present at this site. In this case, service-learning added to what Coleman (1988) calls "social capital" or the quality and depth of relationships between people in a family or a community. Increasing social capital was an important factor in this program's sustainability.

Recommendations for Sustainable Practice

The following three recommendations, gleaned from this study, are directed at sustaining comprehensive service-learning programs.

1. *Promote shared ownership.* Service-learning needs to include critical reflection, student voice and leadership, the fulfillment of community articulated needs, and a critical mass of activities need to be tied to the curriculum with a level of academic rigor. Such qualities ensure that service-learning does not become personality driven, but part of a broadly used pedagogy that engenders a wider sense of ownership and higher potential for sustainability.

2. *Build program sequencing to create a sustaining process.* Service-learning works well and is better sustained when there is a built-in sequencing of activities over time to create a sustaining process. In the systemic structure of this Leader School program, strong service-learning initiatives in the elementary schools built excitement and anticipation about academic learning. Student enthusiasm and parental expectation brought to the middle and high schools both enticement and pressure for other teachers to participate The enthusiasm, expectation, and subsequent pressure rooted in the K–12 sequencing of quality activities were important factors in the institutionalization of service-learning at the high school level.

3. *Integrate the core values of the community.* Service-learning pedagogy is more than an instructional technique. The service component is intrinsically connected to the foundational values and the worldview of the school and its surrounding community. School-based interviews, survey results, and letters of support from community stakeholders highlighted community development as a core value-added outcome of service-learning. Consequently, successful practitioners should develop a sophisticated understanding of the deeper values connected to the teaching and learning process in their respective communities in order to build and sustain quality programs. Practitioners need to ask: What is the collective educational vision of our community and how does service-learning help achieve this goal? Further studies responding to this key question will provide important insight into how sustainable programs are tied to shared community values or cultural/religious apologetics.

CONCLUSION

The curricular integration of service-learning, in conjunction with individualized teacher assistance and administrative commitment, leads to sustainable and institutionalized programs. For this to happen, however, service-learning cannot be narrow in focus and application. It needs to be understood as a comprehensive teaching methodology that connects a variety of stakeholders and allows learning impacts to be extended into a variety of environments. Service-learning can be more fully implemented and sustained when its unique ability to act as this link between the school and its community is supported by program directors and school leaders.

In this case, a variety of constituencies became vested in the innovation because of a shared commitment to the value of community development that it added to the academic curriculum. An ethic of cooperation and care became a context of learning for students through CSL. Other ethical orientations could be ones of social justice, environmental stewardship, or democratic education. Nevertheless, the pioneering passion needed to implement and sustain service-learning initiatives needs to be generated by deeper social, moral, or spiritual values.

At this Leader School, the deep passion and commitment of school leaders, students, teachers, and community members were mediating factors in the institutionalization process. However, it is expected that a lack of funding of such programs at the local, state, and national level will continue to be a threat to sustainability. At some point in the implementation process, once school personnel have put the structural pieces in place, responsibility for the success of service-learning programs will rely on not just school but family and community leadership. Funding helps, but the self-sustaining momentum needed to truly support service-learning rests in the shared commitment and responsibility of all these stakeholders to take their role in the chain of care that ultimately educates the young people of our communities.

REFERENCES

Berman, S. H. (2000). Service as systemic reform. *School Administrator, 57*(7), 20–24.

Billig, S. H. (2000a, March). *The current state of K–12 service-learning research.* Presentation at National Service-Learning Conference, Providence, RI.

Billig, S. H. (2000b). Research on K–12 school-based service-learning: The evidence builds. *Phi Delta Kappan, 81*(9), 658–653.

Billig, S. H. (2000c). The effects of service-learning. *School Administrator, 57*(7), 14–18.

Billig, S. H. (2002). Adoption, implementation, and sustainability of K–12 service-learning. In A. Furco & S. H. Billig (Eds.), *Advances in service-learning research: Vol. 1. Service-learning: The essence of the pedagogy* (pp. 245–267). Greenwich, CT: Information Age Publishing.

Bolman, L. G., & Deal, T. E. (1991). *Reframing organizations: Artistry, choice, and leadership.* San Francisco: Jossey-Bass.

Coleman, J. (1988). *Foundations of social theory.* Cambridge, MA: Belknap Press.

Creswell, J. (1994). *Research design: Qualitative and quantitative approaches.* Thousand Oaks, CA: Sage.

Hargreaves, A., & Fink, D. (2000). The three dimensions of reform. *Educational Leadership, 57*(7), 30–33.

Huberman, A. M., & Miles, M. B. (1984). *Innovation up close.* New York: Plenum Press.

Kendall, J. (1990). Combining service and learning: An introduction. In J. Kendall & Associates (Eds.), *Combining learning and service: A resource book for community and public service: Vol. I.* (pp. 1–33). Raleigh, NC: National Society for Internships and Experiential Education.

Levison, L. M. (1994). *Community service programs in independent schools* .New York: Garland Publishing.

Light, P. (1998). *Sustaining innovation.* San Francisco: Jossey-Bass.

Lincoln, Y. S., & Guba, E. G. (1985). *Naturalistic inquiry.* Thousand Oaks, CA: Sage.

Louis, K. S., & Miles, M. B. (1990). *Improving the urban high school: What works and why.* New York: Teachers College Press.

Melchior, A. (1999). *Summary report: National evaluation of Learn and Serve America* Waltham, MA: Brandeis University, Center for Human Resources.

Miles, M. B. (1983). Unraveling the mystery of institutionalization. *Educational Leadership, 41*, 14–19.

Rogers, E. M. (1962). *Diffusion of innovations.* New York: The Free Press.

Toole, J. (2000, April). *Framing the role of social trust in school reform: Case studies of service-learning.* Presentation at AERA, New Orleans, LA.

PART IV

THE ROLE OF COMMUNITY IN SERVICE-LEARNING

CHAPTER 6

FINDING THE COMMUNITY IN SERVICE-LEARNING RESEARCH
The 3-"I" Model

Melinda Clarke

"How should an evaluation model be designed in order to acknowledge, measure, and reflect the dynamic community impact of service initiatives, and specifically, service-learning programs?" By design, the 3-"I" Model answered the research question by offering a new approach to community impact evaluation. The 3-"I" Model intentionally included three distinct yet related dimensions in order to evaluate community impact as a process. The first "I", the Initiator dimension, considered goal setting, partnership development, shared understandings, and the development of a knowledge base to facilitate the change process; the second "I", the Initiative dimension, addressed the initiative implementation process, measures, indicators, and community involvement and participation; and the third "I", the Impact dimension, considered implementation strategies and results, intended outcomes and goals, and the flow of the impact knowledge back to the Initiator dimension. This impact-as-a-process research framework guided the research design and directed the methods, data gathering and piloting, which

Deconstructing Service-Learning: Research Exploring Context, Participation, and Impacts
A Volume in: Advances in Service-Learning Research, pages 125–146.
Copyright © 2003 by Information Age Publishing, Inc.
All rights of reproduction in any form reserved.
ISBN: 1-59311-071-5 (hardcover), 1-59311-070-7 (pbk.)

unfolded in ways that proved the model's capacity to meet its research objective. The 3-"I" Model involved both quantitative and qualitative research and was tested in a community where multiple projects of a university service-learning program were underway. The triangulation of the multiple sources of evidence proved the presence of community impact as well as the community impact process by demonstrating (a) initiator and community commitment to a utilization-focused service initiative based on community relevance and utility, (b) collaboration and goal sharing between the initiators of the service and the community, (c) positive and negative impact factors, (d) strategies that served the intended goals, (e) impact goals achieved, (f) community changes that occurred as a result of the service initiative, and (g) extent to which results were shared in order to improve future performance.

INTRODUCTION

In *A Service-Learning Research Agenda* for the Next Five Years, Giles and Eyler (1998) cited the community impact of service-learning as one of the "Top Ten Unanswered Questions in Service-Learning Research" (p. 65). In *The Michigan Journal of Community Service Learning* article, *Strategic Directions for Service-Learning Research*, Cruz and Giles (2000) asked the question "Where's the community in service-learning research?" (p. 28), and in *"Building Sustainable Partnerships: Linking Communities and Educational Institutions,"* Sigmon (1998) wrote:

> Programs that attempt to combine effective learning with meaningful service are experiencing unprecedented growth, are being questioned in some circles, and face challenges of deepening meaningful partnerships between educational institutions and communities... at the present time there is a lack of information about effective processes for building meaningful, reciprocal partnerships in service-learning programs... (p. 2)

Traditional evaluation approaches, based primarily on quantitative data measuring one time results have historically lacked the capacity to capture the process of community impact or the establishment of the community partnership. This gap in the service-learning research, coupled with the numerous evaluation attempts of practitioners who find that traditional methods do not capture the process of community impact leads to the research question: "How should an evaluation model be designed in order to acknowledge, measure, and reflect the dynamic community impact of service initiatives, and specifically, service-learning programs?"

THE NEED FOR NEW EVALUATION DESIGN

In summarizing an imperative for future evaluations, Weiss (1995) contended that practices must change from standard, quantitative measures on "available indicators of outcome" to strategies that "fit the complexity of the new community initiatives and the knowledge needs of their practitioners and sponsors" (pp. 65–66). Leaders of comprehensive community initiatives have developed new approaches to evaluation; however, they too express a "lack of fit" between current evaluation methods and the need to effectively measure the community impact of service (Connell, Kubisch, Schorr, & Weiss, 1995, p. viii). In fact, Weiss (1995) asserted that the nature and magnitude of the problems associated with evaluating community service initiatives require new evaluation paradigms and contended:

> We cannot limit our research questions and programmatic approaches to those for which random assignment demonstration research is best suited. We are prepared to redefine standards of certainty in a search for meaningful answers to more relevant, complex, and multi-dimensional questions, and we need your help... (p. 17)

In *Building Community: Social Science in Action,* Nyden, Figert, Shibley, & Burrows (1997) stressed the need for collaborative research approaches and affirmed the method's ability to capture community impact. The authors stated, "collaborative research involves researchers in the 'real' world with the opportunity to see their research efforts used by communities to improve the quality of life of its members" (p. 11).

A review of the evaluation literature also reveals that evaluators indicate that evaluation has become theoretically and methodologically static (Rebien, 1997). Evaluators from diverse areas of the evaluation field concur that evaluation work requires a continued focus on improving and advancing evaluation designs, methods and measures (Blair, 1998; Henderson & McAdam, 1998; Holloway, 1997; Kretzmann & McKnight, 1993; Patrizi & McMullan, 1998; Rebien, 1997; Salzer, Nixon, Schut, Karver, & Bickman, 1997). Although there is an increasing need for improved evaluation methods, evaluating community initiatives remains challenging to evaluators because of the complexities, contexts, and outcomes that accompany them (Connell et. al, 1995).

3-"I" MODEL OFFERS STRATEGIC EVALUATION RESPONSE

Responding to the call for new evaluation strategies that are designed to reflect the process of community impact of service initiatives (Connell et al., 1995; 1998; Weiss, 1995) and the mandate to integrate collaborative models (Giles, Honnet, & Migliore, 1991; Nyden et al., 1997), the 3-"I" model offers a strategic evaluation approach by considering impact at different stages, from different perspectives, while using different measures. The 3-"I" model reflects a review of the literature on evaluation, service-learning, community impact, and comprehensive community initiatives. The model is a response to voices from the field, including foundations, education, and the nonprofit community. The model is a process model that reflects a collaborative community impact framework and offers an alternative approach to assessing community impact by considering community impact from the inside out.

In order to employ a collaborative approach that focuses on the *process* of community impact, the model includes three dimensions that represent:

1. The **Initiators** of the service;
2. The community service **Initiative**; and
3. The community **Impact** of the service.

The 3-"I" dimensions were established due to their significance in the literature, their presence in practice and their value in evaluation and assessment.

Two of the most applicable and most promising evaluation methods that surfaced from research and the evaluation literature are theory-based evaluation and utilization-focused evaluation. When intentionally combined, these two evaluation methods serve as complementary lenses that each focus on specific functions of the impact process, revealing specific pivotal points that lead to the ultimate presence of community impact. The 3-"I" Model employed both utilization-focused evaluation and theory-based evaluation practices as operational constructs for evaluating the community impact of service-initiatives. Both of these evaluation methods incorporate participatory research methods and were chosen because they complement the research objective and have also been used successfully in community impact evaluations.

THEORY OF CHANGE EVALUATION AND THE 3-"I" MODEL

Patrizi and McMullan (1998) asserted that foundation boards were asking, "What has changed?" instead of "What have we done?" (p. 4). This increased focus on change and the need to know why and how programs are working are two reasons why theory-based evaluation and particularly theory-of-change evaluation approaches may provide effective evaluation results.

Rebien (1997) also asserted that a "lack of theory and observance to underlying assumptions have been identified as central weaknesses" of current evaluation practice (p. 2). This assertion finds agreement among both evaluation researchers and practitioners. Weiss (1997) acknowledged the frustrations evaluators' experience because of the "lack of theory" in many evaluations (p. 501). She suggested theory-based evaluation as a possible solution for evaluation designs, specifically evaluations involving communities and service initiatives (Weiss, 1995). Other evaluation researchers such as Chen and Rossi (1987) and Patton (1997) concurred with Weiss and also suggest theory-based evaluation approaches.

Weiss (1995) defined theory of change as the process that explains and gives insights into how and why evaluations work. She asserted that theory of change evaluation is good practice for evaluators concerned with community and service initiatives because:

- It concentrates evaluation attention and resources on key aspects of the program;
- It facilitates aggregation of evaluation results into a broader base of theoretical and program knowledge;
- It asks program practitioners to make their assumptions explicit and to reach consensus with their colleagues about what they are trying to do and why; and
- It may have more influence on both policy and popular opinion by addressing the theoretical assumptions embedded in programs. (p. 69)

In support of theory-based evaluation and more specifically, theory of change evaluations, Fulbright-Anderson, Kubisch, and Connell (1998) added that a theory of change approach is a valuable evaluation method because it is a "systemic and cumulative study of the links between activities, outcomes and contexts in an initiative" (Fulbright-Anderson, Kubisch, et al., 1998, p. 16). Connell and Kubisch also asserted that the theory of change approach acknowledges the community by involving community stakeholders, a key aspect of the theory of change method.

According to Weiss (1995) theory of change is unique in its capacity to bring community and service stakeholders together to openly contemplate and discuss potential outcomes. She wrote: "Theory of change asks participants to be as clear as possible about not only the ultimate outcomes and impacts they hope to achieve, but also the avenues through which they expect to achieve them" (Weiss, 1995, p. 17). Gambone (1998) asserted that theory of change evaluation strategies are intended to aid evaluators in the measurement of effects, progress, and contexts by

- Assessing the effectiveness of the initiatives in achieving the outcomes as specified;

- Providing information for monitoring and reporting on the progress made by initiatives in implementing the activities expected to result in change in the community; and
- Developing a knowledge base about the circumstances that facilitate or hamper positive or negative outcomes in the initiative. (p. 151)

In addition, Connell, Aber, and Walker (1995) expressed the valuable contribution theory of change evaluation can make as a research framework. They explained that its value is found in its capacity to contribute to the evaluation knowledge base by addressing the following:

- Making explicit the theories of change that are guiding the initiatives;
- Specifying the operational strategies that are being implemented to initiate and maintain changes;
- Identifying the external conditions that facilitate or undermine the effectiveness of operational strategies; and
- Projecting the future supports that will permit short-term effects to lead to longer-term outcomes. (p. 121)

For these reasons, this research study incorporates a theory-based evaluation approach because this methodology complements the conceptual synthesis research objectives of the 3-"I" Model due to its capacity to serve as both "a systematic and cumulative study of the links between activities, outcomes and contexts of the initiative" (Fulbright-Anderson et al., 1998, p. 16).

The theory of change approach is also a recommended method for evaluating community impact because the approach "allows the evaluation to be shaped by the ideas, values and aspirations of stakeholders at all levels and at many points" (Fulbright-Anderson et al., 1998, p. 16). Good theory of change should be:

- Plausible, rooted in evidence and common sense;
- Do-able, feasible considering economic, technical, political, institutional, and human resources; and
- Testable, specific, and complete enough to be evaluated in credible and useful ways (Fulbright-Anderson et al., p. 19).

Each of these characteristics is present in the 3-"I" Model.

Utilization Focused Evaluation and the 3-"I" Model

Another effective evaluation alternative with the capacity to reflect the process of change while focusing on practical outcomes that can inform and improve programming is found in utilization-focused evaluation. Patton (1997) defined utilization-focused evaluation as:

> Program evaluation is the systemic collection of information about the activities, characteristics, and outcomes of programs to make judgments about the program, improve program effectiveness, and/or inform decisions about future programming. Utilization-focused program evaluation (as opposed to program evaluation in general) is evaluation done for and with specific, intended primary users for specific intended users). (p. 23)

He also suggested the utilization-focused evaluation because of its "multilevel stakeholder structure and process" (p. 53). Patton also strongly proposed the involvement of the primary users in evaluation methods decisions in order to gain valuable insights into utility and function. In addition, he asserted that the fundamental premises of the initiative and subsequently, the evaluation should be clearly articulated. Utilization-focused evaluations are developed from a framework consisting of six different elements, including: a specific participant or target group, the desired outcome(s) for that target group, one or more indicators for each desired outcome, details of data collection, how results will be used, and performance of targets

For each element, Patton (1997) recommended certain issues for consideration. In the initial identifying specific participant or client target group phase, he advised "it is important...to make sure an intended outcome is meaningful and appropriate for everyone in the identified population" (p. 159). When specifying desired outcomes, he suggested the careful use and explanation of language in order to provide a clear statement of the "targeted change in circumstances, status, level of functioning, behavior, attitude, knowledge, or skills" (p. 159). When determining outcome indicators, he declared, "the key is to make sure that the indicator is a reasonable, useful and meaningful measure of the intended client outcomes" (p. 161). Details of data collection are a "distinct part of the framework...but they shouldn't clutter the focused outcome statement" (p. 163).

In utilization-focused evaluation, methods are guided by the research goals, which in this case, are community impact and the development of a knowledge base that can inform and refine service-learning initiatives. As Patton (1997) stated: "In utilization-focused evaluation, methods decisions, like decisions about focus and priority issues, are guided and informed by our evaluation goal: intended use by intended users" (p. 241). He professed: "Relevance and utility are the driving forces in utilization-focused evaluation; methods are employed in the service of relevance and use, not as their master" (p. 250). Further, Patton said that utilization-focused evaluation requires different types of measures: ". . .prefer to have soft or rough measures of important goals rather than highly precise, quantitative measures of goals that no one much cares about" (p. 161).

The 3-"I" Model incorporates and adapts elements from Patton (1997) who recommended developing measurements through the utilization of a format that incorporates goals, indicators, implementation strategies, and outcomes. Each aspect of the format was addressed in the indicators developed for each of the 3-"I" Model dimensions, including Initiator, Initiative, and Impact.

Evaluators of comprehensive community initiatives have utilized theory-based evaluation as a successful method of identifying and measuring important impact goals. For these reasons, theory-based evaluation was also integrated into the 3-"I" Model.

SYNTHESIS OF "GOOD PRACTICES" ENHANCE 3-"I" MODEL FRAMEWORK

The 3-"I" Model research framework integrated the tenets of utilization-based evaluation (Patton, 1997) with the principles of theory-of-change evaluation (Fulbright-Anderson et al., 1998; Gambone, 1998). When combined, these specific elements served as a set of *good practices* for the evaluation of the community impact as reflected in Exhibit 1.

Research Framework

In Exhibit 2 questions adapted from the literature and probes that operationalize the 3-"I" Model Research Framework and serve as indicators of community impact are illustrated. The Exhibit shows the way the 3-"I" model integrated utilization-focused evaluation and theory-of-change principles. This framework attempts to capture the process of impact by focusing on variables, indicators, measurements, and research probes that were developed specifically to reflect each of the 3-"I" dimensions of the community impact *process*.

Pilot Test of the 3-"I" Model

Following the development of the 3-"I" Model, a pilot test was implemented. Because the 3-"I" Model involves the construction and refinement of a new model as well as aspects of the additional conditions under which pilot testing is recommended, the pilot test of the 3-"I" Model employed the case study method. The chief purpose of the case study was description focused on the model, its dimensions, and its utility.

EXHIBIT 1
Synthesis of 'Good Practices' Incorporated in a 3-"I" Model

3-"I" Model Research Framework

Initiator ➤ *Measuring Utilization-Focus*

- Initiators employed a utilization-focus.
- Initiators identified the goals of the initiative.
- Initiators considered community relevance and utility as two of the driving forces of the initiative.

Measuring Theory-of-Change Principles

- Initiators considered context (Historical, geographical, economical, political).
- Initiators served as active collaborators.
- Initiators identified intended outcomes.
- Initiators shared intended outcomes with community stakeholders.
- Initiator collaborations resulted in shared intended outcomes.
- Initiators developed a knowledge base.

Initiative ➤ *Measuring Utilization-Focus*

- Initiative included indicators of intended goals.
- Initiative implementation was documented.
- Initiative indicators were tightly coupled with the initiative goals.

Measuring Theory-of-Change Principles

- Initiative activities were measured.
- Initiative progress was measured.
- Initiative impact activities were implemented.

Impact ➤ *Measuring Utilization-Focus*

- Implementation strategies served intended outcomes (Impact).
- Impact goals were achieved.
- Impact goals were evaluated for future relevance and application

Measuring Theory-of-Change Principles

- Community impact resulted from the service initiative.
- Changes occurred within the community as a result of the service initiative.
- The community impact of the service initiative was measured.
- Community impact results were shared with initiators of service as well as community stakeholders in order to improve future service initiatives.

EXHIBIT 2
Research Variables, Indicators, Measurements, and Probes

Initiator

Variable	Indicators	Measurements
Community Impact inclusion in establishment of intended outcomes	Community Collaboration, Involvement, and Awareness in establishment of goals and intended outcomes	Interview with Initiators Community focus group Review of extant data

Research probes:

- Were intended outcomes established?
- What were the intended outcomes?
- Who established the intended outcomes?
- Did initiators collaborate with community stakeholders?
- How were community stakeholders identified?
- What input was sought from community stakeholders?
- In what ways did input from the community shape the intended outcomes?
- What type of implementation knowledge base was established?

Initiative

Variable	Indicators	Measurements
Community Impact inclusion in service initiative implementation	Community Impact implementation indicators, such as inclusiveness, participation, and community perception of implementation	Interview with Initiators Community focus group Review of extant data Survey

(continued)

EXHIBIT 2
(Continued)

Research probes:

- How did community residents participate in the service initiative?
- Did the service initiative maintain its focus on intended outcomes?
- What about the initiative worked within the community as planned?
- What about the initiative did not work within the community?
- How was progress in the community measured during the initiative implementation?
- What challenges surfaced in the community?

Were relationships established during implementation?

Impact

Variable	Indicators	Measurements
Community Impact inclusion in actual outcomes	Community Impact indicators including: capacity building, partnerships, community satisfaction, and economic value	Interview with Initiators Community focus group Observations Review of extant data Survey

Research probes:

- What community impact resulted from the service initiative?
- What changes occurred within the community as a result of the initiative?
- How did the program work for the community?
- Why did the program work for the community?
- Did the community perceive the university as a community partner? (community asset)
- How sustainable is the relationship?
- Were community stakeholders satisfied with the outcomes of the service initiative?
- What was the economic value of the services provided by the initiators and the initiative?

Unit of Analysis and Sample

The community was the unit of analysis for the study. Connell et al. (1995) stated that although "the term 'community' is a social rather than a geographical unit," communities do serve as units for measurement (p. 174). For the purpose of this research, the community was described as *neighborhoods,* which are in turn, defined according to a degree of social cohesion that results from shared institutions and space (p. 174).

In an effort to reflect accurately the perceptions of the *community*, the sample was approximately 40 community members and leaders who were listed on the community association's list. Both the Initiator and the community association president suggested that this pool represented the approximate number of people served by the initiative.

Site

The site of the research included a university campus and a community in which the university operated its service-learning programming. The pilot site was chosen because a number of service initiatives involving the community and the faith-based university were underway. These service-learning initiatives had not been evaluated or even described or considered from a community impact perspective. For the purposes of this case study research, the pilot site is considered a single-case holistic design (Yin, 1994, pp. 38–39; p. 56).

Some of the service-learning opportunities in this diverse neighborhood included:

- After-school tutoring programming involving education students;
- Elderly aid programming involving nursing students;
- Tax preparation programming involving accounting students; and
- Reading programming involving English majors.

Additional service activities included civic education initiatives wherein students taught the community about government, including practical advice on how to contact city officials for everything from road repairs to voter registration. In addition, a particularly helpful service included the creation of a community assets publication, which noted the names, occupations, and areas of expertise of all the residents of the community. As a result of this publication, residents expressed feeling a new sense of safety and empowerment in the knowledge that they were surrounded by neighbors with skills that were previously unknown.

Data Collection

Data gathering incorporated research and data collection protocol from Yin's (1994) *Case Study Research: Design and Methods,* and multiple sources of evidence were considered, including observations, interviews and surveys, focus groups, and review of extant data. Observations took place onsite and provided rich insights into the perceptions of the residents of the neighborhood. Interviews were conducted with the university initiator of service while community leaders and participants were interviewed as a focus group. A survey of the community included a 70 percent ($n = 28$) return rate and the extant data was reviewed and analyzed.

Analysis

In *Qualitative Data Analysis,* Miles and Huberman (1994) recommended the development and utilization of a "prestructured case outline" (pp. 84–85). The outline for the case unfolds as detailed in Exhibit 3.

This triangulation of the different data sources provides construct validity because the "multiple sources of evidence essentially provide multiple

EXHIBIT 3
Prestructured Case Outline*

I.   Initiator: The Story of Planning
   a.   Utilization Focus Factors
   b.   Theory of Change Focus Factors
   c.   Community Impact Inclusion in Establishment of Intended Outcomes
II.   Initiative: The Story of Implementation
   a.   Utilization Focus Factors
   b.   Theory of Change Factor
   c.   Community Impact Inclusion in Service Initiative Implementation
III.   Impact: The Story of Impact
   a.   Utilization Focus Factors
   b.   Theory of Change Factors
   c.   Community Impact Inclusion in Actual Outcomes
* Adapted from Miles & Huberman, 1994

measures of the same phenomenon" (Yin, 1994, p. 92). In this research, each of the multiple sources measures the community impact of the service initiative.

The model was based on the proposition that certain theoretical community impact *good practices* could be operationalized in the 3-"I" Model and could serve the research objective. Yin (1994) stated that the original propositions not only help to organize the case study, but also provide insights and answers into "how" and "why" questions which guide the case study analysis (p. 104). Because description is one of the primary purposes of conducting case study research, the data analysis included a descriptive approach in order to identify an explanation of the pilot study.

The analytic strategy for this description of the case study was found in the use of analytic techniques for qualitative data analysis (Miles & Huberman, 1994; Yin, 1994). This approach included designing a matrix of different categories and assigning the evidence gathered from the observations, interviews, surveys, focus groups, and review of extant data into the matrix of categories. Following this categorization of the data and a review of the data, codes were assigned. Codes were established for each variable category as well as for each *good practice* for data analysis.

RESULTS

The prestructured case outline linked each source of evidence (observation, interview, focus group, survey, extant data) with the appropriate 3-"I" dimension of the model. Different codes were established for each good practice from each "I" and an analysis matrix was formed. Each source of evidence was analyzed for the presence of each good practice from the evaluation synthesis and then coded to a dimension in the model, depending on its occurrence in the process of community impact. In addition to expert panel confirmation of the 3-"I" model, additional affirmation for the model was demonstrated during analysis including:

- Descriptive statistics and the means and standard deviations for the survey responses were used to describe the sample;
- The frequencies and percentages of responses to the survey;
- Cronbach's alpha test for internal consistency reliability;
- Independent Samples *t* test: Leader vs. Member;
- Independent Samples *t* test: Gender.

The internal consistency (reliability) analysis of the 3-"I" research probes designed to capture the process of community impact that were translated into survey items (Cronbach's alpha) was an encouraging .92. The outline reflected the results of the 3-"I" Model pilot and included three dimensions: Initiator, Initiative, and Impact.

"Initiator" Findings

The Initiator category captured the story of planning and included the good practice issues represented in utilization focus factors and theory of change factors. The Initiator category also measured the extent to which stakeholders were involved in the development of intended outcomes and addressed the inclusion of community impact in the establishment of intended outcomes. Specifically, this aspect of the model provided vital insight and information regarding the initiative's

- Initial objectives;
- Intended outcomes and goals;
- Stakeholder consideration, involvement, and collaboration; and
- Development of a knowledge base and served as a crucial step in understanding the ultimate community impact of the service initiative.

For example, results from the Initiator dimension of the case study revealed that the university initiators of service did not initially solicit the opinions of the community nor administer any form of needs assessment prior to the service-learning program. Interviews with the university initiator and the community stakeholders (using the Initiator probes from the model) also indicated that once the initiative was underway, the university initiator did respond to community stakeholders and dramatically altered the original intended outcomes of the service to reflect the real needs of the community. This change in direction was the pivotal point that allowed the service to move from being remotely related to tightly linked to community needs. Exhibit 4 provides sample survey results.

"Initiative" Findings

The Initiative category involved the story of implementation and included implementation issues surrounding the utilization focus factors and the theory of change factors. In addition, this category addressed the inclusion of community impact in the service initiative implementation and the extent to which activities were measured. This aspect of the model proved effective in

EXHIBIT 4
Sample Survey Results from Items Specifically
Probing for "Initiator" Dimension

	Frequency	Percent	Valid Percent	Cumulative Percent
Item1: Clear idea why university was involved with community				
Strongly Disagree	1	3.6	3.6	3.6
Disagree	1	3.6	3.6	7.1
Uncertain	4	14.3	14.3	21.4
Agree	17	60.7	60.7	82.1
Strongly Agree	5	17.9	17.9	100.0
TOTAL	28	100.0	100.0	
Item 2: One of the project's goals was to serve community				
Uncertain	3	10.7	10.7	10.7
Agree	14	50.0	50.0	60.7
Strongly Agree	11	39.3	39.3	100.0
TOTAL	28	100.0	100.0	
Item 3: Community participated in setting project goals				
Disagree	1	3.6	3.6	3.6
Uncertain	4	14.3	14.3	17.9
Agree	18	64.3	64.3	82.1
Strongly Agree	5	17.9	17.9	100.0
TOTAL	28	100.0	100.0	

- Its capacity to capture the extent to which activities remain linked to intended outcomes during implementation;
- The extent to which change was measured during implementation; and
- The extent to which collaboration among stakeholders took place, including the establishment of the community/campus partnership.

For example, results from the Initiative dimension of the model's case study revealed how and why implementation did or did not work. The probes from this aspect of the model helped to identify problem areas as well as aspects of the service initiative that were key to its success. A noteworthy example is the evidence from the Initiative dimension that documented the establishment and growth of the university/community partnership that developed during the process of the service initiative. Exhibit 5 provides sample survey results from the Initiative dimension.

EXHIBIT 5
Sample Survey Results from the "Initiative" Dimension

	Frequency	Percent	Valid Percent	Cumulative Percent
Item 4: University project helped community reach its own goals				
Disagree	1	3.6	3.6	3.6
Uncertain	3	10.7	10.7	14.3
Agree	13	46.4	46.4	60.7
Strongly Agree	11	39.3	39.3	100.0
TOTAL	28	100.0	100.0	
Item 5: Project worked well in the community				
Uncertain	1	3.6	3.6	3.6
Agree	13	46.4	46.4	50.0
Strongly Agree	14	50.0	50.0	100.0
TOTAL	28	100.0	100.0	
Item 6: Community was served				
Uncertain	1	3.6	3.6	3.6
Agree	12	42.9	42.9	46.4
Strongly Agree	15	53.6	53.6	100.0
TOTAL	28	100.0	100.0	
Item 7: Community/university partnership improved				
Uncertain	2	7.1	7.1	7.1
Agree	12	42.9	42.9	50.0
Strongly Agree	14	50.0	50.0	100.0
TOTAL	28	100.0	100.0	

Impact" Findings

In the Impact category, the model included good practice factors surrounding utilization focus and theory of change as they relate to impact. In addition, the Impact category addressed the extent to which community impact occurred. Specifically, this phase of the model demonstrated:

- The extent to which results met intended outcomes;
- The extent to which change occurred in the community;
- The extent to which the impact process unfolded; and
- The extent to which knowledge was recorded and shared for improving future service initiatives.

Results from the Impact dimension of the model case study employed the impact probes and reflected an overall summary of the project with a focus on the extent to which intended outcomes were achieved. The most beneficial outcome of this aspect of the model was found in its capacity to help establish a knowledge base that offered both formative and summative evaluation opportunities. The impact probes not only revealed the extent to which the service goals were met, but also captured additional outcomes during the interview and survey that were not initially known by the initiators of the service. Sample items are presented in Exhibit 6. Exhibit 7 shows mean values for survey items.

EXHIBIT 6
Sample Survey Results from the "Impact" Dimension

	Frequency	Percent	Valid Percent	Cumulative Percent
Item 9: Community satisfied with student project				
Disagree	2	7.1	7.1	7.1
Uncertain	1	3.6	3.6	10.7
Agree	10	35.7	35.7	46.4
Strongly Agree	15	53.6	53.6	100.0
TOTAL	28	100.0	100.0	
Item 10: Project gave something of value				
Strongly Disagree	1	3.6	3.6	3.6
Disagree	1	3.6	3.6	7.1
Uncertain	1	3.6	3.6	10.7
Agree	11	39.3	39.3	50.0
Strongly Agree	14	50.0	50.0	100.0
TOTAL	28	100.0	100.0	
Item 11: Community now perceives university as source of help				
Disagree	1	3.6	3.6	3.6
Uncertain	1	3.6	3.6	7.1
Agree	14	50.0	50.0	57.1
Strongly Agree	12	42.9	42.9	100.0
TOTAL	28	100.0	100.0	
Item 12: Helped me become active in community				
Strongly Disagree	1	3.6	3.6	3.6
Disagree	2	7.1	7.1	10.7
Uncertain	3	10.7	10.7	21.4
Agree	13	46.4	46.4	67.9
Strongly Agree	9	32.1	32.1	100.0
TOTAL	28	100.0	100.0	

(continued)

EXHIBIT 6
(Continued)

	Frequency	Percent	Valid Percent	Cumulative Percent
Item 13: Helped residents feel more in control of their own community				
Strongly Disagree	1	3.6	3.6	3.6
Disagree	2	7.1	7.1	10.7
Uncertain	6	21.4	21.4	32.1
Agree	13	46.4	46.4	78.6
Strongly Agree	6	21.4	21.4	100.0
TOTAL	28	100.0	100.0	
Item 14: Helped community/university relationship				
Disagree	1	3.6	3.6	3.6
Agree	14	50.0	50.0	53.6
Strongly Agree	13	46.4	46.4	100.0
TOTAL	28	100.0	100.0	
Item 15: Community gained access to new resources				
Disagree	1	3.6	3.6	3.6
Agree	9	32.1	32.1	35.7
Strongly Agree	18	64.3	64.3	100.0
TOTAL	28	100.0	100.0	

EXHIBIT 7
Survey Item Mean Values

	N	Minimum	Maximum	M	SD
Item 1: Clear idea why university involved	28	1	5	3.86	.89
Item 2: Project had goal to serve community	28	3	5	4.29	.66
Item 3: Community participated in goals	28	2	5	3.96	.69
Item 4: Project helped community meet goals	28	2	5	4.21	.79
Item 5: Project worked well	28	3	5	4.46	.58
Item 6: Community was served	28	3	5	4.50	.58
Item 7: Community/university partnership Improved	28	3	5	4.43	.63
Item 8: Desire additional student projects	28	2	5	4.50	.69
Item 9: Community satisfied	28	2	5	4.36	.87
Item 10: Project gave something of value	28	1	5	4.29	.98
Item 11: University source of help	28	2	5	4.32	.72
Item 12: Helped me become active	28	1	5	3.96	1.04
Item 13: Helped residents with control	28	1	5	3.75	1.00
Item 14: Helped relationship with university	28	2	5	4.39	.69
Item 15: Community gained access to resources	28	2	5	4.57	.69

CONCLUSIONS

The case study pilot test of the 3-"I" Model effectively proved the utility of the model. Specifically, the pilot demonstrated the capacity of each "I" to capture its distinct area of the community impact process. The good practice factors derived from utilization-based evaluation and theory-of-change evaluation served as effective indicators in each phase of the process. One of the most affirming forms of community impact evidence was found in the fact that the model clearly demonstrated the community impact process and not just the outcomes. The 3-"I" model provided a framework with which to consider community impact as a process that developed throughout the service initiative.

Indications of the community impact process were present throughout the pilot evidence. For example, evidence from the Initiator interview and the focus group indicated that the establishment of the partnership between the university and the community was a process. Additional process evidence was found in the development of programming that acknowledged and met the community's needs. Process evidence was also indicated in the collaboration that led to the implementation of service projects and activities. Additional evidence of the process approach was found in the extant data that revealed a clear change in the nature of the relationship, with changes in the goals moving from university-driven to community-focused.

Finally, the survey evidence, which indicated the community's opinions on the project, demonstrated strong support for the initiative and a belief that the new partnership with the university and the service initiative offered something of value to the community. This evidence of impact and satisfaction was a result of the process that resulted in community impact.

In summary, the pilot demonstrated the 3-"I" Model's capacity to provide an applicable way of considering impact as a process, which contributes both formative and summative evaluation opportunities. The evidence demonstrated that the community impact process and community impact outcomes are intertwined rather than separate. This evidence helps to redefine and reconceptualize impact as a process rather than only an outcome.

Future Research

The pilot results indicate a need for further research on the community partnership as the unit of analysis. While the pilot demonstrated the 3-"I" model's capacity to capture the establishment and development of the partnership, perhaps an isolated application on this impact aspect alone would be a promising area of further research. In addition, future research could test the model's applicability to different educational institutions and different community settings.

REFERENCES

Blair, R. (1998). Strategic planning for economic development: A suggested model for program evaluation. *Public Administration Quarterly, 22*(2), 331–348.

Chen, H., & Rossi, P. (1992). *Using theory to improve program evaluation.* New York: Greenwood Press.

Connell, J. P, Aber, J. L., & Walker, G. (1995). "How do urban communities affect youth?" Using social science research to inform the design and evaluation of comprehensive community initiatives. In J. P. Connell, A. C. Kubisch, L. B. Schorr, & C. H. Weiss (Eds.), *New approaches to evaluating community initiatives, Vol. 1: Concepts, methods and contexts* (pp. 93–127). Washington, DC: The Aspen Institute.

Connell, J. P., Kubisch, A. C., Schorr, L. B., & Weiss, C. H., (Eds.). (1995). *New approaches to evaluating community initiatives, Vol. 1: Concepts, methods, and contexts.* Washington, DC: The Aspen Institute.

Cruz, N. I., & Giles, D. E., Jr. (2000, Fall). Where's the community in service-learning research? *Michigan Journal of Community Service Learning,* Special Issue. Retrieved online July 3, 2003, from http://www.umich.edu/~mjcsl/

Fulbright-Anderson, K., Kubisch, A., & Connell, J., (Eds.). (1998). *New approaches to evaluating community initiatives: Theory, measurement, and analysis.* Washington, DC: The Aspen Institute.

Gambone, M. (1998). Challenges of measurement in community change initiatives. In K. Fulbright-Andersen, A. C. Kubisch, & J. P. Connell, (Eds.), *New approaches to evaluating community initiatives, Vol.2: Theory, measurement, and analysis* (pp. 149–165). Washington, DC: The Aspen Institute.

Giles, D. E., Jr., & Eyler, J. (1998). A service-learning research agenda for the next five years. *New Directions for Teaching and Learning, 73,* 65–72.

Giles, D. E., Jr., Honnet, E., & Migliore, S. (1991). *Research agenda for combining service and learning in the 1990s.* A report from 1991 Wingspread Conference. Raleigh, NC: National Society for Internships and Experiential Education.

Henderson, J., & McAdam, R. (1998). A more subjective approach to business improvement and organizational change evaluation. *Total Quality Management, 9*(4/5), 116–120.

Holloway, J. (1997). An effective product/program evaluation for today's schools. *National Association of Secondary School Principals NAASP Bulletin, 81*(589), 112–114.

Kretzmann, J. P., & McKnight, J. L. (1993). *Building communities from the inside out: A path toward finding and mobilizing a community's assets.* Chicago: Asset-Based Community Development Institute.

Miles, M. B., & Huberman, M. (1994). *Qualitative data analysis.* Thousand Oaks, CA: Sage

Nyden, P., Figert, A., Shibley, M., & Burrows, D. (1997). *Building community: Social science in action.* Thousand Oaks, CA: Pine Forge Press.

Patton. M. Q. (1997). *Utilization-focused evaluation: The new century text.* Thousand Oaks, CA: Sage.

Patrizi, P., & McMullan, B. (1998). *Evaluations in foundations: The unrealized potential.* Retrieved online July 3, 2003, from http://www.wkkf.org/Pubs/Tools/Evaluation/Pub773.pdf

Rebien, C. (1997). Development assistance evaluation and the foundations of program evaluation. *Evaluation Review, 21*(4), 438–460.

Salzer, M., Nixon, C., Schut, J., Karver, M., & Bickman, L. (1997). Validating quality indicators: Quality as relationship between structure, process, and outcome. *Evaluation Review, 21*(3), 292–309.

Weiss, C. H. (1995). Nothing as practical as good theory: Exploring theory-based evaluation for comprehensive community initiatives for children and families. In J. P. Connell, A. C. Kubisch, L. B. Schorr, & C. H. Weiss (Eds.), *New approaches to evaluating community initiatives, Vol. 1: Concepts, methods, and contexts.* Washington, DC: The Aspen Institute. Retrieved online July 3, 2003, from http://www.aspeninstitute.org/Programt3.asp?bid=1272

Weiss, C. H. (1997). How can theory-based evaluation make greater headway? *Evaluation Review, 21*(4), 501–524.

Yin, R. K. (1994). *Case study research: Design and methods.* Thousand Oaks, CA: Sage.

CHAPTER 7

ETHICAL RELATIONSHIPS IN SERVICE-LEARNING PARTNERSHIPS

**Marjorie A. Schaffer, Jenell Williams Paris, and
Kristin Vogel**

This exploratory study analyzed ethical problems experienced in service-learning partnerships. The researchers used ethical inquiry in
semi-structured interviews with five faculty members, five students, and three
community partners who had participated in service-learning partnerships
associated with five private liberal arts colleges. Analysis yielded six categories
of ethical problems and a description of participants' resolutions and rationale for their decisions. The authors discuss implications for reducing ethical
conflict and resolving ethical problems in service-learning relationships, and
for working with students.

What ethical problems are experienced by teachers, students, and community partners in service-learning partnerships? How do ethical perspectives
guide the thinking and actions of participants involved in service-learning?
There are many decision points in a service-learning experience that may
involve ethical problems, that is, conflicts about the right thing to do. Situ-

Deconstructing Service-Learning: Research Exploring Context, Participation, and Impacts
A Volume in: Advances in Service-Learning Research, pages 147–168.
Copyright © 2003 by Information Age Publishing, Inc.
All rights of reproduction in any form reserved.
ISBN: 1-59311-071-5 (hardcover), 1-59311-070-7 (pbk.)

ations in which conflict may occur include decisions on how much responsibility to give to students, expectations for community partner contributions to student orientation, how to assess service-learning outcomes, and determining the potential impact on vulnerable populations.

Many service-learning researchers have addressed how participation in community service contributes to student moral development and civic engagement (Astin & Sax, 1998; Boss, 1994; Eyler & Giles, 1999; Giles & Eyler, 1994; Gorman, 1994; McEwen, 1996; Myers-Lipton, 1996; Nnakwe, 1999; Rockquemore & Schaffer, 2000). The widely recognized guidelines, "Principles of Good Practice for Service-Learning Pedagogy" (Eyler & Giles, 1997; Howard, 2001), suggest strategies to increase student learning and benefit communities. These guidelines can be viewed as advice for ethical service-learning practice. However, there has been little exploration of how faculty, students, and community partners experience ethical challenges in their service-learning partnerships.

The purpose of this exploratory study is to identify and describe ethical conflicts, resolutions, and rationale of participants in service-learning partnerships. The study contributes to an understanding of the diverse perspectives and experiences that lead to ethical problems in service-learning and ways to resolve them. Research on the ethical problems encountered in service-learning partnerships emphasizes the ongoing processes rather than the outcomes of service-learning. In this way, the research process is used to sustain collaboration between institutions of higher learning and communities (Cruz & Giles, 2000).

BACKGROUND

Ethical Theory and Perspectives

Ethics is defined as "the branch of philosophy that investigates and creates theories about the nature of right and wrong, duty, obligation, freedom, [and] virtue" (Pence, 2000, p. 19). Volbrecht (2002) addressed the importance of ethics within in a community when she stated ethics is a process that involves dialogue about "what communities value and what they should do in light of these values" (p. 1). Three categories of ethical theory and perspectives identified by Volbrecht are:

1. Rule ethics, which encompasses right and wrong actions, moral obligations, and moral rules;
2. Virtue ethics, which emphasizes character; and
3. Feminist ethics, which focuses on how relationships and society can be restructured to eliminate power imbalances.

Rule Ethics, strongly influenced by utilitarian and Kantian theory, guide action based on rules for ethical behavior (Volbrecht, 2002). Principles illustrating rule ethics include autonomy, beneficence, nonmaleficence, and justice (Beauchamp & Childress, 1994). Autonomy emphasizes self-determination. Beneficence promotes good and preventing harm, while nonmaleficence specifically focuses on avoiding harm for anyone. Justice involves being fair and promoting equality. Rule ethics emphasizes reason and the application of abstract and universal rules to specific cases (Volbrecht, 2002).

Virtue Ethics, which originated with Aristotle, emphasize strength of character and development of an ethical community (Volbrecht, 2002). Examples of virtues are compassion, courage, and integrity. Virtue ethics are person-centered and focus on relationships, interconnectedness, and actions in the context of community (Gilligan, 1982; Noddings, 1990, Taylor, 1998; Volbrecht, 2002). Cameron (2000) wrote that ethical caring means

> we behave ethically when we act in ways that maintain relationships. We affirm and protect the most vulnerable individuals. The best resolution to ethical conflict accounts for everyone's needs. Behavior is unethical when it breaks bonds among people and sacrifices one person for another one's agenda. (p. 18)

Six characteristics of an ethical relationship are appropriate boundaries, caring, fairness, integrity, respect, and trust (Cameron & Moch, 2000). When any one of these characteristics is lacking in relationships in the service-learning partnership, one or more participants may experience ethical conflict.

Proponents of *Feminist Ethics* are committed to ethical practice that eliminates or reduces systemic subordination of women and other oppressed groups. In the 1970s and 1980s, Western feminists critiqued traditional ethical approaches for gender bias that devalued women's experience and contributions (Gilligan, 1982). *Care ethics* emphasize that the moral experience of women should be considered worthy of respect as a guide to ethical decision making; however, feminist ethics primarily focus on systemic oppression (Volbrecht, 2002). A feminist ethical approach aims to analyze societal patterns to determine strategies for reducing oppression, power imbalances, and barriers to development and well being, such as racism and sexism.

Many professions have codes of ethics for guiding professional practice. These codes are based on the ethical principles of autonomy, beneficence, nonmaleficence, and justice (Parsons, 2001). Standards for informed consent, confidentiality, professional relationship boundaries, and competent professional behavior, essential to the professions, are also relevant to ethical service-learning practice. In addition, service-learning partnerships may involve formal or informal contracts that specify the service-learning activities, the duties of each participant, and the relationship between the academic institution and the community agency. Breaking the contract or breaching professional ethics may contribute to ethical conflict in service-learning partnerships.

Ethical Decision Making Models

Ethical decision making models can be effective tools for using ethical theory and perspectives to help resolve ethical problems encountered in relationships between individuals and groups. A number of ethical decision making models are based on ethical principles (rule ethics) such as beneficence, justice, autonomy, and truth-telling (Beauchamp & Childress, 1994; Frankena, 1973; Thiroux, 1986). Cameron (1993) developed the Caring and Justice Ethical Decision Making Model, which balances the caring ethical perspectives of advocacy, compassion, values, and virtue with the justice perspectives of autonomy, fairness, universalizability, and utility.

The Value, Be, Do Ethical Decision Making Model, developed by Cameron (2000), is relevant to ethical decision making in service-learning partnerships. The model incorporates a variety of ethical principles and perspectives in the exploration of three questions:

1. What should I value?
2. Who should I be? and
3. What should I do?

The questions proposed in this model facilitate personal reflection on important values, one's character, and relationships with others. The third question, "What should I do?" encourages the decision maker to balance right action with good consequences. The model is easy to use and is flexible enough to incorporate different cultural values into ethical decision making. In a practice application, Schaffer, Cameron, and Tatley (2000) used the Value, Be, Do Ethical Decision Making Model to resolve a common ethical conflict experienced by school nurses. They found the model provided a strategy for effective resolution and ethical nursing practice. Because the model is straight-forward, practitioners from a variety of disciplines can easily use the model to resolve ethical problems they encounter in practice.

Previous research revealed a basic structure to ethical problems that is useful in this study. Studies of nursing students (Cameron, Schaffer, & Park, 2001), persons with AIDS (Cameron, 1993), and older persons (Cameron, 2002) found the nature of participants' ethical problems consisted of three components: a conflict of values, a resolution to the conflict, and a rationale for the resolution.

Ethics and Service-Learning

Scholars have addressed ethical service-learning practice through principles of good practice, pedagogy applied to service-learning, and partnership development. Sigmon (1979), in his seminal work on service-learning principles of good practice, addressed the importance of control of the service by those being served and control of those who are serving over their learning. This is consistent with the ethical principle of autonomy or self-determination. Eyler and Giles (1997) commented that a quality service-learning experience allows students to explore their interests in service-learning placements. This approach to service-learning promotes student autonomy. The "Principles of Good Practice for Service-Learning Pedagogy" (Howard, 2001) are likely to promote good (beneficence) and prevent potential negative consequences (nonmaleficence) in service-learning partnerships. Faculty members are encouraged to be prepared for a loss of control in the learning environment, which is consistent with promoting greater autonomy for students and community partners. Justice is represented by the service-learning good practice principle that encourages faculty members to promote purposeful civic learning. A focus on community partner assets, including resources and strengths, versus a problem-focused approach (Howard, 2001) promotes an egalitarian community-campus partnership.

To use service-learning ethically as pedagogy, the faculty member is obligated to be competent, assist the student in dealing with sensitive topics, and attend to student development (Tellez, 2000). Pedagogical competence requires that the faculty member is knowledgeable about the context of the service-learning, has relevant experience, and engages in service along with the students. Faculty members are obligated to assist students in addressing difficult and uncomfortable topics, such as child protection issues. Although the faculty member is expected to guide student development, controversy may exist about whether the focus should be on intellectual development or on moral education. In addition, the lack of uniformity in service-learning experiences suggests it is difficult to treat students fairly regarding expectations for amount of work and learning. Tellez (2000) expressed concern that universities and colleges might emphasize service-learning in curricula in order to advance the institution in becoming a better "citizen of the community" (p. 74). Unless student growth results from service-learning, the institutional interests may take priority over the best interests of students.

Partnership development requires attentiveness to reciprocity, collaboration, and diversity (Mintz & Hesser, 1996), which are foundational to *high investment, high trust relationships* in service-learning (Langseth, 2000). Langseth also suggested that harm could be avoided in service-learning partnerships by recognizing and challenging the belief that the academic side of the partnership possesses greater wisdom. Green (2001) discussed the conflict that occurs when race and class differences are experienced. The reduction of power differentials through respect and recognition of the community partner's assets are consistent with the goal of feminist ethics. Welch (2000) conceptualized the reduction of the power differential as moving from an ethic of control to an ethic of risk. An ethic of risk is characterized by respect, uncertain outcomes, and working *with* others, rather than doing good *for* someone. For academic institutions, an ethic of risk involves relinquishing control and learning new ways of thinking and doing. An ethic of control for the community partner or the academic institution can create a power imbalance, which is likely to lead to ethical conflict.

Authors have proposed a variety of guidelines for ethical practice for faculty members, practitioners, and college students (Linzer, 1999; Murray, Gillese, Lennon, Mercer, & Robinson, 1996; Parsons, 2001; Strike & Moss, 1997). However, few have explored the ethical perspectives of community partners, students, and faculty members specifically for service-learning practice. This exploratory study contributes to ethical practice by considering the experiences of service-learning partners.

METHOD

Most research on ethical inquiry consists of descriptive ethics that explores definitions of ethical problems; normative ethics, which examines the right way to resolve a conflict; and/or metaethics, which consists of analyzing the meanings of ethical reasoning (Beauchamp & Childress, 1994; Frankena, 1973). The research presented here focuses on descriptive ethics. The study employed research methods that would yield richly descriptive results, including semi-structured interviews and narrative analysis.

Researchers interviewed 13 participants (five students, five faculty members, and three community partners) who had been involved in service-learning partnerships. Participants were recruited from five private liberal arts colleges in a large metropolitan area. Members of the research team developed a snowball sample based upon their professional contacts (Berg, 1998).

The five student participants were European-American women, representing three of the colleges and a variety of majors. The students were in their early 20s and had participated in at least one semester of service-learning. Faculty members included three European-American females, one European-American male, and one African-American male. Faculty members were from four of the colleges and their academic disciplines were nursing, business, psychology, and sociology. Their years of experience with service-learning ranged from 3 to 23. Community partners, which included a European-American male, an African-American male, and a European-American woman, each had several years of service-learning experience. The community partners had each worked with several academic institutions, representing all five colleges. The sample reflects the racial and ethnic composition of the colleges. The focus on service-learning experience was the only criterion for participation in the study.

Interviews took place in offices, private homes, and public spaces at colleges, and lasted from 30 to 60 minutes. After obtaining a signature of informed consent, each participant was asked, "What situations in your service-learning experiences have caused you conflict about the right thing to do?" Each semi-structured interview covered four key topics (experience with service-learning, identification of ethical problem, resolution, and rationale), and the interviewer was free to improvise or reword questions in the context of the interview (Berg, 1998). Interviews were audiotaped and transcribed.

Narrative analysis was employed to identify emerging themes and patterns in the data. Researchers used focused coding to organize transcripts (Coffey & Atkinson, 1996). Based on research that describes how people experience ethical conflict, researchers developed four codes: experience with service-learning, ethical problem, resolution, and rationale. After completing focused coding, the researchers used open coding to allow themes to emerge from the problem, resolution, and rationale sections (Esterberg, 2002; Strauss & Corbin, 1990).

An ethical problem was defined as the experience of a conflict about the right thing to do in a service-learning situation. The resolution was the participant's decision about what to do. The decision could be an action, a change in thinking about the service-learning experience, or a choice not to act. Rationale was the reasoning participants gave for their decisions or responses to ethical problems. Rule, virtue, and feminist ethical perspectives were used to analyze the reasoning given by study participants.

RESULTS

Ethical Problems Experienced by Students, Faculty Members, and Community Partners

Six themes emerged from analysis of 24 ethical problems identified by participants:

1. Prioritizing interests;
2. Meeting community needs;
3. Responding to unmet expectations;
4. Dropping the ball;
5. Considering the impact on community/society; and
6. Breaking "rules" or promises.

As shown in Exhibit 1, participants identified a range of one to four ethical problems.

EXHIBIT 1
Categories of Ethical Problems Identified by Participants

Prioritizing Interests (7 problems)

- Tension between needs (requirements) of college and needs of community (S)*
- Service did not meet course goals for learning (F)**
- Abandoning the service-learning project in order to prioritize student learning could jeopardize the professor's relationship with the community partner (F)
- Whether to invest time in informing community residents of faulty information given in service-learning project that was determined to make little difference in outcome (F)
- Tension between keeping relationship with agency and lack of learning for students (F)
- Tension between meeting course needs and treating community partners respectfully (telling agency to create service-learning projects) (F)

Meeting Community Needs (5 problems)

- Did not want to repeat an established event that did not meet community needs (S)
- Concern about taking photographs at project site (S)
- Questioned whether service was wanted or was being done because "we thought it would be a good thing for them" (S)
- Concern about expectation for project that meets course goals but is not useful to community (CP)***
- Community wants something other than what college is offering (CP)

Responding to Unmet Expectations (3 problems)

- Experienced disappointment, frustration, and powerlessness in repeated attempts to serve the clinic and communicate with community partner (S)
- Expectations for agency personnel spending time with professor, the professor supervising students closely, and how agency personnel should receive feedback from students (CP)
- Experienced frustration and a sense of wasted time when students did not complete project as expected and professor was non-communicative (CP)

(continued)

EXHIBIT 1
Continued

Dropping the Ball (4 problems)

- Observed inadequate client care provided at agency (S)
- Incorrect data was provided and used for the student activity (F)
- Agency did not have programs ready for students and agreed upon roles for students were not available (F)
- Neither the students or professor communicated enough about the activity with the community partner, resulting in an action that was useless to the agency (CP)

Considering the Impact on Community/Society (2 problems)

- Concern about white middle class students' responses to service-learning and extent of learning needed to do effective service (S)
- Concern about coming in to do a research project in a "poor" community when students were known as wealthier middle class white people (S)

Breaking Rules or Promises (4 problems)

- Following through with commitment when the kind of help they needed was "not what I could give them" (S)
- Student in course who was concerned that agency expectations for assigned task could be harmful to recipients had to decide whether or not to break commitment to agency (F)
- Decision on breaking commitment with agency that asked students to perform tasks beyond their competence (F)
- Decision on breaking a community partner's rule in order to enhance student learning (F)

Notes: *S = Student, **F = Faculty Member, ***CP = Community Partner

Prioritizing Interests

The following question summarizes ethical conflict in this category: "With numerous relationships involved in service-learning partnerships, whose interests do I consider most in making a decision?" Six ethical problems, five from faculty members and one from a student, involved prioritizing whose interests were most important in service-learning partnerships.

Two faculty members described a similar conflict when course objectives were not being met in the service-learning projects in their classes. One faculty member who teaches a tax accounting course, said, "I had some clear objectives for the course and part of the objectives were to be met by doing the service work, but increasingly the students were not meeting those objectives." Both faculty members reported feelings of tension and anxiety about the risk of breaking relationship with a community agency in order to prioritize student learning.

A faculty member described feeling that he was coercing community partners to create service-learning projects. He said, "I will take advantage of my friendships and . . .I'll push harder than I should. People will create something or will do something just because 'somebody from [the college] asked,' and [the agency will say] 'we really should' or 'we really cannot say no.'" This faculty member experienced conflict because he needed service-learning placements ready at the beginning of the semester as well as reciprocal relationships with community partners. These two priorities frequently came into conflict for him.

Meeting Community Needs

Ethical problems in this category can be summarized by the question, "How can we develop a service-learning project that truly meets community needs?" Five ethical problems were identified in this category, three from students and two from community partners. One student experienced this type of conflict when she developed an Earth Day festival for an immigrant community, based on her own environmental commitments. After the festival, she said, "I felt guilty, like I followed this model of community service that I'm totally against . . . just coming in from the outside and not organizing within the community, just superimposing some big social service thing that really has nothing to do with what people want." This conflict was long-lasting, because during the subsequent academic year, she had to decide whether or not to organize a second Earth Day festival. Another student asked, "Are we doing this because they want it or because we think that it would be a good thing for them?" She went on to say, "It gave me kind of a negative feeling about service-learning . . . whether it is really service if you are not volunteering . . . but we are required to do it [for a class]."

A community partner described the tension of collaborating on a project that met course goals but was not useful to the community. She said, "The dilemma came in how usable would the product be at the end. Was it more that they had to prove they had jumped through those hoops, or was it that they had actually taken it and tried it out with some young people and refined the product along the way?"

Responding to Unmet Expectations

Ethical problems in this category pertained to the question, "What is the right thing to do when expectations are unmet?" Of the three ethical problems in this category, one was described by a student and two were provided by community partners. A nursing student worked at a clinic and had expectations regarding the quality of patient charts. When she found incomplete and missing patient charts, she felt she was observing unethical practice, but was "powerless and helpless" in her role as student. This student also expected her community supervisor to return phone calls and meet with the students, and experienced frustration and disappointment when these expectations were unmet.

In a different interview, a community partner said that his colleagues expected positive results from a student-generated qualitative research report on levels of racism in community agencies. "When the students finished and handed in the report, some folks were able to receive it as it was, and some received it defensively . . . saying the students don't know that much about the neighborhood . . . the information is distorted." This community partner experienced conflict in formulating straight-forward responses to both students and his community colleagues.

Dropping the Ball

The question summarizing this category is, "What is the right thing to do when one member of a service-learning partnership "drops the ball"? This category includes four ethical problems, one from a student, two from faculty, and one from a community partner. A student gave examples of a lack of information on records that she felt was necessary to provide services. She said, "I think they are not doing what they should to do fulfill their purpose." A faculty member described a concern about the unavailability of community programs for student involvement: "There was really nothing there and at the same time [they were] not really started on the project and [had] no organization or plans . . . We wanted to tell the agency, 'I am sorry. You just really have to get your act together before we do anything together.'" A community partner struggled with determining fault for a student activity that was not useful to the community and expressed concern about the lack of communication from both the faculty member and the students.

Considering the Impact on Community/Society

Two students expressed concern that their service-learning projects could negatively impact the community. This category addressed the question, "What is the right way to do service-learning in a stratified society?" A student described a trip to an economically-disadvantaged community that focused on environmental justice issues. She expressed the concern that service-learning could be "voyeuristic" on the part of the white middle class students. She said, "People understand there are a lot of problems in the world, but they don't understand how to get through the guilt that surrounds looking at them." She questioned the ethics of service-learning that involves people from multiple socioeconomic levels especially when service does not significantly impact the problem. It was a challenge to this student to build strong relationships with communities because of the commitment and time requirements. In the service-learning experience, reciprocity with the community was missing. The student commented that service activities would be more appropriate if the community identified the needs that service-learning students should address.

Breaking Rules or Promises

Ethical problems in this category are represented by the question, "When is right to break a rule or promise?" Four ethical problems comprise this category, one from a student and three from faculty members. A student provided English tutoring to fulfill a service-learning requirement for a language class. She questioned her ability to provide adequate tutoring, but also felt the obligation to follow through with her commitment. A faculty member struggled with how to help a student resolve the conflict. The faculty member brought the problem to the entire class for discussion: "As a group, we were . . . stumped about how [she could] be ethical in regards to her contract and still feel okay about what she was doing." A faculty member described conflict that occurs when an agency, which has been promised a service, asks students to complete tasks that are beyond the students' competence. She described the challenge "both in terms of duty [to see that] students have the skills they need to be able to serve the organization well and does the organization have the skills to provide good supervision to the student." Another faculty member described the anguish of breaking an agency rule in order to enhance student learning. The agency had established a rule that students should not enter a client's room in a shelter. The faculty member contemplated entering the client's room with the students to provide a health intervention. "I think it is going to be a very rich experience for the students, but am I breaking a rule? . . . This is really bad that I am breaking a rule because I want to have a good relationship in all ways with the institution, yet I want the students to have a good learning experience. I always feel like I am balancing those two."

Resolution of Ethical Problems

Students, faculty members, and community partners resolved their ethical problems in the following ways:

1. For 10 ethical problems they decided to end the partnership, remove themselves from the service-learning activity, or accept the outcome and acknowledge frustration after attempts resolve the problem.

2. For 7 ethical problems they decided to use a different approach to the service-learning activity from their original plan or identified changes they would incorporate for future projects (i.e., a student who chose an alternative service-learning experience and a community partner who decided to invest more time in getting students involved in the project).

3. For 4 ethical problems they reframed or affirmed their thinking about the nature of service-learning. These participants accepted the service-learning activity as it had occurred or continued with their current approaches. For example, a faculty member reframed her thinking when she decided to revise the course goals to justify the service-learning activity.

4. For 3 ethical problems they decided not to take any action.

Ethical Decision Making Rationale

For this study, a rationale that involved having good relationships was considered to be consistent with virtue ethics. Concerns about power differences were considered to be consistent with feminist ethics. Emphases on beneficence, nonmaleficence, or autonomy were considered to illustrate rule ethics. In their rationale, community partners primarily used virtue ethics and feminist ethics, faculty members used rule ethics and virtue ethics most often, and students used all three ethical approaches. Participants sometimes blended approaches, using more than one ethical approach in their rationale. Responses are summarized in Exhibit 2.

EXHIBIT 2
Ethical Approaches Used by Participants (n = 13)

	Rule ethics	*Virtue ethics*	*Feminist ethics*
Students	4	5	5
Faculty	9	7	1
Community Partners	0	3	2

Notes: Some participants described more than one ethical problem, and some participants used more than one approach in their rationale for ethical decision making.

Virtue Ethics

In relationships, participants focused on *who should I be* and expressed a desire to preserve relationships in service-learning (virtue ethics). A faculty member said, "It [the students' project] was not what I had in mind, but the people in the organization were pleased." When her plans for student learning did not work out, she reframed the meaning of service-learning as exchanging good will. A student talked about wanting to be the kind of person who tried to resolve problems as she justified repeated attempts to initiate communication with a community partner who did not respond. A community partner discussed the importance of ongoing communication for building healthy relationships, a willingness to trust one another, and the resulting *stretching* that occurs with continued communication in partnerships. Another community partner, disappointed with the product of the students' work, was reluctant to communicate her feelings because of the potential negative effect on the relationship with the college. She rationalized what had happened when she said, "I'm sure at the end of the semester professors are a little too busy so they just don't have extra time to make phone calls."

Integration of Virtue and Rule Ethics

Two faculty members integrated virtue ethics and rule ethics in their decision making. One faculty member described how service-learning experiences designed to be consistent with student abilities (competence) would also preserve the relationship with the agency. Competence, which addresses the obligation to do no harm, reflects rule ethics. This faculty member provided extensive information about service-learning sites and required students to have weekly meetings with the agency supervisor to promote both student competence and good relationships with agencies. The faculty member who struggled with breaking a rule in order to benefit student learning decided that the good for the student was more important than the duty to uphold the contract with the agency. However, her action was also guided by virtue ethics when she described her concern about her relationship with the agency. Since she valued being an honest person, she told her community partner what had occurred.

The student concerned about the quality of care in a clinic used professional ethics to describe the obligation that professionals have to their clients. She also used the caring response of virtue ethics as she explained how lack of economic resources and the high degree of activity in the clinic contributed to the situation.

Rule Ethics

Participants used rationale consistent with rule ethics when they described decision making based on the wish to do no harm to the community, promoting student learning (beneficence), or duty or obligation. The student who decided not to organize the Earth Day festival said, "By

not doing the Earth Day festival, then I wouldn't do any harm at all . . ..
The biggest justification is that I know by doing nothing and just continuing with the stuff I know was positive, I'd have no effect, and at least no
effect is better than a negative effect." A faculty member justified the decision to discontinue the service-learning activity when he said, "The learning was not there, so even though it was a valuable service . . .the learning
was quite minimal." In supporting the choice to pull back from a commitment to an agency, another faculty member said, "Well, the right thing to
do was to change agencies because . . .they were not sufficient in meeting
the needs of the students."

Participants described their responsibility in the partnership as directly
related to their roles. Faculty and students prioritized student learning,
and in situations that were frustrating or unresolved, they focused on the
learning that was accomplished. A student who felt powerless to influence
the situation commented that the problem was not her responsibility. This
response reflects the lack of authority in the student role. The student,
who struggled to balance her commitment to provide tutoring with the
uncertainty of her ability to do so, used the student role as rationale to
resolve the ethical conflict. She said, "Because it was for a class, for credit, I
had to finish it, or I would fail the class." Community partner comments
indicated that they valued the benefits that resulted for the community in
addition to the partnership.

Feminist Ethics

Feminist ethics provided a broad understanding about systemic influences on service-learning experiences. A student expressed concern about
the oppression of a community when she commented, "This neighborhood was used so often by [the college], and people just were not very
responsive." Another student expressed concerns that community service
could perpetuate inequality. One community partner indicated one of the
purposes of service-learning was to help students understand the effects of
systems on the lives of people in the community. He was also concerned
about the impact of service-learning on the community. He said, " I feel a
lot of times like we start from scratch with a lot of groups," and "Is it really
true that we are at the mercy of any group that wants to come in and work
with us?" One community partner reflected on how partnership development between the college and community was impeded by different
understandings of power and other system influences.

DISCUSSION

Consideration for relationships was important to all participants in their
ethical decision making. Most ethical problems either originated in a rela-

tionship or had implications for the quality of relationships. Participants had strong and consistent expectations for what a good service-learning relationship is: it should be collaborative, reciprocal, honest, and involve good will. Behaviors that break these relationships, or that may be perceived by others as disrupting the relationship, could cause an ethical problem. These professional relationships depend on trust, promise, and commitment. Breaching trust is one of the most damaging things that may happen in these relationships.

Participants expressed concerns about upholding their own integrity, respecting one another's needs and views, and the need for trust in the relationship. These responses are consistent with the characteristics of ethical relationships suggested by Cameron and Moch (2000). The consideration of the question "Who should I be?" in a service-learning relationship appears to be an important part of resolving an ethical problem.

Participants described the relationship between colleges and communities as a partnership that should be characterized by reciprocity, open communication, mutual benefit, and attentiveness to the power dynamics in the relationship. Partnerships are always dynamic, as faculty, students, and community partners pursue overlapping, yet distinct agendas. Even as they cared for the partnership as a whole, faculty often prioritized student learning, students prioritized their course progress, and community partners prioritized the community. Because these priorities are sometimes complementary but sometimes competing, ethical problems may arise.

Participants reported time constraint as a significant barrier to successful resolution of ethical problems. Students face the demands of coursework, jobs, and social schedules; community partners often work to address overwhelming community need without adequate staff or funding; and faculty balance their service-learning course with the rest of their academic load. In addition, time conflicts occur because faculty and students live with an academic calendar, while community partners do not. Faculty and students become less willing to invest time in relationships when schedules become busy at the end of a term, and sometimes see the end of a term as a fairly clear end of their service-learning responsibilities. Because the calendars of community partners and colleges do not correspond, efforts to communicate, invest time, and resolve problems are often difficult to coordinate.

Only two students reported ethical problems regarding whether and how to do service-learning in a stratified society. These students were experiencing social stratification and were beginning to see their own social situation during their service-learning experience. For students, service-learning may raise these ethical issues in a fresh way. Faculty and community partners often referred to power and social inequalities as they talked about the college-community partnership and students' experiences in encountering community people. They did not, however, define these issues as ethical problems. Faculty and community partners referred to social inequalities as an inevitable part of the context of service-learning, rather than as a problem they faced in a specific situation. This carries important implications for pedagogy, for while faculty and community partners work with these issues in their daily work, students may experience injustice in a more personal and immediate way than faculty during a service-learning course.

Participants in all categories showed a need for closure, even if the problem itself was not resolved. Many participants extended good will to others, imagining why other people made certain choices. When a person failed to return phone calls, missed appointments, or did not follow through on commitments, the offended person often created favorable scenarios to explain the failure. Common reasons involved time and financial resources. A second way that people created closure was to discuss strategies for the future to avoid the reoccurrence of the problem. These processes seemed to serve two purposes: comforting the person who experienced an ethical problem and allowing partnerships to continue. While some participants seemed willing to try again with an agency or individual with whom they experienced an ethical problem, others might not be willing to invest the time and effort needed to resolve the situation. They might become disillusioned with service-learning or they may enter into a partnership with another organization, seeking a more satisfying experience.

Service-learning partnerships might be strengthened when participants acknowledge and understand the differing ethical perspectives used by faculty members, community partners, and students. Faculty members used rule ethics as a justification for their ethical decision making more often than community partners. Certainly, both professional and academic ways of knowing are grounded in the principles of rule ethics. Community partners, who frequently serve vulnerable and oppressed populations, provided explanations for their decisions that were often consistent with feminist ethics. Students used all three ethical approaches, possibly because they have not yet been socialized by typical professional or community ethics.

Need for Further Research

While this exploratory research yielded rich detail of how 13 people in liberal arts colleges experienced ethical conflict in service-learning, the generalizability of these findings is limited in several ways. A larger sample size, including greater racial and ethnic diversity of participants, could contribute to an understanding of a fuller range and context of ethical problems in service-learning. In addition, research could explore other locales (i.e., universities and community colleges as well as liberal arts colleges), and include administrators as participants. An analysis of the perspectives of triads of a faculty member, student, and a community partner in the same partnership could lead to a greater understanding of how ethical problems emerge in service-learning partnerships. Since two faculty members and a senior student conducted the research, the addition of a community partner to the research team could enrich the interpretation of the findings. Future research could address how teaching an ethical decision making model to service-learning participants could contribute to the reduction of ethical conflict or effective resolution of ethical problems.

IMPLICATIONS FOR SERVICE-LEARNING PRACTICE

Reducing Ethical Conflict

Faculty members, students, and community partners may experience diverse ethical problems at different points in the service-learning partnership. It is important to anticipate this diversity by including time for processing unmet expectations and frustrations throughout the experience. A good orientation will sensitize participants to the possibility of these differing perspectives. Clarification of expectations for the contributions of each participant and articulation of responsibilities and roles may be necessary to avoid ethical conflict. Ongoing dialogue can help participants realize that their experience and interpretation of ethical problems is not always mutual. To diffuse this problem, participants can share the missions of their organizations, discuss expectations for time management and communication strategies, and talk about expected benefits for both community members and students.

Participants can reduce ethical conflict by deliberately acknowledging and discussing perceived power inequalities. Power dynamics are sometimes a source, and generally always part of the context for ethical problems. Each partner can consider their social location and their role in the service-learning project as they communicate and serve across differences in power. This mindfulness can help participants reduce power differences in service-learning relationships.

Resolving Ethical Problems

Anticipation of ethical conflict, that is, viewing it as an expected and usual part of service-learning, can help resolve ethical problems. Participants can both identify the conflict and reframe their expectations when ideal partnerships are not realized. Anticipation can also assist participants in the resolution of ethical conflict since recognizing and resolving any ethical problems will then become the norm for service-learning partnerships.

All participants can encourage a "good will" mindset in their service-learning relationships. In this study, participants who assumed the best about others' motivations and behaviors were likely to continue with the service-learning partnership and plan future strategies for resolving ethical problems. Participants also sought to understand one another's experiences and viewpoints. Acknowledgement of difficulties and frustrations might be uncomfortable initially, but could result in clearer communication and a commitment to continuing the partnership.

The Value, Be, Do Ethical Decision Making Model (Cameron, 2000) could be used to help resolve ethical problems encountered in service-learning partnerships. The model could be included in an orientation to service-learning. A systematic examination of one's values, one's character, and relationships with others as promoted by the questions of the Value, Be, Do Model could reduce frustration and facilitate dialogue about ethical conflict. Faculty, students, and community partners could use the model to identify and explain their respective values. A discussion of differing values at the outset of a project could potentially lead to a consensus on what is important in the service-learning experience.

Working With Students

Faculty members need to be available and supportive of students as they work through ethical conflict experienced in service-learning, particularly in confronting social inequalities. Students may not be committed to the partnership to the same extent as faculty members and community partners. In addition, the pressure of receiving a grade may influence students to follow through with a service that raises confusion or ethical problems for them. When students are unable to resolve their ethical conflict, they might develop negative attitudes, reinforce their stereotypes about communities, and/or experience disinterest in future involvement in service-learning. Dialogue about the purpose of service-learning and the value of partnership can facilitate student engagement. Reconsideration of the project goal, activities, and time commitment might be needed to make expectations reasonable for all partners.

CONCLUSION

In summary, faculty members, students, and community partners experience a variety of ethical problems from perspectives consistent with their roles and responsibilities in service-learning partnerships. These ethical problems decrease satisfaction with service-learning experiences and may lead to either revised expectations or discouragement followed by decreased participation. Participants can use an ethical framework for understanding and resolving conflicts that are likely to occur in service-learning practice. Approaches are suggested for resolving ethical conflict that can contribute to rewarding service-learning partnerships.

REFERENCES

Astin, A., & Sax, L. (1998). How undergraduates are affected by service participation. *Journal of College Student Development, 39*(3), 259–63.

Beauchamp, T. L., & Childress, J. F. (1994). *Principles of biomedical ethics.* New York: Oxford University Press.

Berg, B. L. (1998). *Qualitative research methods for the social sciences* (3rd ed.). Boston: Allyn & Bacon.

Boss, J. A. (1994). The effect of community services on the moral development of college ethics students. *Journal of Moral Development, 23*(2), 183–198.

Cameron, M. E. (1993). *Living with AIDS: Experiencing ethical problems.* Newbury Park, CA: Sage.

Cameron, M. E. (2000). Value, be, do: Guidelines for resolving ethical conflict. *Journal of Nursing Law, 6*(4), 15–24.

Cameron, M. E. (2002). Older persons' ethical problems involving their health. *Nursing Ethics, 9*(5), 537–556.

Cameron, M. E., & Moch, S. D. (2000). Ethical relationships among nurses. *Journal of Nursing Law, 7*(1), 13–20.

Cameron, M. E., Schaffer, M., & Park, H. (2001). Nursing students' experience of ethical problems and use of ethical decision-making models. *Nursing Ethics, 8*(5), 432–447.

Coffey, A., & Atkinson, P. (1996). *Making sense of qualitative data: Complementary research strategies.* Thousand Oaks, CA: Sage.

Cruz, N. I., & Giles, Jr., D. E. (2000). Where's the community in service-learning research? *Michigan Journal of Community Service Learning*, Special Issue, 28–24.

Esterberg, K. (2002). *Qualitative methods in social research.* Boston: McGraw Hill.

Eyler, J., & Giles, Jr., D. (1997). The importance of program quality in service-learning. In A. S. Waterman, *Service-learning applications from the research* (pp. 57–76). Mahwah, NJ: Lawrence Erlbaum Associates.

Eyler, J., & Giles, D. E. (1999). *Where's the learning in service learning?* San Francisco: Jossey-Bass.

Frankena, W. K. (1973). *Ethics* (2nd ed.). Englewood Cliffs, NJ: Prentice-Hall.

Giles, D. E., & Eyler, J. S. (1994). The impact of a college community service laboratory on students' personal, social and cognitive outcomes. *Journal of Adolescence, 17*, 327–339.

Gilligan, C. (1982). *In a different voice: Psychological theory and women's development.* Cambridge, MA: Harvard University Press.

Gorman, M. (1994). Service experience and the moral development of college students. *Religious Education, 89*(3), 422–431.

Green, A. E. (2001). "But you aren't white:" Racial perceptions and service-learning. *Michigan Journal of Community Service Learning, 8*(1), 18–26.

Howard, J. (Ed.). (2001). Service-learning course design workbook. *Michigan Journal of Community Service Learning,* Companion Volume. The University of Michigan: OCSL Press.

Langseth, M. (2000). Maximizing impact, minimizing harm: Why service-learning must more fully integrate multicultural education. In C. R. O'Grady (Ed.), *Integrating service-learning and multicultural education in colleges and universities* (pp. 247–262). Mahwah, NJ: Lawrence Erlbaum Associates.

Linzer, N. (1999). *Resolving ethical dilemmas in social work practice.* Needham Heights, MA: Allyn & Bacon.

McEwen, M. K. (1996). Enhancing student learning and development through service-learning. In B. Jacoby and Associates (Eds), *Service-learning in higher education: Concepts and practices* (pp. 53–91). San Francisco: Jossey-Bass.

Mintz, S. D., & Hesser, G. W. (1996). Principles of good practice in service-learning. In B. Jacoby and Associates (Eds.), *Service-learning in higher education: Concepts and practices* (pp. 26–52). San Francisco: Jossey-Bass.

Murray, H., Gillese, E., Lennon, M., Mercer, P., & Robinson, M. (1996). Ethical principles for college and university teaching. In L. Fisch (Ed.), *New directions for teaching and learning* (pp. 57–63). San Francisco: Jossey-Bass.

Myers-Lipton, S. J. (1996). Effect of service-learning on college students' attitudes toward international understanding. *Journal of College Student Development, 37*(6), 659–68.

Noddings, N. (1990). Review symposium: A response. *Hypatia, 5*(10), 120–126.

Nnakwe, N. E. (1999). Implementation and impact of college community service and its effect on the social responsibility of undergraduate students. *Journal of Family and Consumer Sciences, 91*(2), 57–61.

Parsons, R. D. (2001). *The ethics of professional practice.* Boston: Allyn & Bacon.

Pence, G. (2000). *A dictionary of common philosophical terms.* New York: The McGraw-Hill Companies.

Rockquemore, K. A., & Schaffer, R. H. (2000). Toward a theory of engagement: A cognitive mapping of service-learning experiences. *Michigan Journal of Community Service Learning, 7,* 14–25.

Schaffer, M. A., Cameron, M. E., & Tatley, E. B. (2000). The value, be, do ethical decision-making model: Balancing students' needs in school nursing. *Journal of School Nursing, 15*(5), 44–49.

Sigmon, R. (1979). Service-learning: Three principles. *Synergist, 8,* 9–11.

Strauss, A., & Corbin, J. (1990). *Basics of qualitative research: Grounded theory procedures and techniques.* Newbury Park, CA: Sage.

Strike, K. A., & Moss, P. A. (1997). *Ethics and college student life.* Needham Heights, MA: Allyn & Bacon.

Taylor, C. R. (1998). Reflections on "nursing considered as moral practice." *Kennedy Institute of Ethics Journal, 8,* 71–82.

Tellez, K. (2000). Reconciling service-learning and the moral obligations of the professor. In C. R. O'Grady (Ed.), *Integrating service-learning and multicultural education in colleges and universities* (pp. 71–91). Mahwah, NJ: Lawrence Erlbaum Associates.

Thiroux, J. P. (1986). *Ethics: Theory and practice* (3rd Ed.). New York: Macmillan.

Volbrecht, R. M. (2002). *Nursing ethics: Communities in dialogue.* New Jersey: Prentice Hall.

Welch, S. D. (2000). *A feminist ethic of risk.* Minneapolis, MN: Fortress Press.

PART V

IMPACT OF SERVICE-
LEARNING ON STUDENTS

CHAPTER 8

USING WRITTEN PROTOCOLS TO MEASURE SERVICE-LEARNING OUTCOMES

Pamela Steinke and Peggy Fitch

This paper reports on the development of a written protocol for measuring two academic outcomes of service-learning: intellectual development and cognitive learning. Coding schemes are described along with measures of reliability and validity. A theoretical model is presented to further understanding of the possible intersections between student intellectual development and cognitive learning in service-learning courses. Suggestions for the use of the protocol as a tool for reflection are also provided.

Problem solving protocols have been used extensively by social, cognitive, and educational researchers to assess both performance on cognitive tasks (e.g., Ericsson & Simon, 1985) and understanding of real-life issues (e.g., Voss, 1988). Such protocols also show promise for measuring cognitive or intellectual outcomes of service-learning (Eyler & Giles, 1999; Steinke & Buresh, 2002). Eyler and Giles (2002) noted that ideally these protocols

Deconstructing Service-Learning: Research Exploring Context, Participation, and Impacts
A Volume in: Advances in Service-Learning Research, pages 171–194.
Copyright © 2003 by Information Age Publishing, Inc.
All rights of reproduction in any form reserved.
ISBN: 1-59311-071-5 (hardcover), 1-59311-070-7 (pbk.)

would be used in an interview format to allow respondents to offer their full understanding and to avoid inherent problems, such as lack of seriousness and hasty responses, with administering surveys in class. However, given that interviews are time consuming and expensive, there is merit in developing a written protocol that can be easily administered and integrated into reflection activities (Rama, Ravenscroft, Wolcott, & Zlotkowski, 2000), and can provide instructors with feedback about their students' level of understanding and problem solving abilities.

This chapter reports on the development, reliability, and validity of academic outcome measures coded from such a protocol and presents a number of ways both practitioners and researchers can benefit from using written protocols. Specifically, the chapter demonstrates how the same written problem solving protocol can be used to code for both course-specific cognitive learning outcomes based on the cognitive psychological research on expertise and knowledge structure representation, and used to code for more general critical thinking skills indicative of epistemological beliefs based on the research on student intellectual development. A theoretical model is presented to help explain the possible intersections of cognitive learning and student intellectual development in service-learning courses. For researchers or practitioners who are not interested in coding for these two specific outcomes, other uses of the protocol as a tool for reflection and discussion are presented.

DEVELOPING THE WRITTEN PROBLEM SOLVING PROTOCOL

Recommendations for the development of written protocols follow a number of basic guidelines. First, in order to provide a good measure of cognitive learning, such protocols need to retain the course-specific nature of Eyler and Giles' (1999, 2002) problem solving interviews yet still be comparable across very different courses. Research on expertise suggests that expert knowledge is detailed, deep, and well organized and able to be easily accessed in the right context (Bransford, Brown, Cocking, Donovan, & Pelligrino, 2000). However, expert knowledge is also domain-specific, suggesting that measures of student learning also need to be related to specific course content. Domain-independent measures of students' thinking skills may be relevant to institutional academic goals, but say little about whether students' knowledge structures for a specific subject have been developed in a meaningful way. In addition, domain specific questions require students to use knowledge gained from the course. Assessing prior knowledge is an important part of learning and in part accounts for why experts are better able to remember new information in their field. A measure that assesses use of knowledge can provide a good indicator of cognitive learning. For example, the role of accessing prior knowledge in order to enhance science learning has been of particular interest to educational researchers (Edmondson, 2000).

Second, the content of the protocols works best when students are asked to apply their knowledge to solving real-world problems. Given the fact that expert knowledge is "conditionalized" to reflect its use in appropriate contexts (Bransford et al., 2000), outcome measures must also demonstrate that students can appropriately use the knowledge they have to solve novel problems. Therefore, it is important to develop cognitive outcome measures that are closely aligned with productive outcomes of learning or the development of knowledge structures useful to solving real world problems (Thomas & Rohwer, 1993). Students' ability to solve novel problems is an important indicator of their ability to transfer what they have learned to new contexts, or adaptive flexible learning (Bransford et al., 2000).

Third, in order to provide a good measure of student intellectual development, protocols should also provide an opportunity for students to apply their critical thinking and problem solving skills to important issues and to consider the basis of their claims. This reflection needs to go beyond using indirect measures that are based on students' impressions of what they have learned or how they have improved their thinking skills. Students clearly believe that they have learned and grown intellectually from involvement in service-learning (Litke, 2002). Students' reflections of what they have learned can provide a good measure of their beliefs and can enhance service-learning outcomes, so this type of reflection is recommended as a pedagogical tool (Steinke, Fitch, Johnson, & Waldstein, 2002). Students' reflections are not, however, as useful as a direct measure of student intellectual outcomes (Steinke & Buresh, 2002). Assessments of student learning applied to a content area provide more direct measures of intellectual or epistemelogical development. For example, much scientific thinking is problem solving in nature and as Kuhn (1997) noted, the relationship between cognitive skills, epistemological beliefs, and science education highlights the important relationship between scientific thinking and more general intellectual skills.

Fourth, to ensure that written protocols accurately assess cognitive learning and intellectual development outcomes, instructors must provide more time and more specific instructions than with checklists or rating scales. Moreover, students must perceive that the exercise is meaningful. These challenges might be alleviated by integrating written protocols into the classroom as reflection tools. Students may find the exercise more personally meaningful if it is used as an in-class reflection tool or method of evaluation. Students must also be given ample time for the completion of the protocol. Instructors who commit time in class can emphasize the importance of answering the items completely and explain why this procedure is important. Doing so will increase the likelihood that students will find the exercise meaningful because they view the purpose of the study as being aligned with their commitment to service-learning or educational reform research.

USING THE PROTOCOL TO MEASURE COGNITIVE LEARNING AND INTELLECTUAL DEVELOPMENT OUTCOMES

As part of a larger study, 110 service-learning students from 12 private colleges in Iowa answered written post-test questions about an applied issue that was relevant to the course material. The format was adapted from interview protocols developed by Eyler and Giles (1999). Researchers worked with instructors to develop issues that were relevant to students' service-learning projects but did not explicitly make reference to the projects. For example, students in *Changing the World,* a Philosophy/Religion class, volunteered weekly in several organizations in a small Iowa town. Their assignment was "to participate in the life of the town, via various volunteer organizations, while consciously reflecting on the structures that underlie its ordinary view of itself" (taken from the course syllabus). The written protocol for this course posed the following problem for students: "The real problem today is people failing, or feeling unable, to take responsibility for what needs to be changed in the world." Students then answered the following questions about the issue:

- What are the consequences of this problem?
- What do you think causes this problem?
- What are some other opinions about the causes of this problem?
- What do you think should be done to try to solve this problem?
- What are some other opinions about possible solutions to this problem?
- How would you personally go about getting something done about this problem in your community?

Protocols were administered in class at the end of the semester to students in 12 service-learning courses representing a variety of disciplines.

Responses were coded separately using two different coding schemes. First, the coding scheme for cognitive learning provided a measure of expertise by assessing the similarity between knowledge structure representations of students as novices and the instructor as expert based on a knowledge structure approach used in text comprehension and question answering (Graesser & Clark, 1985) and causal inferencing (Steinke, Long, & Wilkins, 1996). Two independent coders identified the individual knowledge statements generated in response to the specific questions about consequences, causes, and solutions, and judged whether they matched with statements identified from responses provided by the instructor. For exam-

ple, the student who answers that one of the consequences of people failing to take responsibility for changing the world is that things "will
continue to be more and more of a problem" would be coded as having a
shared knowledge statement or node with the instructor's response that
"the basic infrastructure . . . continues to deteriorate." The total number of
shared statements across the responses to the consequences, causes, and
solutions questions was used as a shared knowledge score for each respondent.

Second, responses were coded using a scheme adapted from Eyler and
Giles (1999) as a measure of problem solving. The scheme assessed both
the locus and complexity of consequences, causes, and solutions to the
problem and the sophistication of personal action strategies. The coding
scheme for locus of consequences, causes, and solutions (see Exhibit 1)
measured the degree to which respondents identified individual, systemic,
or combined individual and systemic factors in each answer.

The following are examples of coding for causal locus in response to the
problem that people do not take responsibility for changing the world:

Level 1—Lack of motivation. Learned helplessness. (focus on individual
   mental state, etc.)

Level 2—Lack of unity, of opportunity to take action. Also part of our
   morals/values; needs to be instilled at an early age. (focus on members of a social group/system)

Level 3—Government somewhat hides problems of world. (focus on system, not explained)

Level 4—Lack of thought about the world's responsibility to fix its problems. It is seen all over T.V. that it is cool to add towards the corrup-
   tion of society and completely odd that one would try to change the
   world. (focus on system with explanation)

Level 5—The problem is that focus is on self-absorbed resolution. An
   individual is seen as just that and not part of the greater good and
   the role they have in it. The problem might be that we are failing
   ourselves because we do not abide by a moral code of sorts. We have
   lost the will to abide by a conduct of ethics. (focus on individuals
   within contexts of systems, including causal connections)

As shown in Exhibit 2, the coding scheme for complexity of consequences, causes and solutions measured the degree of differentiation and
elaboration in each answer.

Examples follow of coding for solution complexity in response to the
problem "In the U.S., poverty is a gendered issue" used for a women's studies course:

EXHIBIT 1
Problem Analysis Coding Categories (Revised from Eyler and Giles coding categories):
Locus of Consequence, Cause, and Solution

A. Consequence Locus	B. Causal Locus	C. Solution Locus
• missing data/leaves the response blank (use even if they have answered other questions in the same protocol)	• missing data/leaves the response blank (use even if they have answered other questions in the same protocol)	• missing data/leaves the response blank (use even if they have answered other questions in the same protocol)
0. no consequences; does not view the problem as stated as having consequences; answer given does not address consequences; states "don't know"	0. no problem locus; does not identify a problem; does not think there is a problem; gives an answer that does not answer the question about cause; states "don't know"	0. no solution locus; does not feel a solution is needed; gives an answer that does not answer the question; states "don't know"
1. consequences to individual mental state/ individual behavior; focus on consequences to individuals who may make up a group; if the group is mentioned the focus is on individual mental states, behaviors and characteristics of the individual group members	1. individual mental state/individual behavior/ characteristic of the individual even if not intentional (e.g., genetic endowment); focus is on individual differences among people in general or a specified group of people	1. solution focused on addressing individual mental state/individual behavior/individual failure/immediate needs of individual/individual differences in how people respond to situations
2. consequences to group of which individual is a member (e.g., family, community, cultural group); focus on consequences to group/shared characteristics; identifies subgroups that have different consequences; reference to character- istics of group of which the individual is a member	2. individual focus with some placement within broader social group or system of which the individual is a member (e.g., culture, family, proximity); refer- ence is to the group of individuals/ shared characteristics of members of a group; different groups may be con- trasted to make the point or the reader can easily generate groups that could be contrasted	2. solution focused on meeting needs of individuals as members of a social group (e.g., family, nation, neighborhood, com- munity, occupation) but not connected to an established system; focus is on needs of the group as a whole; different groups may be contrasted to make the point or the reader can easily generate groups that could be contrasted

3. consequences to broader system (e.g., political, educational, financial, occupational) identified but not developed/explained/ elaborated; reference to characteristics of broader systems

4. consequences to broader system identified and further developed or explained/ elaborated; if individual is mentioned there is no development or explanation/elaboration

5. consequences to both individuals and systems identified and developed or explained/ elaborated with causal connections but causal connections need not be between the systemic and individual

3. systemic locus (e.g., political, educational, financial, occupational) identified but not developed/explained/ elaborated

4. systemic locus identified with development/ explanation/elaboration; explanation given for why the system causes a problem; greater specificity about what part of the system causes the problem or how the problem came to be

5. combined individual/systemic locus developed/explained/elaborated with causal connections; both individual and systemic must be explained

3. systemic solution (e.g., political, educational, financial, health, occupational) identified but not well developed/ explained/elaborated; solution focused on changing, expanding, or pointing out what is right or wrong with an established system

4. systemic solution developed/ explained/ elaborated; reference to broader principle (e.g. reciprocity; equity); explanation as to why or how the system should be changed or expanded

5. integrated individual/ systemic solution developed/ explained; both individual and systemic solutions integrated into a well elaborated solution; no causal connectivity required

Notes: If multiple loci are identified within one response, the locus with the highest score will determine the code for that response unless the multiple loci are connected in a way that meets the criteria for coding the entire response as a "5."

EXHIBIT 2

Problem Analysis Coding Categories (Revised from Eyler and Giles coding categories): Consequence, Causal, and Solution Complexity

A. Complexity of Consequences	B. Complexity of Cause	C. Complexity of Solution
• missing data/leaves the response blank (use even if they have answered other questions in the same protocol)	• missing data/leaves the response blank (use even if they have answered other questions in the same protocol)	• missing data/leaves the response blank (use even if they have answered other questions in the same protocol)
0. no consequences; states "don't know"	0. no cause given; does not view as a problem; response does not identify a problem; states "don't know"	0. no solution given; states "don't know"
1. Low: simple; no context; one consequence even if that consequence has two related parts (e.g., occupation as defined by both work and school, affects two sides of the same issue, affects development of social and cognitive); low elaboration of reasons for consequence	1. Low: simple; no context; one cause; low elaboration of reasons for problem; if two causes are identified, they are highly related to each other and not explained	1. Low: noncontextualized: naïve; often individual action without analysis; unconnected to current service infrastructure; only a single solution offered

2. Medium: more elaboration of single consequence; at least two very different consequences identified either representing two different perspectives/types of people or clear differences within the same perspective (e.g., both short-term and long-term consequences, both individual and social consequences, specific consequences identified for two different environmental contexts); different consequences identified for different subgroups

3. High: at least two consequences from the same perspective explained/elaborated and situated in context with causal connections but there need not be a causal connection between the two consequences; multiple perspectives explained/elaborated

2. Medium: some context; may mention need to gather more information; some awareness of current efforts; mention of how solution is connected to a current program or service infrastructure with reference to established sites (e.g., hospitals, schools) or direct reference to recognized professions at established sites (e.g., nurses, teachers); may cite current program as model; more than one solution offered

2. Medium: more extensive elaboration of a single cause usually with causal connectivity; at least two very different causal loci identified

3. High: at least two loci identified and elaborated/situated in context with causal connections within at least one of the explanations; loci representing multiple perspectives integrated with causal links

3. High: systemic approach; connected to causes and systematic needs assessment; multiple solutions or complex solutions; contextualized; supported with analysis; well elaborated

Level 1—Share the wealth. (low: simple; no context; one solution)

Level 2—Welfare reform, increase minimum wage. (medium: two different solutions)

Level 3—Well, get people educated in poverty areas so that these people can get better paying jobs and get out of poverty. Get people into programs to learn ways to get out of poverty. (high: at least two solutions that are elaborated, situated in context)

The coding scheme for sophistication of personal action strategy (see Exhibit 3) measured the degree of contextualization and specificity of strategy, and awareness of current processes and programs.

Examples are shown below of coding of responses to the problem "Minority and disadvantaged youth often have difficulties with mathematical concept development" posed for an elementary education course to prepare mathematics teachers.

EXHIBIT 3
Problem Analysis Coding Categories (Revised from
Eyler and Giles coding categories): Sophistication of
Personal Action Strategy

- missing data/leaves the response blank (use even if they have answered other questions in the same protocol)

0. no personal strategy; would not do anything; states "don't know" (Note: If a strategy that does not seem personal but rather implies a person would have to be in a different role in order to implement it, the response should still be coded as if the person was in that situation/role)

1. Low: noncontextualized; naïve; unaware of current programs; unaware of practical processes for connecting with programs and community (e.g., "just tell them" or "I'll start a program")

2. Medium-low: unclear or noncontextualized strategy but recognition of a need for a process to gather more information or to identify a strategy; no specific program identified but strategy/role for working with an unspecified program mentioned or mention of need to develop strategy/role to work with an established system

3. Medium: aware of current programs and need to work with others and/or need to do a systematic needs assessment of the community; realistic practical guidelines; strategy/role connected to a current specified program

4. High: Highly contextualized; aware of volunteer and policy process; targeted plan; systematic approach; clearly practical awareness of community; characterized by clear, detailed knowledge of processes and programs; very specific role with a clearly defined program; several levels to strategy including at least two different roles and programs identified

Level 1—Increasing the lines of communication (low: noncontextualized; naïve).

Level 2—Volunteer time as a tutor (medium-low: strategy/role given though no specific program identified).

Level 3—Educating other teachers on creative projects I have done that have been successful (medium: aware of current programs and need to work with others).

Responses from the one question on consequences were coded for locus and complexity of consequences, the combined responses from the two questions on cause were coded for locus and complexity of cause, the combined responses from the two questions on solutions were coded for locus and complexity of solutions, and responses from the one question on personal action strategy were coded for complexity of personal action strategy. Scores from each category were added together to obtain a total score for each respondent. Two raters together created the adapted coding scheme using pilot data from another research project and separately coded 20 percent of the sample, reconciling differences through discussion. One coder then completed the sample, in consultation with the other coder.

RELIABILITY AND VALIDITY OF PROTOCOL MEASURES

Reliability

The correlation between the two coders for shared knowledge statements was $r(110) = .66$, $p < .001$. Previously Steinke and Harrington (2002) found good interrater reliability between two independent coders for shared knowledge [$r(183) = .86$, $p < .001$] on a different set of data using the same shared knowledge structure coding procedure. Due to differences between the classes and the issues posed for each class, the original scores on the shared knowledge coding of the protocols were transformed into z-scores for each class. The course-specific nature of the measure calls for z-score transformation because the course-specific issues elicited differing amounts of information. For example, the number of shared propositions in one course ranged from zero to two, whereas for another class this range was from one to seven. Clearly, it is not necessarily the case that students in the second class had more expertise in their subject matter than students in the first class. By transforming the raw scores into z-scores for each class, the resulting score indicates how much and in what direction each individual deviated from the class average.

By adding the scores for consequence locus (0 to 5), consequence complexity (0 to 3), causal locus (0 to 5), causal complexity (0 to 3), solution locus (0 to 5), solution complexity (0 to 3) and personal action strategy complexity (0 to 4), the possible range of total scores on the problem solving measure was 0 to 28. The actual range of scores for the sample was 6 to 26. The correlation between the two coders for the problem solving measure was $r(23) = .77$, $p < .001$.

Validity

To assess the validity of the measures as indicators of cognitive learning and of intellectual development, a confirmatory factor analysis was computed using AMOS 4.0 Structural Equation Modeling (SEM) software. Intellectual Development and Cognitive Learning were treated as latent variables. Latent variables are variables that represent a single concept yet are not directly observed or measured. Each latent variable can have several observed or measured variables as indicators. Shared knowledge was one indicator of the latent variable cognitive learning and problem solving score was one indicator of the latent variable intellectual development.

Other indicators of the latent variable cognitive learning were items taken from a self-report scale. Self-report measures are the most widely used and have produced the most positive findings on cognitive learning outcomes of service-learning (Steinke & Buresh, 2002). Several studies have found students in service-learning courses report greater learning benefits from their service-learning experiences than non-service-learning students report from alternative, traditional assignments (e.g., Berson, 1997; Markus, Howard, & King, 1993). The self-report scale used has consistently demonstrated good validity as an outcome measure of service-learning predictors (Steinke et al., 2002; Steinke & Harrington, 2002). Items are rated on a 5-point scale (1 = strongly disagree, 5 = strongly agree) and were adapted from Eyler and Giles (1999) with additions for a total of eight items, listed below. A pre-test version of the scale uses the stem, "Typically, course requirements that go beyond participation in class and assigned readings..." The post-test version of the scale reported here uses the stem, "In this course, course requirements that went beyond participation in class and assigned readings..."

- Helped me to make connections between the ideas and questions I encounter in different classes and/or fields of study.
- Did not teach me how to apply things I learned in class to real problems. (reverse coded)
- Did not greatly enhance my learning in the course beyond what I gain from reading the text and attending class. (reverse coded)
- Helped me to spontaneously generate my own examples of principles and concepts I am learning about in class.
- Helped me to see the complexity of real life problems and their solutions.

- Did not provide me with a greater understanding of the social and ethical issues in that field. (reverse coded)
- Did not enhance my understanding of the logic behind various perspectives about controversies in that field. (reverse coded)
- Allowed me to gain a much deeper appreciation of the importance of things I am learning about in class.

The post-test items demonstrated good scale reliability (Cronbach's alpha = .87).

Other indicators of the latent variable intellectual development were subscale scores from a self-report rating scale and scores from Knefelkamp and Widick's Measure of Intellectual Development (MID) (as cited in Moore, n.d.), an open-ended essay-type instrument that is coded by trained raters and measures Perry's (1999) scheme of intellectual and ethical development. Perry's scheme describes how college students' conceptions of knowledge, truth, learning, and commitment evolve through nine positions within four broad stages, from Dualism (i.e., all knowledge is known by the "right" Authorities and it is black and white; thus, Truth is absolute) through Multiplicity (i.e., knowledge includes some "gray" areas and things we do not' know yet; authorities disagree, thus any opinion is as good as another) and Contextual Relativism (i.e., knowledge is constructed by learners in specific and limited contexts; the best opinions are supported by quality evidence, thus standards exist to judge the adequacy of opinions) to Commitment Within Relativism (i.e., commitments that reflect one's identity—to an area of study, a career, a relationship, a value system—must be made within an essentially relativistic world). The particular version of the MID used here asked students to write about their ideal learning environment.

> **Instructions:** Please answer the questions below about your ideal learning environment. Again, there are no right and wrong answers. What is important is the way you think about learning. Please be as specific and complete in your answer as possible. Feel free to use the back of the page if needed.
>
> If you were to design a course that would embody the best learning environment for you, what would it look like? What types of assignments would be given? How would your performance be evaluated? What types of demands would the course include? What would the professors be like? What would the class "atmosphere" be like? What would be your role as a student in the course? (© Knefelkamp & Widick. Available from Moore [n.d.])

MID essays were scored independently by two trained raters. To score the essays, raters use a manual of prototypical statements or cues that reflect each Perry position and the transitions between positions. Essays are given a three-digit score that represents the rater's judgment of the dominant position and, if applicable, a transition between positions. For example, an essay that received a score of 223 indicates that the writer is reasoning primarily from Position 2 (Dualism), but is in transition to Position 3 (Early Multiplicity); an essay rated 233 indicates primarily position 3 with traces of Position 2 reasoning. Each digit represents one-third of a stage. Thus, the two ratings in this example are in agreement within one-third of a stage. Interrater reliability for the MID was 76 percent for agreement within one-third of a stage.

Three additional indicators of the latent variable intellectual development were subscale scores from a self-report rating scale that was administered at the beginning and end of the semester/block. As shown in Exhibit 4, the scale included a subset of 12 items selected from the Learning Environment Preferences (LEP, Moore, 1989), a checklist measure of the lower

EXHIBIT 4
Indicators of Intellectual Development: LEP Subscale Items

Dualism (Position 2)

- The classroom atmosphere and activities would consist of lectures (with a chance to ask questions) because I can get all the facts I need to know more efficiently that way.
- As a student I would study and memorize the subject matter -- the teacher is there to teach it.
- The teacher would teach me all the facts and information I am supposed to learn.
- Evaluation procedures would consist of objective-style tests because they have clear-cut right or wrong answers.

Early Multiplicity (Position 3)

- As a student I would participate actively with my peers in class discussions and ask as many questions as necessary to fully understand the topic.
- The teacher would be not just an instructor, but more an explainer, entertainer, and friend.
- The classroom atmosphere and activities would include a lot of projects and assignments with practical everyday applications.
- Evaluation procedures would be based on how much students have improved in the class and on how hard they have worked in class.

Late Multiplicity (Position 4)

- Evaluation procedures would consist of thoughtful criticism of my work by someone with appropriate expertise.
- As a student I would expect to take learning seriously and be personally motivated to learn the subject.
- The classroom atmosphere and activities would include research papers, since they demand that I consult sources and then offer my own interpretation and thinking.
- The teacher would challenge students to present their own ideas, argue with the position taken, and require evidence for their beliefs.

positions on Perry's scheme of intellectual development. Time constraints prevented administration of the complete LEP.[1]. Four of the 12 items reflected Dualism (Position 2), four reflected Early Multiplicity (Position 3), and four reflected Late Multiplicity (Position 4). In response to the stem, "In my ideal learning environment . . . ," students rated their agreement with each item on a 5-point scale (1 = strongly disagree; 5 = strongly agree). The four items for each position were summed to obtain three position scores for each student on the pre-test and the post-test. Only the post-test scores were used in the SEM analysis reported here.

The estimated standardized regression weights and probability levels for each indicator are presented in Exhibit 5. Correlated errors were assumed for measures taken from the same scale or instrument. All indicators of the latent variables intellectual development and cognitive learning were significant at the .05 level except the problem solving measure and most were significant at the .001 level. The estimated relationship between the two latent variables, intellectual development and cognitive learning, was also significant ($b = .44$, $p = .004$). The means and standard deviations of the all indicators of the latent variables are presented in Exhibit 6.

EXHIBIT 5
Estimated Standardized Beta Weights and Probability Levels for
Intellectual and Cognitive Learning Indicators

Intellectual Development		
Indicators	*Estimated Standardized*	*p value*
Dualism/Position 2	-.54	.003
Early Multiplicity/Position 3	.62	< .001
Late Multiplicity/Position 4	.46	.001
Perry/MID	.55	.013
Problem Solving	.24	.076
Cognitive Learning		
Shared Statements/Nodes	.22	.039
Connections Between Classes	.62	< .001
Teach to Apply	.64	< .001
Enhanced Learning	.70	< .001
Generate Examples	.78	< .001
Complexity of Problems	.76	< .001
Social/Ethical Understanding	.69	< .001
Logic of Perspectives	.70	< .001
Appreciation of Importance	.48	< .001

EXHIBIT 6
Mean and Standard Deviation of Intellectual
Development and Cognitive Learning Indicators

Intellectual Development		
Indicators	M	SD
Dualism/Position 2	11.51	2.93
Early Multiplicity/Position 3	16.46	2.08
Late Multiplicity/Position 4	15.64	2.13
Perry/MID	3.15	.38
Problem Solving	14.18	3.75
Cognitive Learning		
Shared Statements/Nodes[a]	.00	1.00
Connections Between Classes	3.92	.88
Teach to Apply	3.97	.87
Enhanced Learning	3.96	.94
Generate Examples	3.93	.73
Complexity of Problems	4.01	.86
Social/Ethical Understanding	3.89	.93
Logic of Perspectives	3.87	.82
Appreciation of Importance	4.12	.74

Notes: [a] Mean of zero and standard deviation of one due to z-score transformation

These results suggest that the measures used indeed captured two separate assessments of cognitive learning and student intellectual development. They also suggest, however, that the written protocol needs further improvement as the two protocol measures, problem solving and the z-score for shared knowledge statements or nodes, were the weakest indicators of the latent variables. The main problem in the model is that the problem solving measure is only a very modest indicator of intellectual development.

THEORETICAL MODEL OF THE RELATIONSHIP BETWEEN INTELLECTUAL DEVELOPMENT AND COGNITIVE LEARNING

A model of the intersections between student intellectual development and cognitive learning outcomes is being developed to help understand the theoretical relationship between these two concepts in the context of service-learning courses (Steinke & Fitch, 2001). The model, as shown in

Exhibit 7, suggests that both characteristics of instruction and characteristics of the service-learning project are processed through the student's level of intellectual development, providing a focus for the inevitable expectation failures that occur during the learning process (Schank, Berman, & Macpherson, 1999). Characteristics of instruction (e.g., discussing projects with faculty, giving speeches, applying current course material) and characteristics of the service-learning project (e.g., challenging tasks, freedom to develop ideas, meeting community needs) combine to provide a certain level of challenge and support for the student engaged in service-learning. Previous research found that both types of characteristics were related to academic outcomes (Steinke et al., 2002). Depending on the presence of these characteristics and the student's level of intellectual development, the student tends to focus failed expectations for learning solely on the material learned which enhances cognitive learning but does not necessarily enhance intellectual development; solely on the self as learner which enhances intellectual development but does not necessarily enhance cognitive learning; or on the self as learner in the context of the material learned which enhances both intellectual development and cognitive learning. Furthermore, due to the intellectual growth encouraged by the enhancement of both outcomes, the latter focus should produce synergistic effects.

The importance of service-learning in this model is that service-learning uniquely allows students to experience current classroom material in the context of a real world setting in which the community is looking to the

EXHIBIT 7
Theoretical Model of Intersections Between Student Intellectual Development and Cognitive Learning

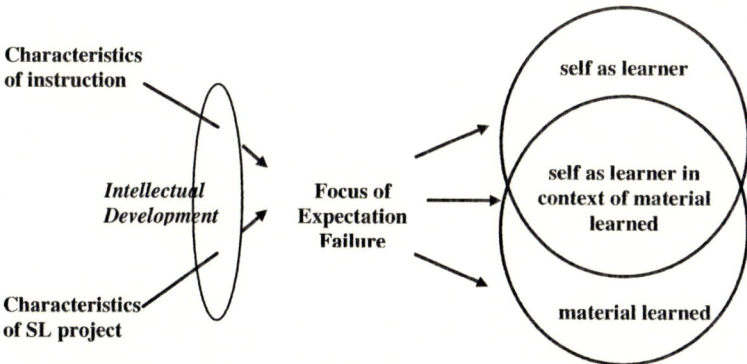

individual student learner as a provider. As a result, service-learning courses typically encourage the focus of learning to be on the self as learner in the context of the material learned more than do non-service-learning courses. The importance of expectation failure in this model is that optimal expectation failure, which occurs when challenge and support are in balance, encourages the focus of expectation failure to be on the self as learner in the context of material learned. The potential for reaching this balance is greater in service-learning courses than with the use of most traditional pedagogies.

The importance of intellectual development as a lens in this model is that students will be challenged and supported by different characteristics of instruction and of the service-learning project depending on their level of intellectual development. Students at higher levels of intellectual development will be more likely to focus on the self as learner in context of material learned than will students in Dualism who will focus more on the material or students in Multiplicity who will focus more on the self. Equally important is that intellectual development theory has implications for how to design service-learning experiences in ways that promote intellectual development.

The problem solving protocol provides a measure not only of cognitive learning but also of intellectual development specific to course content. Both academic outcomes should be enhanced when the focus of the student's expectation failure is on the self as learner in the context of material learned as it is in well-designed service-learning courses. Improvements are needed to determine whether the coding of the problem solving protocol for locus and complexity is not measuring the concept of intellectual development per se but rather a related concept, or whether the protocol just needs more work to improve its validity as a measure of intellectual development.

RECOMMENDED IMPROVEMENTS TO THE WRITTEN PROTOCOL

The current problem solving measure does not go far enough to reflect student intellectual development fully. Future efforts should focus on refining the problem solving measure and coding scheme to better assess personal epistemological beliefs more specifically by asking questions that get at students' beliefs about the nature of knowledge (Hofer, 2001; Kuhn, 2001) as has been assessed in the interview format. For example Eyler and Giles' (1999) problem solving interview asked for students' justifications for their answers, their certainty, and the basis for their judgments about the adequacy of their opinions (e.g., How do you know that it/those is/are the cause(s)? On what do you base your view? Can you ever know for sure that your position is correct? [p. 259]). They also included probes to assess students' perspectives on why people disagree and how they would evaluate different opinions/evidence (e.g., Why do people have different points of view about the factors related to this problem? How do you decide which view is right when experts disagree? [p. 259]). These types of questions are not included in the current version of the problem solving protocol and are at the heart of understanding students' personal epistemological beliefs and assessing their intellectual development (Kuhn, 2001; Moore, 2000). In an attempt to address this problem, the authors' most recent revision of the written protocol has included the questions: "Why is your opinion about the cause of this problem better than some other opinions?" and "What are the limitations of your proposed solution to this problem?"

Another recommended improvement to the written protocol involves the way issues and questions are framed, particularly the probes used to elicit elaboration from students. The written protocol should frame the initial problem in a way that is easy for students to understand and, though open-ended, should not be subject to a wide range of interpretation. Instructions and the questions students are asked to write about in response to the problem should emphasize the importance of taking the time and care to answer as completely as possible because the written protocol does not allow for additional probes to "say more about that" as does the interview. For example, the instructions given earlier in this chapter for the MID essay indicate that "there are no right and wrong answers" and ask the student to "be as specific and complete in your answer as possible."

The problem solving coding scheme may need additional revision. The current version of the coding scheme shown in Exhibits 1, 2, and 3 was adapted from Eyler and Giles (1999) and gives more weight to consequences, causes, and solutions that consider the systemic nature of the issue (e.g., political, educational, financial, occupational) over those that refer only to individual considerations (e.g., mental states, behaviors, characteristics, differences). The highest scores are given to protocols that integrate systemic and individual considerations and elaborate on causal connections. It makes sense to give higher scores to more integrative and elaborated responses because they reflect a more complex understanding of the issue. Potential problems can arise in the lower part of the coding scheme; however, if the content or framing of the issues generates more individual or more systemic responses. For example, the problem "Individuals often do not receive support or feedback for their fitness improvement efforts" is likely to generate more responses at the lower end of the coding scheme; whereas the problem "When different organizations meet to address a community issue, they often have different agendas, purposes and goals" is likely to generate more responses in the middle of the coding scheme. Revisions on the coding scheme and the content and framing of the issues are needed to resolve this problem.

Related to the framing of issues is a consideration of the number of issues needed to get valid assessments of cognitive learning and intellectual development outcomes. In the most recent revisions of the protocols, we have introduced two issues for each class; one issue presented from an individual perspective and one issue presented from a systemic perspective. For example, students in a child and adolescent development class responded to the following two issues: "Parents in the U.S. are often frustrated in their efforts to find affordable, quality childcare" (individual) and "The field of developmental psychology has historically overstated the influence that parents have in creating individual differences among children" (systemic). Analogously, Moore (n.d.) describes the development of the MID that initially included essays on three separate issues: classroom learning, decision making, and career planning. Currently the MID focuses primarily on students' epistemological beliefs about classroom learning, and the other two essays are available separately as assessments of the complexity of students' reasoning about these two domains.

In addition, in the most recent revisions of the protocol students are asked to answer questions about "issues" rather than problems, then are asked to generate why these may be considered problems. This format provides a greater opportunity for students to identify the specific problems inherent in complex issues as is relevant to problem solving abilities and to come closer to a measure of whether students can spontaneously apply course content to a real-world problem (Thomas & Rohwer, 1993). This format, however, does not go far enough, to allow for a measure of whether students can spontaneously generate problems through the contextual details of a complex issue. It does not allow for a measure of whether students can spontaneously transfer what they have learned to new domains (Bransford et al., 2000). Future revisions should include lengthier descriptions of issues in which several problems are embedded that can be identified by the student including problems with analogous structures to allow for measures of problem identification and knowledge transfer.

Finally, the knowledge structure coding scheme does not go far enough in capturing knowledge structure representations. Beyond assessing shared knowledge, the problem solving protocol allows for the development of a conceptual representation of the knowledge structures. As adapted from work by Graesser and Clark (1985) on reading comprehension, statement nodes could be categorized as ongoing states, events, goals, or manner specifications then connected by categorized and directed arcs. The arc categories would describe the relationships that exist between the statement nodes (e.g., reason, consequent, outcome). The knowledge structures between experts (instructors) and novices (students) and the knowledge structures between students in the same course could then be compared. Concept maps, which are similar to knowledge structure representations except that they are mapped by the student, have been used to assess student understanding by both comparing novices and experts and by comparing the maps of students in the same course (Edmondson, 2000). Based on research using concept maps to assess student understanding, knowledge structure comparisons could be made both qualitatively by comparing diagrams and quantitatively by scoring the diagrams for specific criteria such as number of concepts, relationships, branchings, hierarchies, cross-links, and examples (Markham, Mintzes, & Jones, 1994; Novak, 1998).

USING THE PROBLEM SOLVING PROTOCOL AS A CLASS REFLECTION TOOL

Further work is also needed to develop the problem solving protocol as a class reflection tool. The protocol itself encourages student application and reflection of course material in the context of real world problems, suggesting a number of options for its in-class use. This use extends beyond end of the course reflection exercises to exercises prior to and during the service-learning project.

A number of possible uses of the protocol as a class reflection tool are evident. First, even without coding the protocols, the instructor can use them either as part of the course evaluation or separate from evaluation to gain a better understanding of students' comprehension and problem solving skills. For example, as part of the final exam instructors could choose relevant issues that ask students to apply course content to identifying and solving real-world problems. This could be done either in class or as part of a take-home exam. If instructors do not want to use responses to the protocols as part of formal evaluation, they could also be completed as part of a developmental tool to provide feedback for instructors on their students' ability to apply course content as the instructors consider future course revisions. Students could also be given a potential problem related to their service-learning project to write about at the beginning, in the middle, and at the end of their project so instructors could observe the development of students' course-related knowledge and its application in the context of their project.

Second, whether students complete the protocol in the written format or not, this exercise could provide a starting place for class discussion and reflection. For example, prior to beginning their service-learning projects, students could be asked to write about or discuss their expectations for problems or challenges their agency or its constituents might encounter, and at the end they could be asked to reconsider these expectations in light of their service-learning experience. Asking students to share their responses with other students in the class would have the additional advantage of helping students to see multiple perspectives on a complex issue.

CONCLUSION

The results presented here suggest that two distinct academic outcomes of great interest to service-learning faculty, cognitive learning and intellectual development, potentially can both be measured using the same written protocol. Further work in this area should focus on improvements to the reliability and validity of the coding schemes and on clarifying the relationship between cognitive learning and student intellectual development more broadly in the context of service-learning. Service-learning experiences that focus on both cognitive outcomes and intellectual development will produce a synergistic effect. A model of how this works was developed, but this model needs to be tested more directly. Further work is needed to understand how the unique pedagogical elements of service-learning contribute to the relationship between intellectual development and cognitive learning, and how reflection activities can enhance both of these intellectual outcomes.

NOTE

1.   The title of the LEP implies that it might assess learning style; however, as can be seen by the items listed in Exhibit 4, the scale actually measures epistemelogical or intellectual development. That is, it measures students' conceptions of knowledge as dualistic and learning as simply information exchange through their recognition of knowledge as pluralistic and their appreciation of the need for evidence to evaluate arguments.

REFERENCES

Berson, J. S. (1997). *A study of the effects of a service-learning experience on student success at an urban community college.* Unpublished doctoral dissertation. Florida International University, Miami.

Bransford, J. D., Brown, A. L., Cocking, R. R., Donovan, M. S., & Pellegrino, J. W. (Eds.). (2000). *How people learn: Brain, mind, experience, and school.* (Expanded ed.). Washington, DC: National Academy Press.

Edmondson, K. M. (2000). Assessing science understanding through concept maps. In J. J. Mintzes, J. H. Wandersee, & J. D. Novak (Eds.), *Assessing science understanding: A human constructivist view* (pp. 15–40). San Diego, CA: Academic Press.

Ericsson, K. A., & Simon, H. A. (1985). Protocol analysis. *Handbook of discourse analysis,* (Vol. 2, pp. 259–268). London: Academic Press.

Eyler, J., & Giles, D. E. (1999). *Where's the learning in service-learning?* San Francisco: Jossey-Bass.

Eyler, J., & Giles, D. E., Jr. (2002). Beyond surveys: Using the problem solving interview to assess the impact of service-learning on understanding and critical thinking. In A. Furco & S. H. Billig (Eds.), *Advances in service-learning research: Vol. 1. Service-learning: The essence of pedagogy* (pp. 147–160). Greenwich, CT: Information Age Publishing.

Graesser, A. C., & Clark, L. F. (1985). *Structures and procedures of implicit knowledge.* Norwood, NJ: Ablex.

Hofer, B. K. (2001). Personal epistemology research: Implications for teaching and learning. *Journal of Educational Psychology Review, 13*(4), 353–383.

Kuhn, D. (1997). Constraints or guideposts? Developmental psychology and science education. *Review of Educational Research, 67,* 141–150.

Kuhn, D. (2001). How do people know? *Psychological Science, 12*(1), 1–8.

Litke, R. A. (2002). Do all students "Get It?" Comparing students' reflections to course performance. *Michigan Journal of Community Service Learning, 8*(2), 27–34.

Markham, K. M., Mintzes, J. J., & Jones, M. G. (1994). The concept map as a research and evaluation tool: Further evidence of validity. *Journal of Research in Science Teaching, 31*(1), 91–101.

Markus, G., Howard, J., & King, D. (1993). Integrating community service and classroom instruction enhances learning: Results from an experiment. *Educational Evaluation and Policy Analysis, 15*(4), 410–419.

Moore, W. S. (n.d.). *The Measure of Intellectual Development: An instrument manual.* Olympia, WA: Center for the Study of Intellectual Development. Available from the author at CSID, 1505 Farwell CT. NW, Olympia, WA 98502 wsmoore51@attbi.com

Moore, W. S. (1989, November). The *Learning Environment Preferences*: Exploring the construct validity of an objective measure of the Perry scheme of intellectual and ethical development. *Journal of College Student Development, 30,* 504–514.

Moore, W. S. (2000). Understanding learning in a postmodern world: Reconsidering the Perry scheme of intellectual and ethical development. In B. K. Hofer & P. R. Pintrich (Eds.), *Personal epistemology: The psychology of beliefs about knowledge and knowing* (pp. 17–35). Mahwah, NJ: Lawrence Erlbaum Associates.

Novak, J. D. (1998). *Learning, creating, and using knowledge.* Mahwah, NJ: Lawrence Erlbaum Associates.

Perry, W. G. (1999). *Forms of intellectual and ethical development in the college years: A scheme.* San Francisco: Jossey-Bass. (Original work published 1968/1970).

Rama, D. V., Ravenscroft, S. P., Wolcott, S. K., & Zlotkowski, E. (2000). Service-learning outcomes: Guidelines for educators and researchers. *Issues in Accounting Education, 15*(4), 657–692.

Schank, R. C., Berman, T. R., & Macpherson, K. A. (1999). Learning by doing. In, C. M. Reigeluth (Ed.), *Instructional-design theories and models* (Vol. 2, pp. 161–181). Mahwah, NJ: Lawrence Erlbaum Associates.

Steinke, P., & Buresh, S. (2002). Cognitive outcomes of service-learning: Reviewing the past and glimpsing the future. *Michigan Journal of Community Service Learning, 8*(2), 5–14.

Steinke, P., & Fitch, P. (2001, March). Intersections between cognitive outcomes of service-learning and student intellectual development. Paper presented at the annual American Association of Higher Education conference, Washington, DC.

Steinke, P., Fitch, P., Johnson, C., & Waldstein, F. (2002). An interdisciplinary study of service-learning predictors and outcomes among college students. In S. H. Billig & A. Furco (Eds.), *Advances in service-learning research: Vol. 2. Service-learning research through a multidisciplinary lens* (pp. 73–102). Greenwich, CT: Information Age Publishing.

Steinke, P., & Harrington, A. (2002). Implementing service-learning in the natural sciences. [Electronic version] *National Society for Experiential Education Quarterly, 27*(3), 4–10.

Steinke, P., Long, D. L., & Wilkins, D. (1996). The effect of verb choice on causal attribution. In R. J. Kreuz & S. MacNealy (Eds.), *Empirical approaches to literature and aesthetics,* (Vol. 52, pp. 53–68). Norwood, NJ: Ablex.

Thomas, J. W., & Rohwer, W. D. (1993). Proficient autonomous learning: Problems and prospects. In M. Rabinowitz (Ed.), *Cognitive science foundations of instruction* (pp. 1–31). Hillsdale, NJ: Lawrence Erlbaum Associates.

Voss, J. F. (1988). Problem solving and reasoning in ill-structured domains. In C. Antaki (Ed.), *Analysing everyday explanations: A casebook of methods* (pp. 74–93). London: Sage.

CHAPTER 9

SERVICE AND MOTIVATION TO SERVE
An Exploration and Model

Christine M. Stenson, Janet Eyler, and Dwight Giles

Using data from Eyler and Giles (1999), this chapter presents a preliminary measure of students' intrinsic motivation to perform community service. This measure is used in a structural equation model to explore whether students' intrinsic motivation is negatively affected by participating in a service-learning course, as cognitive evaluation theory predicts it could be. The results of this analysis suggest that students' intrinsic motivation to serve is not negatively influenced by service-learning. The chapter ends with possible directions for future research concerning intrinsic motivation and its relationship to service-learning.

OVERVIEW

Data from numerous studies provide convincing evidence that participation in service-learning positively affects students' personal development, social responsibility, interpersonal skills, tolerance, and academic learning.

Deconstructing Service-Learning: Research Exploring Context, Participation, and Impacts
A Volume in: Advances in Service-Learning Research, pages 195–212.
Copyright © 2003 by Information Age Publishing, Inc.
All rights of reproduction in any form reserved.
ISBN: 1-59311-071-5 (hardcover), 1-59311-070-7 (pbk.)

However, there is evidence from studies of volunteerism that providing extrinsic motivations for service work, such as offering money as a reward, may reduce its intrinsic value (Frey & Goette, 1999). This article raises the question of whether students are reacting to service-learning courses as if they are acting on extrinsic motivations for providing service. It explores the abundant research from the field of psychology on motivation, much of which suggests that extrinsic rewards and punishments given for tasks can reduce the desirability of these tasks. These rewards and punishments may include grades, extra-credits, and requirements. Applying these findings to service-learning suggests that the practice might reduce, instead of increase, the enjoyment of service work for students, lead students to perform minimal service in courses that require it, and perform less service in the future.

This is clearly not an effect that service-learning practitioners intend. To see if such an effect is indeed occurring, a measure of students' intrinsic motivation to perform service is created and explored in this chapter. This measure is tested to determine how well the number of hours of service students perform can be predicted. In addition, this measure is used in a structural equation model to determine whether completing service hours connected to an academic course encourages students to perform future service, regardless of whether or not they are highly intrinsically motivated to perform service before taking the course. The secondary analysis is intended as a beginning of a process of examining motivations to serve and of service-learning's impact on this motivation. Eyler and Giles's (1999) data set was used in this type of exploratory analysis because of its large sample size and number of variables.

LITERATURE REVIEW

Psychologists and other social scientists have been debating the nature that tangible rewards have on people's intrinsic motivations for over 20 years. Intrinsic motivations are defined as inner drives to undertake particular actions, while extrinsic motivations are external inducements to perform, such as money or grades. Several meta-analyses of experimental data find that extrinsic motivations dampen intrinsic motivation to perform tasks under many circumstances (Deci, Koestner, & Ryan, 1999; Rummel & Feinberg, 1988; Tang & Hall, 1995; Wiersma, 1992; see Cameron & Pierce, 1994, for contrary findings).

The reasons for this are debated. One of the best-known theories explaining this effect is cognitive evaluation theory (CET). Intrinsic motivation is defined by CET theorists as "...the process of doing an activity for its own sake...for the sake of the feelings of excitement, accomplishment, and personal satisfaction [it] yields" (Deci, 1995, p. 21). In this view, intrinsic motivation is linked to people's wish to be the origin of their own actions and to attain mastery over their environments. Deci likened intrinsic motivation in adults to the innate desire children show in mastering objects and behaviors, such as learning how to work toys for the sheer pleasure of it. An adult analogy is hobbies for which people are not paid. However, when expected rewards are received for tasks, people often feel controlled by outside forces and intrinsic motivation is decreased (Deci, 1995). For instance, an enjoyable hobby can easily turn into a dreaded paying job. On the other hand, CET theory also posits that rewards may be taken as indicators of personal competence or mastery, in which case intrinsic motivation is not dampened. This is most likely to occur when rewards are administered in a non-controlling manner and when the actor's performance competence is unclear to him or her.

Applied to service-learning, this theory would predict that if service-learning students expect to receive an external reward, such as a grade, a course credit, or even positive regard from the instructor as their primary reason for performing service, they will exhibit a decrease in motivation to serve. The reason for this loss of interest may be due to experiencing service-related behavior as controlled by outside forces. Alternately, students may see high marks, positive feedback, or extra credits as validation of their competence in the performed service, in which case intrinsic motivation will remain unchanged or even increase.

Deci (1995) noted that both processes may be at work in any given situation. Therefore, when examining motivation, researchers must take into account the interest of the task, the nature of the reward, the interpersonal context in which the reward is given, and whether rewards are contingent upon participating in, completing, or excelling in the given task. In general, CET predicts that the more freedom from performance expectations and personal pressure from those who control rewards, that subjects have in performing their tasks, the less likely it is that intrinsic motivation will be dampened.

It is CET theory, though differently named, that Frey and Goette (1999) used to explain their finding that volunteers who were paid small sums for their time worked significantly less than their non-paid counterparts. According to the authors, low-paid volunteers interpreted their wage as the primary reason for giving their time, and thus gave little of it. Well-paid volunteers worked more than low paid and non-paid volunteers. This may be because, when rewards are high enough, extrinsic motivation for tasks replaces intrinsic motivation as the prime driver of task-related behavior.

There have been no studies of service-learning and/or intrinsic motivation that compare to Frey and Goette's work on volunteers. However, many service-learning researchers have held background variables related to motivation constant in studies of the impact of service on participants. Such control variables include high school service activities, religious activity, closeness to faculty members, gender, course load, commitment to participating in community action programs, socioeconomic status (SES), and minority status (for examples see Batchelder & Root, 1994; Eyler & Giles 1999; Myers-Lipton, 1996). However, the less tangible psychological motivations that may be correlated with and logically prior to some of these variables have not been examined.

This is disturbing because McMahon (1998) noted that journal entries show that students sometimes react negatively to service components of courses. More troubling is Parker-Gwin and Mabry's (1998) finding that at the end of the semester, service-learning students in courses requiring a prescribed service-learning project rated the importance of community service significantly less favorably than at pre-test and agreed significantly less often with the statement that adults should give some time for the good of their community. It is just this type of result that Werner and McVaugh (2000) sought to avoid by warning that service-learning practices that undermine student choice and control over their service may dampen students' intrinsic motivation for future volunteer work.

Though the literature on motivation and service-learning is sparse, the literature on motivations to volunteer is voluminous and crosses many disciplines, including psychology, sociology, social work, and organizational sciences. Rather than focus on intrinsic versus extrinsic motivation, this research generally takes a functional approach to determine which motivations habitual volunteers report fulfilling via volunteer work. Functionalist research has a long history, and assumes that human behavior is purposive. Functionalist researchers pay attention to the reasons, plans, and goals that underlie psychological phenomena. They assert that people can and do perform similar actions for different psychological functions (Clary et al, 1998). Applied to volunteerism, functionalism would hold that different people meet different needs by volunteering. Therefore, functionalist studies of motivations to volunteer consist either of discovering individual reasons for volunteering through interviews or surveys, or through factor analysis (Schondel & Boehm, 2000). Those researchers employing factor analysis of survey questions disagree as to how many factors contribute to volunteer motivation.

Bales (1996) presented a four-factor model he holds to measure an attitude of volunteerism-activism, which he tested on survey data from Oxfam volunteers in the United Kingdom. Bales defined an attitude after Oppenheim as "a state of readiness, a tendency to act or react in a certain manner when confronted with certain stimuli" (p. 212). Bales sought to capture readiness or tendency to volunteer in his volunteerism-activism scale, which contains a sense of efficacy (ability to effect change or make a difference), sociability or generalism (a sense that volunteering is a part of one's lifestyle), idealism or philosophical commitment (an orientation towards social justice), and a "feel-good" factor (volunteering helps the volunteer, is rewarding). Clary, Snyder, and Ridge's (1992) six-factor model has one motivation that is similar to Bales' feel good factor: the esteem motivation.

The other five motivations identified in the authors' 30 item Volunteer Functions Inventory (VFI) are: social, such as peer networks that volunteer; value, such as concern for others; career, such as contacts, skills, and career option exploration; and understanding, such as learning more and gaining perspectives. This model was developed by surveying the literature of volunteer motivations, designing a questionnaire, and then testing the items theorized to be a measure of each motivation for internal consistency.

Cnaan and Goldberg-Glen (1991) argued for a one-factor model. They presented volunteers and non-volunteers with a list of 28 motivations for volunteering, gleaned from literature reviews of motivations for volunteering. Subjects ranked these items in importance. Each motivation was found to be present in at least five previous studies. Some motivations had been described in numerous reviewed literature as either altruistic, a desire to something worthwhile; egoistic, such as improving one's own attitude; material, such as gaining job skills; social, such as opportunities for relationships; or religious, such as it is God's expectation. The authors could not validate distinct factors when they attempted to use confirmatory factor analyses for two and three factor models.

Schondel and Boehm (2000) assessed adolescents' motivations to volunteer with the Volunteer Needs Profile, an instrument developed by Francies (1982). This profile measured seven areas of motivational needs: the need for experience, feelings of social responsibility, the need for social contact, responding to expectations of others, the need for social approval, expectation of future rewards, and the need to achieve. When the researchers subjected their data to exploratory factor analyses, they discovered that a three factor model fit best for volunteers at one set of sites, while a four factor model fit best for volunteers at one other site. The three factor model included a desire to help others; social approval and need to achieve; and a need for social contact. The four factor model included a prosocial factor, a growth factor, a social approval factor, and a need to achieve factor.

Clearly, researchers find that there is great diversity in volunteer motivations and how they scale together. Despite this diversity, however, most models contain variables from the following areas: expressing altruistic values, setting or meeting expectations for and of family and friends, gaining work and/or personal experience and knowledge, meeting people and maintaining friendships, and self-esteem or satisfaction. What Clary et al. (1998) called protective factors, such as the need to escape guilt or feel needed, are similar to Schondel and Boehm's (2000) items relating to the need for social approval, but personal efficacy shows up only in Bales' (1996) scale.

Functionalist studies of volunteer motivations generally ignore the distinction between intrinsic and extrinsic motivations. However, Andrews' (1995) dissertation research made it clear that functionalist accounts for volunteering are not inconsistent with the assertion that some motivations are extrinsic while others are intrinsic. His work examined many of the volunteer motivations traditional functionalists have discovered, while distinguishing between them. Intrinsic motives included helping others, seeing the results of work, freedom to decide how to accomplish tasks, opportunities to develop special skills, challenging problems to solve, and opportunities to do what one does best. Extrinsic motives included having opportunities to work with respected staff and organizations, chances to make friends, chances to move to paid employment, volunteer recognition, and adequate reimbursement for expenses. Andrews (1995) also examined the importance of situational variables and social status variables. Intrinsic motives were rated as most important by his sample, and "helping others" was the single most important intrinsic dimension of volunteer work. Both intrinsic and extrinsic motivations were reported by volunteers, though volunteers expressed a preference for intrinsic motivations.

The research reported on below offers an exploration of the intrinsic motivation of service-learning students to serve and examines whether engaging in service-learning undermines this intrinsic motivation. It uses data originally collected by Eyler and Giles (1999) to examine whether performing community service hours in the context of a service-learning course impacts the number of hours students predict they will spend doing future community service after the end of one semester. If service-learning dampens students' intrinsic motivation to serve, students who spend more hours in service-learning should wish to spend less time performing future service, as such action has lost value to them. The variables indicating intrinsic motivation should also decrease after service-learning courses. In contrast, if service-learning does not dampen intrinsic motivation, the number of service hours students perform in concert with service-learning courses should either be unrelated to the number of future community service hours students predict they will perform, or the estimations of future community service hours should increase as performed hours increase.

METHODOLOGY

Subjects

The subjects for this phase of Eyler and Giles' (1999) original study were 2,462 students enrolled in 109 courses offered at 19 colleges and universities during the spring quarter or semester of 1995. Six of the institutions were private universities, five were small liberal arts colleges, and eight were public universities. Colleges and universities were located across the

United States and each had several service-learning options available to students.

Though over 60 percent of the students surveyed were enrolled in arts and science courses, students in education and social work classes were also included in the sample, as were those performing service internships. Students majoring in the humanities, social sciences, math and engineering, education, and business were also represented in the sample.

Students were primarily undergraduates ranging in age from 17 to 25. Seventeen percent of participating students were non-white; 68 percent were women. Students from all college classes were represented in the sample. In this phase of the Eyler and Giles' (1999) research project, 1,544 completed pre- and post-test surveys designed to measure the impact of service-learning on learning, opinions, attitudes, and actions. Of the final sample, 1,131 participated in service, and 404 opted not to perform service as part of their grade or not to take a course for which service was required. The time from pre-test to post-test ranged from three to four months, depending on whether the school was on a quarter or a semester system.

Measurement

The pre-test survey opens with questions about previous community service and levels of parent service. Following these are questions concerning students' opinions, skills, and activities. Questions in this section concerning leadership skills, communication skills, and tolerance were modeled after those developed by the Walt Whitman Center for the Culture and Politics of Democracy as part of their Measuring Citizenship project (see Barber, 1997). With this instrument, Eyler and Giles (1999) validated three of the scales from the Whitman Center's project relating to leadership qualities, tolerance, and communication skills.

Other questions were modeled after measures developed by Markus, Howard, and King (1993) and are not intended to form scales. These include student ratings of how much they value: careers helping others, working in public policy, or being community leaders. Other survey questions also measured single elements, such as the conviction that social justice is a critical issue for communities and beliefs in the importance of impacting political structure and changing public policy.

Items measuring personal and interpersonal development form scales related to citizenship and were first developed by Scheurich (1994). Also included in the pre-test are items that scaled as measures of students' ideas of community problem locus. The post-test measured the quality of the learning experience and reproduced all the questions concerning students' opinions, skills, and activities discussed above. Data from these surveys were analyzed by Eyler and Giles (1999) and Eyler, Giles, and Braxton

(1997) to determine whether students' attitudes and skills had changed as a result of service-learning, and to determine whether the quality of the service-learning experience, such as placement quality and opportunity for reflection, had an effect on students' perceptions and learning.

A principal components analysis was performed to determine which variables formed a scale that represented motivation to serve. This analysis used half the data set so that a confirmatory factor analysis could be performed on the other half of the data. The variables used in this analysis were chosen for two reasons. The first reason for selecting a variable was whether or not it had been controlled for by Eyler and Giles (1999) in their hierarchical regression analyses. These variables included gender; ethnicity; SES; and previous involvement in service, club membership, and parental involvement in service. These variables have been found by many researchers to predict service participation. The second reason for choosing a variable was its similarity to constructs reported to be significant predictors of volunteer motivation (see Andrews, 1995; Bales, 1996; Clary, Snyder, & Ridge, 1992; Cnaan & Goldberg-Glen, 1991; Schondel & Boehm, 2000; Winniford, Carpenter, & Grider, 1995). That is those items that reflected altruistic values, gaining work and/or personal experience and knowledge, sense of efficacy; and self-esteem or satisfaction. More specifically, items from the following scales reported by Eyler and Giles (1999) were included in the PCA: social values, tolerance, personal efficacy, communication skills, leadership skills, career skills, importance of social justice, important to change policy, openness to new views, and systemic problem locus (pp. 212–214, 276–278). Items reflecting the need for social approval, meeting people and maintaining friendships, and setting or meeting expectations for and of family and friends are not included since these questions were not included in the original survey. Standardized scores for the variables were included in the exploratory analysis. Exhibit 1 shows the factor loadings for the three components found to explain the most variance with orthogonal rotation. All have eigen values in excess of one.

The first factor listed above explained approximately 17 percent of the variance when all variables were included in the PCA—more than any other construct explained. A factor analysis performed on the data that were not used in the EFA yielded a Cronbach's alpha of 0.78 for these variables, confirming that they scale together. This factor is hypothesized to be a measure of motivation for service.

The factor loadings show that this particular array of personal values, expectations, and opinions are consistent with intrinsic motivation. They relate to the importance and helping others as a life and career goal (items 1, 2, 4), tempered by a belief that one can do so (item 3) if one has the right skills (items 4, 5).

The construct has face validity for college students. The first two variables listed in the motivation factor "important to me personally to volun-

EXHIBIT 1
Results from the Exploratory Factor Analysis

	Component Matrix (Motivation)	*Factor Loadings[1]*
1.	Important to me personally to volunteer time to help needy	0.7653
2.	Important to me personally-a career helping others	0.701
3.	I can have an impact on solving problems in my community	0.6629
4.	Community service skills valuable to career	0.8142
5.	Community service helps develop leadership skills	0.7046
	Component Matrix (Groups)	
6.	High schools clubs/groups	0.6995
7.	High school junior year community service	0.8053
8.	High school senior year community service	0.8306
9.	College clubs/groups	0.6125
10.	College community service	0.5350
	Component Matrix (Empathy/Tolerance)	
11.	Respecting the views of others	0.6408
12.	Tolerant of people different from me	0.7098
13.	Empathetic to all points of view	0.7384
14.	Think about others before myself	0.6367
15.	Feel responsible for others	0.6316

Notes: [1]Note that the factor loadings shown in this table are drawn from a second principal components analysis (PCA) with orthogonal rotation. Only those variables from the factors listed in the table were included in this PCA.

teer time to help needy" and "important to me personally—a career helping others" are roughly equal to what Andrews (1995) finds is the most important intrinsic dimension of volunteer work, "helping others." Andrews's variable "opportunities to develop special skills" is closely related to both the "community service skills valuable to career" and "community service helps develop leadership skills" variables of this data set. The personal efficacy variable "I can have an impact on solving problems in my community" also corresponds well to Andrews "opportunities to do what one does best." Indeed, the factor is well in line with defines Deci's (1995) assertion that intrinsic motivation is linked to people's wish to attain mastery over their environments (items 3, 4, and 5), and perform actions that are interesting and rewarding to them (items 1 and 2).

The other two factors listed in the table were not used for further analysis. They are listed to indicate factors that explained a significant portion of the variance in this exploratory analysis and that future researchers may find of interest. The groups and experience factors show how closely experiences with clubs and groups are related to service both in high school and in college. The tolerance factor is further described in Eyler and Giles (1999).

Structural Equation Modeling (SEM)

Exhibit 2 shows the path model. This model tests assumptions of CET theory and that the intrinsic motivation factor is valid. It includes only those students who participated in service.

Gender is included in the path model below as a control variable, since gender has been shown by many researchers to predict the number of community service hours students perform (see Astin & Sax, 1998; Eyler & Giles, 1999). Intrinsic motivation at pre- and post-test are theoretically related, so the errors of the variables that compose the construct are allowed to correlate in the path model. Within each of the intrinsic motivation constructs (pre-test and post-test) the errors of the variables measuring perceived benefits of service (leadership and career skills) are also allowed to correlate, as they were included in the survey as part of a single factor.

Pre-test scores of the scale representing intrinsic motivation should predict the number of service hours students report serving for the course. That is to say, the more intrinsically motivated a student is, the more hours he or she should put into the service portion of the course. The left half of the structural equation modeling (SEM) shows that the path from intrinsic motivation to the numbers of hours students perform as part of their course is statistically significant at the 0.05 level.

Intrinsic motivation does predict the number of hours a student will spend in service. The path running from intrinsic motivation at pre-test and at post-test to forecasted future hours of community service also suggest that the intrinsic motivation factor is predictive of performing community service. This provides support for the validity of the intrinsic motivation construct.

The model also tests whether intrinsic motivation is impacted by participating in service-learning. CET theory would predict that if students see their service as determined more by extrinsic motivations, such as getting a good grade or satisfying a course requirement, their intrinsic motivation scores should not predict the number of hours they perform in service-learning and the number of future community service hours they predict they will perform. In addition, their intrinsic motivation scores should decrease from pre-test to post-test as intrinsic motivation is undermined. They do not. This suggests that students' intrinsic motivations related to community service work are not being undermined over the course of a semester of service-learning.

EXHIBIT 2
Path Model

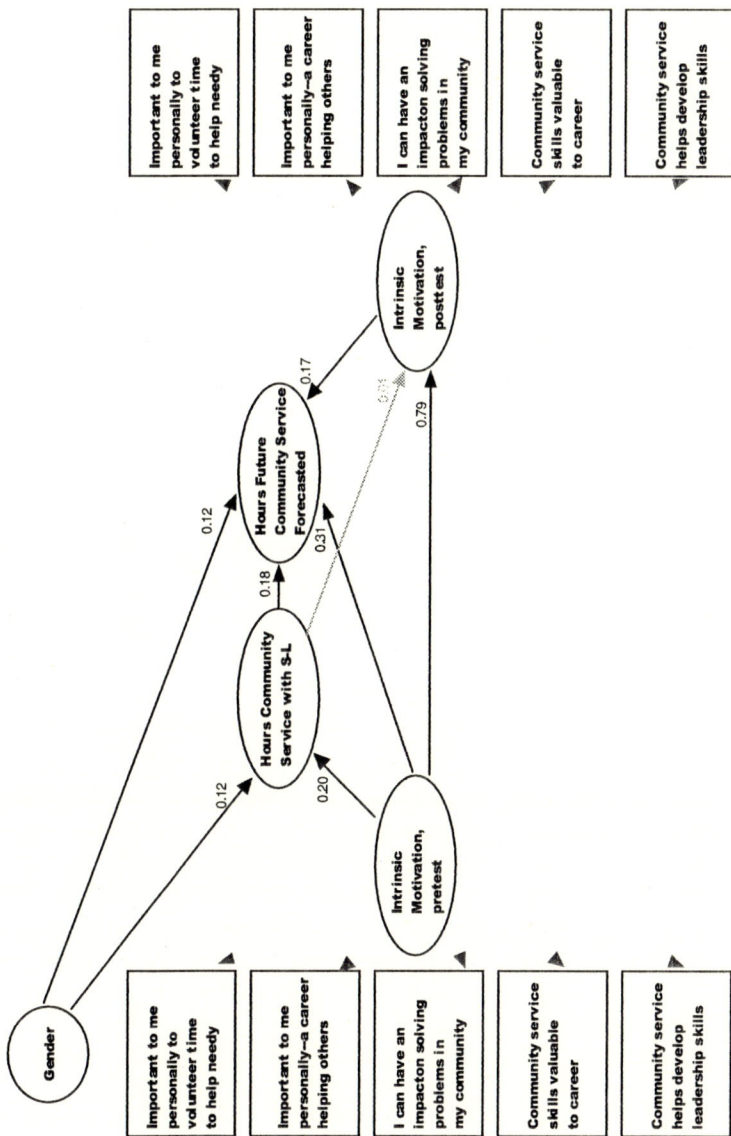

Chi-Square = 162.91, df = 52, P-value= 0.00000, RMSEA = 0.047

CET theory would also predict that if students felt their actions were controlled by extrinsic motivations, students who performed more hours of service as part of the course would show less enthusiasm for future service at post-test. However, if service hours are having no effect on intent to serve, or if they are having a positive effect on this intent, the number of future community service hours students predict they will perform should either be unassociated with increased service hours as part of the course or should increase as a result of increased hours of service in service-learning courses.

The latter scenario fits the results obtained in this path analysis. The more hours of service students perform in service-learning courses, the more community service hours they predict they will serve in the future. This is reflected in the positive significant path showing the relationship between hours of community service in the service-learning course to predicted hours of future community service. This path's significance suggests that students' commitments to performing service are being reinforced, rather than undermined, as a result of increasing numbers of service hours. The variables measuring intrinsic motivation are controlled in this path, so this result cannot be attributed to them.

Finally, the number of hours spent doing service does not negatively (or positively) predict the intrinsic motivation score at post-test. It is the only non-significant path in the model. This result suggests that higher numbers of community service hours do not affect intrinsic motivation in any significant manner.

DISCUSSION

For this study, the construct of intrinsic motivation has been demonstrated to be is valid in that it predicts number of hours that students spend in community service for their service-learning courses. Increased hours of community service in service-learning courses positively impacted future intent to perform community service. Students' enthusiasm for service was thus reinforced through service-learning related community work, and not undermined by it. Intrinsic motivation remained roughly constant from pre-test to post-test, indicating that intrinsic motivation was not changed by the service-learning experience.

This analysis is not a direct test of CET. Rather, it is the beginning of an exploration to determine how service-learning practitioners can conceptualize and understand intrinsic motivation and its effects. These results could mean two things. If CET theory is correct, the results indicate that gaining course credit and grades do not have the effect that Frey and Goette (1999) found volunteer pay had on volunteer motivation. Students do not interpret their grades or course credit in the manner that volunteers come to interpret wages, i.e., as a primary reason for giving time to service, thus giving less time when not highly rewarded. A second possibility is that CET theory is incorrect in its assumption that extrinsic motivations often squelch intrinsic ones. This research is unable to answer which of these propositions is true.

Since the original survey was not concerned with intrinsic and extrinsic motivations, no measure of extrinsic motivations, such as those put forth by Andrews (1995), is included in the path model described above. Possible extrinsic motivations that are relevant to the service-learning experience of students include the wish to make good grades, opportunities to work with more and less respected organizations, positive feedback from professors and other students, and recognition for service performed. In addition, as Werner and McVaugh (2000) noted, practices that undermine student choice and control over their service may dampen students' intrinsic motivation for future volunteer work.

The students in this sample did have choice and control in one key area; all chose to take service-learning courses or chose service options in courses. The results of the path analysis might differ for students taking required service-learning courses. In such cases, the students might interpret this requirement as an external inducement in the same way that Frey and Goette's (1999) volunteers experienced pay. However, CET would predict that even in required service-learning courses, the chance that intrinsic motivation will be dampened would be lessened by letting students have choices. As Werner and McVaugh (2000) noted, this would include granting students a high degree of choice in service assignments, ensuring that autonomy and guidance are balanced in service activities, promoting a sense of ownership of projects, and encouraging reflection on personal values in the context of the service-learning project.

DIRECTIONS FOR FUTURE RESEARCH

Though the fit of this model is good, it should be noted that this study is a post hoc analysis designed as an exploration of how to model intrinsic motivation and how motivation is affected by service-learning. Further studies should be performed to assess the validity of both the motivation construct and the path models presented here. Moreover, the scales used by researchers on motivations to volunteer, especially those by Andrews (1995), should be adopted for use in research on service-learning's impact on student motivations.

Future research should assess the impact of required service-learning courses on motivation to volunteer. The quality of such courses and the degree to which students are granted autonomy and control over their service should also be examined in such studies. A pre-/post-survey could be designed for students taking service-learning courses. Path models require

large datasets, therefore the sample size would need to be roughly equiva-
lent to that reported here or larger. In the pre-test, the items listed in the
intrinsic motivation scale could be included. These are specific to service-learning as opposed to volunteerism. These items are:

1. Is this a required course?; If so,
2. Is service required for it? For the pre-test and post-test the following
    item would be included:
3. How many hours a week do you plan on volunteering next semester.

The rest of the questions to include in a pre-test and post-test would be
drawn and modified from what Andrews found most important in his
work. A section labeled "describing yourself," could include:

4. "It is important that I see the results of my work";
5. "It is important that I do interesting tasks at work, in community
    service, or in classes";
6. "It is important that I have a chance to do the things I do best at
    work, in community service, or in classes."

A section entitled "about community service" Could include these items:
"If I were to perform or when I perform community service, it is important
that:

7. I have the opportunity to work with respected community organiza-
    tions;
8. I have the opportunity to work with a professional staff;
9. I have the opportunity to make friends; and
10. I receive recognition for service."

The post-test could include an item found in Eyler and Giles (1999)
post-test in the "during my community service" section. Such items could
include: "During my community service:

11. I was free to develop and use my ideas."

In addition, the following questions should be added:

12. "During my community service I had choices about the service I
    performed"; and
13. "Compared to courses without a service component, I worried
    about my grade in this course."

Together, these items would provide a measure of how much freedom a
student felt he or she had in the service component of the service-learning
course.

The first step in analyzing these items would be confirmatory factor analyses on the pre-test and the post-test data. Through these analyses, researchers could determine whether the intrinsic motivation scale presented in this paper held when the intrinsic motivation items (items 4 to 6 in the previous paragraphs) adapted from Andrews (1995) were added to it. If the factor were confirmed, a robust measure of intrinsic motivation would be derived. A factor analysis would also confirm or disconfirm an extrinsic motivation scale constructed from the extrinsic motivation items in the pre-test and post-test (items 7 though 10 listed previously).

A scale of items measuring the relative freedom within the course would also need to be confirmed via factor analysis and would include items 11 through 13 listed previously. This factor addresses Werner and McVaugh's (2000) concern that students should be granted a high degree of choice in service assignments. It also addresses Deci's (1995) concern that people be reasonably free from performance expectations for a task to remain intrinsically driven. High levels of grade anxiety in service-learning compared to other courses would be reflective of students' perceiving performance expectations to be high for their community service.

If the factors were confirmed, linear and hierarchical linear multiple regression equations could be used to determine if extrinsic and intrinsic motivations affected outcomes of service-learning over a semester. Positive outcomes found by Eyler and Giles (1999), and Eyler, Giles, and Braxton (1997) might be mediated by levels of intrinsic and extrinsic motivation to serve.

In addition to regression models, a path model would be used to examine the effects of required service, intrinsic motivation, and freedom within the service-learning course on the number of community hours students see themselves performing in the future. This path model is illustrated in Exhibit 3.

Gender is included as a control variable. The paths in the model would test the following propositions:

- Requiring service affects the numbers of hours students will perform in the service-learning course and in the future;
- Intrinsic motivation affects the numbers of service hours students will perform in the service-learning course and in the future, and also predicts intrinsic motivation at post-test;
- Levels of freedom and autonomy affect the numbers of service hours students will perform in the service-learning course and in the future;
- Levels of freedom and autonomy affect intrinsic motivation over the course of the semester;
- The number of service hours students complete in their service-learning course affects the number of service hours students will perform in the future; and

EXHIBIT 3
Possible Path Model

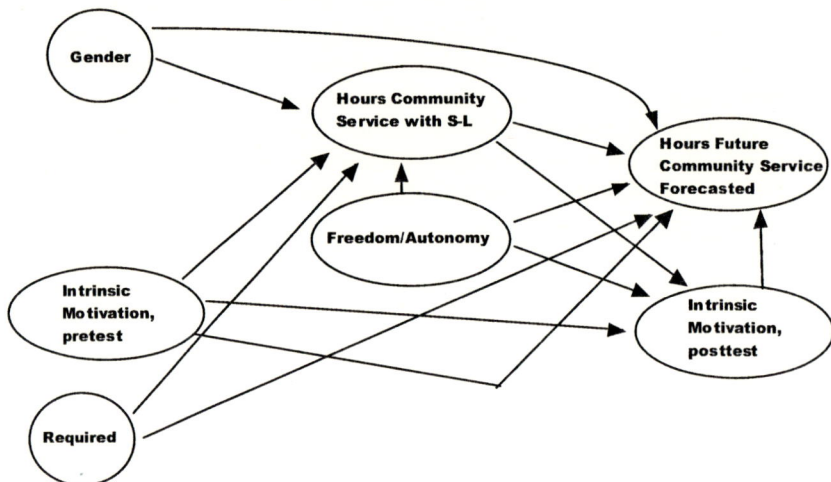

- The number of service hours students complete in their service-learning course affects intrinsic motivation at post-test.

Paths can act as controls for other paths. For example, a path runs from the service-required variable to the variable reflecting the number of service hours students complete. Therefore, the service-required variable is controlled in the path running from the variable reflecting the number of service hours students complete to the intrinsic motivation at post-test construct. Thus any effect of increased service hours on intrinsic motivation is significant whether the course is required or not.

Similarly, there is a path running from the students' freedom and autonomy construct to the variable reflecting the number of service hours students complete in their service-learning course. Therefore, the path running from the variable reflecting the number of service hours students complete to the construct of intrinsic motivation at post-test is free of the effects of the variable reflecting freedom and autonomy.

Two important paths in the model are those from the freedom and autonomy construct to the intrinsic motivation construct and to the number of future community service hours variable. If CET theory is correct, high levels of freedom in courses will predict increased intrinsic motivation. In addition, high levels of freedom should lead students to predict they will spend increased hours performing future community service. If these results were obtained, it would suggest that service-learning practitioners be very careful to plan their courses in such a way as to enhance intrinsic motivation and to increase the likelihood of students' volunteer work.

CONCLUSION

This analysis provides evidence to suggest that intrinsic motivation is not dampened by participating in service-learning courses. In fact, the data presented here imply that service-learning positively impacts students' plans to perform future community service hours, even when intrinsic motivation to serve is controlled for in a structural equation model. This in turn supports the assertion that service-learning be added to institutions' core curricula, as the societal benefits of graduates possessing the will to serve is considerable.

However, since this analysis is post hoc and incomplete, future research should include more explicit measures of intrinsic and extrinsic motivation, and pay attention to whether students have considerable freedom in their service experience. The future research described in this chapter could illustrate one means by which to examine the recursive relationships between intrinsic motivation and the willingness to provide service to others.

REFERENCES

Andrews, G. L. (1995). *Factors affecting volunteer motivation: The importance of intrinsic motives, extrinsic motives, and situational facilities on volunteer work.* Unpublished Dissertation, Kent State University, Kent, OH.

Astin, A. W., & Sax, L. J. (1998). How undergraduates are affected by service participation. *Journal of College Student Development, 39*(3), 251–263.

Bales, K. (1996). Measuring the propensity to volunteer. *Social Policy and Administration, 30*(3), 206–226.

Barber, B. (1997). *Measuring citizenship project, June 1997 Project Report.* Available for purchase at http://wwc.rutgers.edu/mcpindex.htm#ONE

Batchelder, T. H., & Root, S. (1994). Effects of an undergraduate program to integrate academic learning and service: Cognitive, prosocial cognitive, and identity outcomes. *Journal of Adolescence, 17*(4), 341–355.

Cameron, J., & Pierce, W. D. (1994). Reinforcement, reward, and intrinsic motivation: A meta-analysis. *Review of Educational Research, 64*(3), 363–423.

Clary, E. G., Snyder, M., & Ridge, R. (1992). Volunteers' motivations: A functional strategy for the recruitment, placement, and retention of volunteers. *Nonprofit Management and Leadership, 2*(4), 333–350.

Clary, E. G., Snyder, M., Ridge, R. D., Copeland, J., Stukas, A. A., Haugen, J., & Miene, P. (1998). Understanding and assessing the motivations of volunteers: A functional approach. *Journal of Personality and Social Psychology, 74*(6), 1516–1530.

Cnaan, R. A., & Goldberg-Glen, R. S. (1991). Measuring motivation to volunteer in human services. *Journal of Applied Behavioral Science, 27*(3), 269–284.

Deci, E. L. (1995). *Why we do what we do: The dynamics of personal autonomy.* New York: G. P. Putnam's Sons.

Deci, E. L., Koestner , R., & Ryan, R. M. (1999). A meta-analytic review of experiments examining the effects of extrinsic rewards on intrinsic motivation. *Psychological Bulletin, 125*(6), 627–668.

Eyler, J., & Giles, D. E., Jr. (1999). *Where's the learning in service-learning?* San Francisco: Jossey-Bass.

Eyler, J., Giles, D. E., Jr., & Braxton, J. (1997). The impact of service-learning on college students. *Michigan Journal of Community Service Learning, 4,* 5–15.

Francies, G. R. (1982). *The volunteer needs profile: Development and testing of a seven scale model for use in placing volunteers in human service agencies.* Unpublished Master's Thesis, University of Wisconsin, Green Bay WI.

Frey, B. S., & Goette, L. (1999). *Does pay motivate volunteers?* (Working Paper Number 7). Zurich: Institute for Empirical Research in Economics, University of Zurich.

Markus, G. B., Howard, J. P. F., & King, D. C (1993). Integrating community service and classroom instruction enhances learning: Results from an experiment. *Educational Evaluation and Policy Analysis, 15*(4), 410–419.

McMahon, R. (1998, November). *Service-learning: Perceptions of preservice teachers.* Paper presented at the 27th Annual Meeting of the Mid-South Educational Research Association, New Orleans, LA.

Myers-Lipton, S. J. (1996). Effect of service-learning on college students' attitudes toward international understanding. *Journal of College Student Development, 37*(6), 659–668.

Parker Gwin, R., & Mabry, J. B. (1998). Service-learning as pedagogy and civic education: Comparing outcomes for three models. *Teaching Sociology, 26*(4), 276–291.

Rummel, A., & Feinberg, R. (1988). Cognitive evaluation theory: A meta-analytic review of the literature. *Social Behavior and Personality, 16*(2), 147–164.

Scheurich, J. (1994). Citizenship responsibility scales. Unpublished manuscript, University of Texas.

Schondel, C. K., & Boehm, K. E (2000). Motivational needs of adolescent volunteers. *Adolescence, 35*(138), 335–344

Tang, S. H., & Hall, V. C. (1995). The overjustification effect: A meta-analysis. *Applied Cognitive Psychology, 9*(5), 365–404.

Werner, C. M., & McVaugh, N. (2000). Service-learning "rules" that encourage or discourage long-term service: Implications for practice and research. *Michigan Journal of Community Service Learning, 7,* 117–125.

Wiersma, U. J. (1992). The effects of extrinsic rewards in intrinsic motivation: A meta-analysis. *Journal of Occupational and Organizational Psychology, 65*(2), 101–114.

Winniford, J. C., Carpenter, D. S., & Grider, C. (1995). An analysis of the traits and motivations of college students involved in service organizations. *Journal of College Student Development, 36*(1), 27–38.

CHAPTER 10

SERVICE-LEARNING AND RESILIENCE IN DISAFFECTED YOUTH
A Research Study

Nancy Kraft and Jim Wheeler

This chapter examines the relationship between service-learning and resilience in disaffected youth. The study is grounded in a conceptual framework based on Marzano's (1998) theory-based meta-analysis of research on instruction and systems that govern human learning (e.g., the knowledge system, the cognitive system, the metacognitive system, and the self-system).

INTRODUCTION

According to Marzano (1998), the self-system has five categories of beliefs—beliefs about self-attributes, self and others, the nature of the world, efficacy, and purpose—that appear to control all other aspects of human thought and action, and can be both stimulated by teachers and

Deconstructing Service-Learning: Research Exploring Context, Participation, and Impacts
A Volume in: Advances in Service-Learning Research, pages 213–238.
Copyright © 2003 by Information Age Publishing, Inc.
All rights of reproduction in any form reserved.
ISBN: 1-59311-071-5 (hardcover), 1-59311-070-7 (pbk.)

directly altered by specific instructional techniques. This research seeks to understand increased academic performance and service-learning from the perspective of meta-learning theory. Specifically examined is the relationship between students' involvement in service-learning and the self-system.

The setting for this research is a charter school in a Midwestern state, the Youth Learning Cooperative (YLC), that served up to 40 disaffected, behavior disordered, and at risk high school youth from six rural school districts during the 2001–2002 school year. The school, which has existed for four years, is structured around Deweyan pedagogy and a service-learning philosophy, and provides multiple service-learning experiences for students with an emphasis on the environment. Given the nature of the students, this study posits a model for theorizing how service-learning impacts learning and cognition (or academic performance), as well as increases self-efficacy and internal locus of control in a student population traditionally described as "most difficult to reach."

Review of the Literature

A Meta-Theory of Human Learning

The literature on service-learning frequently cites the learning benefits of service in reference to learning academic skills with authentic instruction and hands-on learning (Kraft & Billig, 1997). Newmann and Wehlage (1995) examined determinants of human learning from the perspective of an individual's engagement in knowledge construction, disciplined inquiry, and learning that has value beyond school. Other literature relates aspects of Dewey's educational and social philosophy to the development of service-learning theory, including learning from experience, reflective thinking, citizenship, community, and democracy (Anderson, 1998; Giles & Eyler, 1994). A limitation inherent in these studies is the failure to provide the connections to a larger schema or meta-theory of instruction based on a meta-analysis of existing research.

Marzano (1998) generated a theory of instruction from an extensive meta-analysis of learning research. That research provides an infrastructure to help build an understanding of the complexities of human learning from a broad literature and research base that includes social sciences, neurological sciences, and information processing. Marzano's theory "posits the interaction of four aspects of human thought operating in most, if not all situations:

1. Knowledge;
2. The cognitive system;
3. The metacognitive system; and
4. The self-system" (p. 8).

Exhibit 1 depicts the relationship and interactions of these systems, from the time a task is presented until completion. A task is defined "as any externally generated or internally generated stimulus to change the status quo" (p. 8) and can comprise a student attending to actual instruction or a teacher redirecting students' attention to the task at hand.

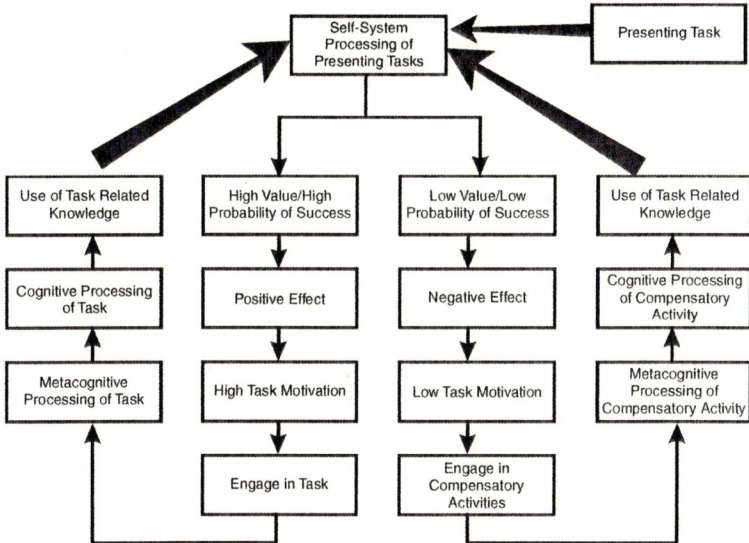

EXHIBIT 1
Theory of Instruction

The elements of human thought, that is referred to as **knowledge**, is comprised of the information, mental processes, and psychomotor processes that are specific to a given subject matter. The processes within the **cognitive system** are organized into four categories:

1. Storage and retrieval;
2. Information processing;
3. Input/output; and
4. Knowledge utilization.

These mental processes act on the knowledge domains providing an individual with access to the information that has been stored in permanent memory and a way of storing new knowledge so that it might be used at a later date.

The **metacognitive system** controls any and all aspects of the knowledge domains and the cognitive system and is believed to be the "engine of learning." For example, Marzano (1998) articulated that if an individual retrieves and executes a specific mathematical strategy from the mental process domain, the overall execution of this process is under the control of the metacognitive system, which has been described as responsible for the "executive control" of all processes.

The **self-system** consists of beliefs and values that allow one to make sense of the world (Markus & Ruvulo, 1990) and is thought to produce the goals that are executed by the metacognitive system. "Specifically, the self-system determines whether an individual will engage in or disengage in a given task; it determines what is attended to from moment to moment" (Marzano, 1998, p. 57). Once the self-system has determined that a presenting task will be accepted, the functioning of all other elements of thought (i.e., the metacognitive system, the cognitive system, and the knowledge domains) are, to a certain extent, dedicated or determined. In addition, the self-system acts as a kind of executive function to evaluate the importance of the presenting task and the probability of success relative to one's beliefs. If the self-system deems a presenting task to be important and determines that engagement would result in a high probability of success, then positive affect is generated and the individual is motivated to engage (Ajzen, 1985; Ajzen & Madden, 1986). Once a determination is made to engage, the other human thought systems contribute to successful completion of the task. The metacognitive system processes information about the nature and importance of goals, plans, resources and their interactions, and designs the strategies for completing a goal once it has been set. The cognitive system processes the information essential to completion of the presented task and utilizes an individual's knowledge base for either employing familiar problem solving strategies or inventing novel approaches for task completion or resolution (Anderson, 1995; Lindsay & Norman, 1977). All four of these systems are involved in effective learning and information processing.

Marzano (1998) used effect size (ES) as a method for determining the efficacy of the research literature with over 4,000 effect sizes from studies that involved over one million subjects. He found relatively strong effects for techniques that employed the self-system and the metacognitive system, and believed that "techniques that utilize these systems have traditionally either been ignored or, at worst, discounted" (p. 105). He admonished those like Hirsch who strongly criticize the use of instructional techniques that rely on meta-cognition, explaining that the findings of this meta-analysis confirm that metacognitive strategies, along with strategies that employ a student's self-system, "are primary ingredients for improving student achievement" (p. 106). Based on his meta-analysis, the five categories of beliefs within the self-system appear to control all other aspects of human thought and action. Additionally, positive self-system beliefs can both be stimulated by teachers and directly altered by specific instructional techniques.

A strong case can be made for the fact that instructional goals that pertain to the self-system should be an educational priority. Marzano (1998) acknowledged that instructional goals that relate to the self-system are highly controversial in public education, citing the controversy over what is commonly referred to as "outcomes-based education" that is focused on the perceived emphasis on self-system related instructional goals. The apparent objection to such an emphasis was that the self-system inherently addresses values that some individuals do not believe are an appropriate target for instruction. Marzano concurred that it is certainly true that the self-system addresses values, particularly those beliefs within the self-system that deal with life purpose. But, given the large effect size that attending to the self-system produces, he believes it is expedient to develop instructional techniques that help students better understand the nature of emotions and how they affect one's behavior.

Resiliency Research

The past 10 years the educational community has engaged in a public conversation regarding children and families at risk, citing societal ills, poverty, and social maladjustment as determinants and predictors of school failure (Benard, 1991). According to Benard, one unintended effect of this dialogue has led to "stereotyping, tracking, and lowering expectations for many students in urban schools, and even prejudice and discrimination" (p. 2). Benard, in a summary of the research on resiliency, indicated that the attitudes and competencies typically associated with resiliency (social competence, problem solving ability, sense of identity, a sense of purpose and future) are not necessarily skills to be taught but rather the outcomes of resiliency. The research indicates that a resiliency-promoting environment includes caring relationships in which adults listen to students, demonstrate kindness and respect (Meier, 1995), and have high and positive expectations for students (Delpit, 1996). The research suggests that service-learning that provides opportunities for students in a high relationship environment to engage in authentic tasks that affords opportunities for participation and contribution will promote resiliency.

Etiologies of At Risk and Disaffected Youth

Providing quality education to meet at risk students' needs has always been a challenging proposition. This challenge is compounded by the increasing numbers of at risk and disaffected students that now account for nearly 25 percent of U. S. students who feel disengaged, disenfranchised, and marginalized from school (Goodman, 1999).

One of the root causes for disaffectedness among youth includes lack of monetary resources caused either by downturns in the economy or the dramatic increases in single parent families, with nearly 13.3 million (19%) of U. S. children living in poverty (Olson, 2000). Disaffectedness can be related to substance abuse issues or youth violence and gangs, or can emerge from the absence of adequate support systems or lack of social capital (Maeroff, 1998). Payne (1998) identified eight categories of resources that she believes can foster a sense of disaffectedness in children and youth when absent: lack of financial, emotional, mental, spiritual, and physical resources; limited support systems; few, in any relationships/role models; and limited or no knowledge of hidden rules.

Disaffectedness that youth experience also can be traced to conditions in school. Poplin and Weeres (1992), in an ethnographic investigation of four schools, found that "a pervading sense of despair" characterized the experiences of students, teachers, and other school staff. Two major themes emerged from their research and have implications for all the other problems identified: the nature of relationships formed between educators and students; and issues of race, culture, and class. The authors found that students in 5th grade reported boredom in school and felt what was being taught had little relevance and meaning to their lives and future. Although students prefer schooling to be exciting, meaningful, and challenging, teachers, who feel increasing pressure of accountability, are resorting to traditional transmission techniques, believing erroneously that drilling the information into students increases their achievement and test scores.

Adolescent Depression and Social and Emotional Adjustment Problems

The incidence of adolescent adjustment problems with "affective disorders" (depression) in a general school population ranges from about 10 percent (McFarlane, Bellissimo, Norman, & Lange, 1994) to more than 25 percent (Sullivan & Engin, 1986), although less than 5 percent are actually diagnosed. Adolescent depression or affective disorder is characterized by maladaptive changes in mood, attitudes, energy level, and physical status. These changes constitute the three basic dimensions of depression. The normal developmental process presents adolescents with many real losses and threats to their sense of adequacy. To a large degree, lack of academic and social successes at school can contribute to a sense of powerlessness, learned helplessness, and lacking a sense of control. As a result, depressed adolescents may have problem behavior, which they act out through temper tantrums, running away, stealing, truancy, and other rebellious or anti-social acts. By the age of 15 or 16, adolescents may exhibit depression through drug abuse, sexual promiscuity, alienation, or suicidal behavior (McFarlane et al., 1994).

Adolescents who are depressed report significantly more internal attributions for negative events and less internal attributions for positive events, evidence more external locus of control, and describe themselves as significantly more hopeless (Pinto & Francis, 1993) Attributional styles are related to self-efficacy and beliefs about one's control over their environment. Individuals who focus on internal causes attribute failure to a lack of ability or insufficient effort. Others attribute failure to external factors, such as bad luck, task difficulty, or discrimination. Attributing failure to external forces can be useful in terms of one's sense of self-confidence, provided the external factors are perceived as controllable and changeable. However, if the external factors are perceived as a given or inherent and uncontrollable, external interpretation of failures can lead to frustration, resignation, and depression. When one attributes failure to unstable internal sources (e.g., lack of effort), the attribution can help to mobilize strengths and increase motivation in future encounters with similar situations. But, attributing failure to stable internal forces can also be damaging to one's self-esteem, perception of self-efficacy, and motivation.

The Social Construction of At Risk and Disaffectedness

More recently, alternative and critical perspectives on the high proportion of disaffected adolescents attempt to "depathologize" the experiences of high risk youth by exploring how complex social processes affect and "construct" their "mental health" (Unger & Teram, 2000). This genre of research joins a growing body of literature that questions the tenets of the "mental health model" and replaces it with a critical analysis of power and control (Foucault, 1972/1980; Ungar & Teram, 2000; Viet & Ware, 1983). Recent research that examines the link between mental health, or a strong sense of self-efficacy, and a struggle for developing a sense of empowerment and control questions the traditional paradigms defining deviance. Ungar and Teram argued that their research with deviant youth suggested, "that it is the capacity to experience power in the social discourses that define them is the most important determinant of their (adolescents') mental well-being" (p. 229). The authors contended that whether behaving as delinquents or scholars, adolescents are in a process of acquiring a sense of well-being by "drifting" toward social discourses where they exercise some degree of power in the self-defining labels attached to them.

> This patterned drift between discourses is the process by which adolescents, their peers, family members, and communities coauthor a youth's personal narrative.... According to the participants of this study, when the stories youth tell about themselves are invested with sufficient power to be widely accepted, mental health is maintained. When youth feel they lack the power to influence the way they are viewed, their mental health becomes threatened and troubling behaviors and symptoms follow. (p. 229)

These co-authored narratives are more than just stories youth tell about themselves; they are the way the self constitutes its identity through inter-subjective experiences in socio-historical contexts (Gergen, 1996). A small number of studies have noted the mental health-enhancing and empowering aspects of delinquent behaviors. Pombeni, Kirchler, and Palmonari's (1990) study of Italian youth pointed out that street groups provide an equally important and helpful juvenile sub-culture as formal groups committed to sports, religious programs, or politics. Simon, Dent, and Sussman (1997) reported that youth who carried weapons to school in southern California did so because they felt vulnerable, and a large number of them carried weapons for defense, to show off, and to feel powerful. These studies showed that youths' perceptions of ways to access power and status within their own sub-group appear to be the main determinant to their at risk identification. This is contrary to what society has traditionally labeled as deviant behavior resulting from mental health maladjustment. Consequently, labels of at risk and disaffectedness in youth may only be social constructions.

Cultural Reproduction Theory

Critical theory offers another framework for understanding and uncovering dominant cultural assumptions. The concept of social capital (Bourdieu & Passeron, 1977) views schools not as neutral institutions but rather as ones where the preferences, behaviors, and attitudes of the dominant class are most valued. This concept was initially used to analyze how culture and education interact, thereby contributing to the social reproduction of inequality (Bourdieu & Passeron, 1977). A discussion of at risk, disaffected youth needs to include an examination of the frequency with which at risk students appear to participate in their own oppression. While service-learning is often considered an intervention strategy to use with at risk students and disaffected youth, the end result is sometimes continued maladaptive and rebellious behavior, even from students who, by conventional standards, should stand to benefit from this intervention.

Landmark studies from sociology and anthropology provide a useful framework for understanding and analyzing this seeming contradiction (Lareau, 1989; Willis, 1977). Willis studied English, working-class youth in British schools and found that their youthful rebellion against schooling may have actually been shaped by the system, with the result being that students from lower class environments tend to perceive schooling differently than other students. According to Willis, schools try to differentiate between students and their appropriate places within society. His analysis was that schools often unwittingly encourage these students to rebel against authority in order to recognize the ways in which they can be controlled and punished by forces greater than them. More simply put, it is beneficial to work the rebellion out of them before they enter the world of work because rebellion by adults is challenging and costly while youthful rebellion is viewed as misguided and immature.

These examples show a type of cultural reproduction at work in which students from socially marginal backgrounds reproduce their culture. As a result, disaffected youth often seem to realize that the system is not meritocratic and the way to gain a sense of pride and self-esteem is by rebelling and buying into a counter school culture that rejects the mainstream values of the educational community; hence, some of the students who feel marginalized by the traditional school experience end up resisting all forms of school and authority. In considering intervention strategies, such as service-learning, and the tenets upon which service-learning is based (i.e., student voice and ownership in their own learning and enabling students to have a sense of control over their own lives), it is critical to understand how a theory of cultural reproduction might come into play in service-learning resulting in less than positive outcomes for highly disaffected youth.

This review of the literature and research gives credence to consideration of Marzano's (1998) classification of the self-system and its sub-components—beliefs about self-attributes, self and others, the nature of the world, efficacy, and purpose—as the primary factor to maximize learning in students, especially those who are considered at risk and highly disaffected. This review also appears to support careful orchestration of service-learning to optimize student potential to gain and benefit from their involvement in service-learning experiences through the collateral use of treatment strategies supported by the research effecting self-system beliefs.

RESEARCH QUESTIONS GUIDING THE STUDY

The question for this research was, "Does service-learning increase students' presence, participation, and academic performance at school?" In researching this question, the study resulted in recommendations that answer a second question: "How should service-learning be structured to maximize the academic, personal, and social development of disaffected youth?"

In this study, service-learning is defined as learning that enables student engagement and application of learning in meaningful contexts through active involvement in solving actual community needs, and is defined operationally as having a high level of consistency with the 11 Essential Elements of effective service-learning practice and 5 components for organizations implementing service-learning (NSLC, 1998). Resilience factors relate to Marzano's (1998) self-system components.

For purposes of this study, presence is defined as students' annual average daily attendance. Participation is defined as students' willingness and active engagement in project-based service-learning, including the school curriculum and students' expression of attitudes and values that indicates attentiveness and high interest concerning their involvement. Participation also refers to students' contribution to a positive school climate and demonstrated good citizenship, attitudes, and skills. Academic performance is defined as growth in the core academic areas that is either equal to or greater than one grade equivalent and as indicated by overall grade-point average and successful promotion to the next grade level. Risk factors include low motivation in traditional school settings, poverty level, and students with moderate to severe social and emotional adjustment problems.

METHODOLOGY OF THE STUDY

This study uses a case-study approach. The unit of analysis was a charter school with 40 students. To understand the relationship between the variables that were studied, multiple qualitative and quantitative methods were used. According to Denzin and Lincoln (1994), the use of multiple methods, or triangulation, reflects an attempt to secure indepth understanding of the phenomenon in question. Objective reality can never be captured (p. 2). Exhibit 2 shows the data sources and instrumentation that were used in this study.

EXHIBIT 2
Data Collection Methods and Data Sources

Method	Brief Description/Use
Methods Used to Determine Academic Growth and Achievement	
Six-Trait Writing	A representative sample of each student's writing was selected at three points during the year: Sep/Oct, Dec/Jan, and Apr/May and assessed using the Six-Trait Writing Scale.
Grade-Point Average	Comparisons of students GPAs, pre- and post-attendance, involvement, participation at the charter school.
Course Grades in Core Content Areas	Course grades in social studies, English, math, science, and fine arts were tracked throughout the year using nine-week progress reports and final grades at the end of each semester. Indices include performance and participation in class, completion of assignments, and mastery of subject matter.
Reading Level Indicator (RLI) (American Guidance Group Assessments)	An un-timed, group-administered, norm referenced reading screener was administered to identify individuals reading at 2nd- to 6th-grade levels. It also identified functional non-readers. The RLI contains 40 multiple-choice questions that assess sentence comprehension and vocabulary items. Twenty-four students used the RLI as a pre- and post-reading assessment.

(continued)

EXHIBIT 2
Continued

Methods Used to Determine Student Participation

Service-Learning and Locus of Control Survey	A survey assessing the relationship between student involvement in service-learning and locus of control was developed based on the Search Institute's 40 Developmental Assets (i.e., external assets focused on support, empowerment, boundaries and expectations, and constructive use of time; and internal assets focused on commitment to learning, positive values, social competencies, and positive identity). In January 2002, 21 students responded to general questions about their perceptions of service-learning and personal value/benefits they derived from their involvement in service-learning. They also responded to an additional 25 items that examined whether or not service-learning had fostered protective factors.
Documentation of Service-Learning Experiences	A detailed report documented student involvement in service-learning and tracked data including the community agency involved, the type of service students performed, the number of hours that students served, and which students participated.
Student Interviews	Fourteen students were interviewed either individually or in groups to learn more about their experiences at the school and perceptions of the value of those experiences. Interviews were taped and transcribed.
Student Climate Survey	A survey designed to assess the learning environment and culture of the charter school included items that addressed students' understanding of service-learning, their perceptions of the value of service-learning, and the degree of voice they believed they had in all decisions concerning the school and their learning. Fifteen 9th- through 11th- grade students completed the survey at the end of the school year.
Student Reflections	Student reflections were collected and included those done throughout the year consisting of required reflections on service-learning experiences and for formal class assignments as well as journals in creative writing and student reflective contributions to the school newsletter and yearbook. Reflections were collected and analyzed.

Methods Used to Determine Student Presence

Attendance Records	Records were kept on a daily basis and compared to students' attendance at their prior schools.

(continued)

EXHIBIT 2
Continued

Methods Used to Determine Student Presence, Participation, and Academic Growth and Achievement	
Quality of Service-Learning Experience Rubric	Student involvement in service-learning was categorized into three levels. Indicators of quality service-learning in Level 1 included: (1) high levels of participation; (2) personal initiative; (3) high degree of student voice; (4) service that reinforces cognitive, developmental, and social learning; and (5) service that displays empathy and caring. Indicators of quality service-learning in Level 2 included: (1) limited involvement, (2) limited participation, and (3) limited academic benefit. Indicators of quality service-learning in Level 3 included: (1) low interest, (2) resistance to participation, and (3) unwillingness to benefit or learn from the experience. All students' service-learning degree of involvement was assessed and determined with this rubric.

In analyzing how service-learning was structured at the YLC and the degree the implemented program resembled the intended design, an important research construct—program fidelity—was determined. Program fidelity is defined as implementing "all the core components of a program at the intended dosage" (Blueprints, 2001, p.1). If programs are not implemented with fidelity to the original model, there is a chance that the expected outcomes will not be realized and the program will prove to be ineffective. Examining the YLC program from the perspective of fidelity of implementation was critical to demonstrating the effectiveness of the program and to establishing reliability of service-learning as a powerful intervention strategy for disaffected youth.

CONTEXT OF THE SETTING

The Mission and Structure of the YLC

The YLC, a publicly authorized charter school in a midwestern state, has existed for four years either as a charter or alternative school, serving highly disaffected and at risk high school youth from six rural school districts. The mission of the YLC is to provide an authentic, nurturing, and academically-challenging learning environment for high school students that connects to the world outside of school, is meaningful, and promotes a positive sense of community, enthusiasm for learning, critical thinking/ problem solving, and social-emotional resiliency. Service-learning, where students are learning and reinforcing educational concepts while performing service that meets real community needs, provides a philosophical as well as practical base for the YLC. To accomplish the mission, the faculty at YLC implemented creative and unconventional instructional techniques and performance-based structures that improved students' academic performance by individualizing learning in the school and community settings. The intent of the school is to promote student enthusiasm for learning and desire to attend.

Accountability of the YLC is connected to the academic goals of increasing student achievement in the core academic areas and demonstrating students' ability to think critically and independently, and to become problem solvers. Accountability is also based on an increased rate of student attendance and participation; their contribution to a positive school climate; good citizenship, attitudes, and skills; increased appropriate personal and social adjustment, knowledge, skills and application; and responsible and independent behaviors. The academic program is structured with six class-period days and rotation between classes. Classes are small, varying in size from 5 to 10 students per class. As service-learning is a major component of the school, much learning takes place at various sites throughout the community with the processing and reflecting occurring at the school. The program also emphasizes authentic instruction so courses, such as science, are often taught in the state-of-the-art greenhouse adjacent to the school. The school is performance- rather than time-based (i.e., students complete a course once they have completed the requirements).

Structure of Service-Learning

Service-learning at the YLC consistently entailed two components:

1. What occurred at the school relating to student voice and choice, extensive pre- and post-reflection, connection to curricular goals, and so on; and
2. An experiential component where students were in the community performing a variety of activities and services that met authentic community needs.

Intensive professional development prior to the 2001–2002 school year focused on Deweyan philosophy as supportive of authentic education and service-learning to facilitate implementation of this philosophy. Service-learning was integrated into much of the curriculum during the 2001–2002 school year and involved numerous community partners with opportunities for students to interact with diverse populations (see Exhibit 3). While most content areas utilized the experiential component of service-learning as a hands-on application of content taught in the classroom, service-learning was not apparent in one section each of English and social studies. Students, especially those who had attended the school for a longer time, understood the essence and value of service-learning as they aptly defined it as, "helping other people while learning at the same time; any project you do to contribute to and help the community and also learn something about it; a hands-on way to learn; and doing service and learning a new skill." Students also reported being able to have voice in decision making concerning classroom learning as well as field experiences.

Student Characteristics

Up to 40 students attended YLC during the 2001–2002 school year with a male-female ratio of 3 to 1. Nine students ranged in age from 13 to 16; 30 students were aged 17 and 18. The mix included 19 seniors, 9 juniors, 4 sophomores, and 7 freshmen. Poverty level was approximately 50 percent. The ethnicity of the students was primarily Caucasian. The class included one bi-racial student and a small percentage of Native American students. Two students had children.

Almost 50 percent of students had legal concerns/problems/issues (i.e., felony charges, property damage, vandalism, physical fighting, and confrontations with other students and/or parents). Several were on diversion; at least eight were in Social Rehabilitative Services custody with supervised probation; and some had informal, unsupervised probation. Nine had histories of truancy with many of the students more than one year behind in credits. Roughly 20 percent of the enrolled students had been caught using drugs or possessing drug paraphernalia; 51 percent admitted to trying marijuana, cocaine, or LSD; 71 percent reported tobacco and alcohol usage; 43 percent reported going to class high on alcohol or drugs; and several had been charged with driving under the influence.

A unique characteristic of many of the students was their extreme disaffectedness or high at-risk status that was attributable to factors, such as poverty, dysfunction in families, and circumstances sometimes beyond their control (i.e., mental illness or depression). From a mental health perspective, about two-thirds of the students at the YLC displayed moderate to severe behavior disorders with many having been diagnosed with "clinically significant" levels of depression and/or "personality disorders," such as opposition and defiance and bi-polar disorder. Forty-four percent of the

EXHIBIT 3
Service-Learning and Connection to Curriculum

Project/Activity	Connection to Curriculum
Environmental Education Classroom	Science: Students worked with Pheasants Forever environmental conservation group to create a 190-acre outdoor classroom. They learned about wildlife conservation, habitat restoration, trail building, plant-life, and water quality.
Domestic Violence Prevention	Women's Issues Class: This project increased female students' knowledge of domestic violence and examined ways to recognize and prevent abuse. Students worked with Women's Transitional Care Services.
Rescue Mission and LINK (area kitchens for the homeless)	English, Creative Writing, and Self-in-Society: Students volunteered to prepare and serve meals at shelters for homeless people. Students toured facilities and interacted with staff and community members. Students wrote about their experiences and learned about issues facing homeless people through research, reading, watching movies, and discussions.
Hunger Awareness Project	Self-in-Society: Students identified hunger and poverty as an issue and coordinated a food drive with area grocery stores to benefit God's Storehouse. They researched and discussed issues of hunger and poverty and wrote reaction papers and an editorial for a local newspaper.
Serenata Farms	English: Students volunteered to assist people with multiple sclerosis to ride horses at a therapeutic horseback-riding farm. They completed academic work involving research about disabilities and careers working with people who have disabilities. Students wrote reaction papers and journals, created photo essays, and gave presentations about their experiences.
Elementary School Tutoring	English and Creative Writing: Students visited an area elementary school to assist 2nd and 3rd graders with reading and writing. They learned effective tutoring skills and journaled their experiences.

(continued)

EXHIBIT 3
(Continued)

Project/Activity	Connection to Curriculum
Habitat for Humanity	English: Students promoted recycling by planning and coordinating a recycling program with several community businesses and collected aluminum cans to recycle as a fundraiser for Habitat for Humanity. Students researched the Habitat for Humanity program and wrote reflection papers about their experiences.
Elementary Career Fairs	Art, Business Leadership, and Career Choices: Students assisted with planning and creating props for three School-to-Career career fairs for regional 3rd- through 5th-grade students. Students also facilitated activities in seven career pathways learning centers for students attending the fair.
Mentoring Program	A select group of students volunteered as mentors at the alternative classroom in an area elementary school. The students visited this classroom eight times throughout the semester, and each student participated in four hours of mentor training. Students earned an extra .5 credit for participation in this project.
Lil' Bees Preschool	Creative Writing: Students visited an area day-care center twice a month to read with the preschool aged students. The charter school (YLC) students also facilitated play activities.

students with IEPs (Individualized Education Plans for students with dis-abilities) addressed social and emotional adjustment goals as well as cogni-tive goals. Eighty percent reported non-participation in organized team sports or membership in clubs and other student activities.

Given the characteristics of YLC students, two issues were problematic. First, the number of students who attended the school increased consider-ably during the year with 24 in attendance at the beginning of the year and 40 at the end. Another challenge for staff and students alike, were students who attended the school on a part-time basis—either attending vocational school programs in the morning or dividing their time between their send-ing school and YLC.

Results

To better understand how service-learning impacted students' presence, participation, and performance levels a rubric, designed by the YLC ser-vice-learning coordinator, categorized student involvement in ser-vice-learning into three levels (see Exhibit 3). Using the rubric as an indicator to identify which students' service-learning participation quali-fied at either Level I, II, or III, the data revealed a high correlation between quality of students' service-learning experience, GPA, attendance, and years at the YLC, as shown in Exhibit 4. Because of the way ser-vice-learning was implemented at the school, with a high degree of fidelity to the Essential Elements, results demonstrated that service-learning posi-tively impacted these three variables. These data reveal that students who attended YLC for longer periods of time generally had a higher attendance rate, a higher quality service-learning experience, and a higher grade-point average. While it is difficult to establish causation, one can surmise that there is a strong correlation between student involvement in service-learn-ing and academic achievement and that possibly service-learning is related to students' wanting to attend school on a more regular basis. Other data, presented in Exhibit 4, provide evidence to support the relationship between these variables. Levels refer to mean scores on the quality assess-ment.

Student Presence

Indicators for increased attendance, identified in the charter, were that the school will have an attendance rate of 95 percent, and that at least 70 percent of the students will improve their annual average attendance. While not meeting the 95 percent goal, attendance was vastly improved

EXHIBIT 4
Quality of Service-Learning Engagement

Level	Quality of Service-Learning	GPA	Attendance	Years at YLC
I	Mean = 1.0	3.3025	88.58%	2.2273
	N	12	12	11
II	Mean = 2.0	2.8308	82.69%	1.6154
	N	12	13	13
III	Mean = 3.0	1.3589	73.50%	1.1500
	N	9	10	10
	Total Mean	2.6009	82.09%	1.6765
	N	33	35	34

over students' prior attendance rates at their previous schools, which were sometimes as low as 30 percent to 40 percent. Nearly 25 percent of the entire student population had histories of truancy. Of the students for whom data were available, eight attended more than 94 percent of the time; 11 had an 85 percent to 93 percent attendance rate; 10 had an attendance rate of 70 percent to 84 percent; and nine a rate of less than 70 percent. Given the problematic issue of student enrollment, with an increase of more than half of the student body at the YLC throughout the year, it appears that overall, there was an improvement in attendance rate. This research found a positive correlation between the length of time enrolled in the school, participation in service-learning, and increased attendance.

Student Participation

Findings revealed that 32 students participated for 960 hours in the experiential component of service-learning with more than 10 community agencies. A further analysis of the data showed that most of the service-learning activities were ongoing, with students participating on a monthly basis throughout the entire year. Some activities required weekly commitments.

The majority of students, even those who had not been at the school for as long a period of time as many of the seniors, also seemed to "buy-in" to the concept of service-learning. On a school climate survey, 93 percent of 9th- through 11th-grade students reported that they either strongly agreed (33%) or agreed (60%) with the statement, "I understand how service-learning relates to my academic work." When students were asked to express their attitudes, feelings, and perceptions about the school and service-learning, responses indicated that students had high engagement in service-learning and valued their experiences.

A major service-learning project in which students engaged was the creation of a 190-acre outdoor classroom that included building handicapped accessible hiking trails, planting up to 2,000 trees, and creating wildlife habitats. Student comments concerning this project were positive: *It's close and eventually we will be able to see what we've done; We got to work outside and do something helpful for people and wildlife;* and *I love the outdoors and I like to build things.* Another student, who had been involved at the equestrian therapy farm, responded, *I like to help the elderly, and I love horses.* Several who participated in an early childhood program indicated that they liked working with children. Others who were involved at the nursing home said that they liked to help old people. Another who was involved in the Rescue Mission (a soup kitchen for homeless persons) commented, *I would just like to help the homeless out so bad* [sic] . . . *but at least feeding them and talking to them is good, but it's not good enough. I wish I could do more.*

In comparing his prior schooling experience to his experience at the YLC one student said,

> At my old school they did not have a program like service-learning. At YLC, I have learned some valuable lessons that will carry me through life. Working in the service-learning program has taught me that the grass is not always greener on the other side. I feel strongly that my life will be better because of this experience that I have encountered. These experiences have made me a better person now and forever.

Another student responded similarly, indicating how service-learning had enabled him personally, to feel positively about school and himself. He said,

> YLC has been a very good experience for me this year because it has opened my eyes to new things. I have been involved in so many activities that it makes me feel good about myself, which I have not felt in such a long time.

One more student, when interviewed, internalized the value and benefits of his participation in service-learning at the YLC through his response,

> One way that YLC has helped me is through service-learning. This is the first semester I have participated in service-learning. Some of the projects that I have been involved with are helping people with multiple sclerosis ride horses, tutoring elementary students and making handicapped accessible trails. I also gave blood in response to the September 11 attacks. Another project that I did independently was making a piñata for a little girl's birthday because her mother had recently been killed in a car wreck. Along with my science class, we worked with Streamlink to test the water in a nearby creek. We will be monitoring that creek throughout the school year to make

sure it is not polluted. At the beginning of the year, I participated in Youth/ Adult partnership training. This training helped me work and interact with adults and students better.

There was a high correlation between service-learning and student resilience for the vast majority of the students, indicated by responses on the Service-Learning and Locus of Control survey. Eighty-one percent of the students responding felt that service-learning enabled them to form relationships with other caring adults, and 72 percent believed that service-learning had enabled adults to see them as having something valuable to offer others. Fifty-seven percent of the students believed that involvement in service-learning made them feel good about themselves. Also, 52 percent indicated that service-learning enabled them to see that they had something valuable to offer others and to see themselves as a positive role model for others; motivated them to do well in school in their other classes; and caused them to become more responsible. Approximately 50 percent felt that service-learning caused them to think about getting involved in worthy causes outside of school, helped them to think about other constructive activities to do outside of school, and caused them to stand up for and support their beliefs.

Even with the positive participation that service-learning engendered in students, not all felt the same way or were consistently positive about their involvement in service-learning. At mid-year, when asked about their perceptions of service-learning, several students responded, "[they] *didn't know*," and "*it was a 'pain in* ...." In an end-of-the-year survey, to a similar question, six of fourteen 9th- through 11th-graders responded, "*smoke break*," "*I don't care*," "*it's not fun*," and "*nothing*." Several of the students taking this survey had been at the school less than nine weeks. While in the minority, comments such as these confirm the validity of the "Quality of Service-Learning Experience" rubric that shows a negative relationship between a Level III service-learning experience, grade-point average, attendance, and length of time at the school. Comments such as these also reveal the extreme anger, rage, and frustration that some of these students feel. Another explanation is that some of these disaffected youth may be drifting toward social discourses where they can exercise some degree of power and do not want to "lose face" with their peers.

The last indicator of participation measured students' contribution to a positive school climate and assessed how they demonstrated good citizenship, attitudes, and skills. In responding to a survey that assessed how service-learning enabled students' protective factors, student comments revealed a strong sense of personal efficacy and feelings of having a purpose in life. Comments included such responses as, "*Involvement in a Christmas service-learning project has made me feel good to know that I was able to give and expect nothing in return, only to know that I was able to contribute what I could.*" Reflecting on his experience of being a mentor to an elementary child with severe emotional problems, one student commented,

> I think that by going (to the mentoring service-learning site) and being on my best behavior makes the school look good. It helps me because it can help me help care about somebody else. It could impact other persons because they could be like—Wow—"He's a bad kid like me and he's doing something. Maybe I should try that."

Other student comments included: "*Service-learning has filled a void in my life. Before I was involved in service-learning I was always getting in trouble with the law,*" and "*Service-learning has showed me what I want to do with my life.*" Another student shared the value of service-learning as giving him a sense of purpose in life, "*The experience at the equestrian therapy farm has changed me because later in life if there is a chance for me to help any age group of people with any kind of therapy or if they just want a friend around I will do my best to help them.*"

Student Academic Performance

Measures used to determine gains in student achievement included six-trait writing assessment, the Reading Level Indicator, grade-point average, and course grades in core content areas. While a variety of assessments were used in math, social studies, and science, pre- and post-assessments were not administered so there was no baseline established against which growth could be determined. Improving students' writing abilities was a major academic goal of the school, and teachers used reflection connected to service-learning as the primary means to facilitate students' writing and critical thinking skills. This occurred most frequently in the Creative Writing Class, English, and Self-in-Society, as shown in Exhibit 3 that illustrates how service-learning connected to the curriculum. Analyzing students' writing against the Six-Trait Writing Scale, results in Exhibit 5 reveal a statistically significant difference in scores from fall of 2001 to spring of 2002.

EXHIBIT 5
Results of Writing Assessment

	N	*Mean*
Fall 2001	29	16.5517
Winter 2001	33	19.5152
Spring 2002	29	20.1724

Due to the nature of student enrollment, that increased throughout the year, the primary indicator of reading improvement was based on reading scores of 24 students who were administered both a pre- and post-assessment using the Reading Level Indicator tool. The mean score of the 24 students went from 28.46 to 30.88, an increase of 2.42 (a statistically significant difference). The range of the scores was from 4th to post 12th grade. The independent reading level increased by one grade, from the 5th to 6th grade, and instructional reading levels increased from the 9.5 grade level to the 12.2 grade level. The increase seems to be attributable to: (a) interventions that teachers are making in the program, and/or (b) increased student motivation and willingness to demonstrate ability. Using Marzano's (1998) meta-theory of instruction, particularly the self-system, one can surmise that service-learning, which is so central to the culture of the school, had a positive impact on students' participation and/or willingness to succeed in the school.

Students' grade-point average is based on letter grades that teachers assign and is determined by several indices: student performance and participation in classes, completion of assignments, and mastery of the subject matter. Grades are tracked on a nine-week basis and are recorded as progress reports and semester grades. Exhibit 4 compares quality of service-learning experience, attendance, length of time at the school, and grade-point average for 33 students. The Exhibit shows a significant increase in students' GPA, from an average GPA of 1.3589 for students categorized at a Level III quality of service-learning, to an average GPA of 3.3025 for students categorized at a Level I quality of service-learning. What is especially significant about this finding is the fact that the average GPA of all students coming to the YLC is between a 1.5 and 1.9. Being able to raise their GPA from a D+/C- to a B-, B, or a B+ average GPA, indicates that something is impacting learning for these students, of which service-learning seems to be contributing factor.

CONCLUSION

This study defined service-learning and documented its implementation as aligned with the Essential Elements of Service-Learning. Various qualitative and quantitative data sources were used as indicators of student presence, participation/engagement, and academic performance in order to search for patterns that can be explained by the conceptual (theoretical framework) and related research.

Utilizing multiple measures and a converging evidence frame of reference, it is possible to conclude that service-learning, as practiced at YLC, was able to meld the best characteristics of democratic classrooms, project-based learning, authentic pedagogy, and a type of "group therapy" similar to cognitive behavior modification or cognitive restructuring. In this context, service-learning became more than simply a setting for trying to teach academic concepts in a hands-on manner. Rather it was expanded to include affective and therapeutic components that were instrumental in stimulating positive beliefs related to the self-system.

The frequent and varied service-learning activities, largely selected by students, also provided an excellent venue the teachers used to engage in dialogue, discussions, and reflections with students that were similar to another technique reviewed by Marzano (1998) that had a large effect size (ES .68) (e.g., techniques involving the rational examination of emotions).

In terms of achievement, students clearly made significant progress in reading and writing and in school adjustment and general resiliency. Their attendance and participation rates increased, as did their GPAs and positive attitude toward themselves and school. Students who were judged by their teacher to be more engaged in service-learning had better school attendance (presence), reported more positive outcomes from their presence and participation and had higher grade-point averages.

As evidenced by student interviews and self-report data, service-learning at the YLC appeared to engage many of the students in more appropriate behavior, better academic performance, and school attendance. Service-learning also seemed to positively impact student resilience in a number of areas increasing their personal sense of efficacy and locus of control. The review of the related literature, theories of adolescent adjustment/treatment, resiliency research, and Marzano's (1998) meta-theory of learning can help to explain these positive outcomes.

To attain the benefits and outcomes with disaffected youth, as evidenced in this study, it is critical that service-learning be an integral part of the school and not just an add-on activity or perceived merely as an opportunity for hands-on application of curriculum being taught. Instead, to maximize academic, personal, and social development in youth, teachers, administrators, and staff need to come to understand service-learning as more than pedagogy and embrace it as a philosophy and a way to "do" schooling. Because there was such a high degree of program fidelity to the Essential Elements at the Youth Learning Cooperative, it was difficult to separate out which outcomes were attributable to service-learning and which were attributable to other factors at the school, as one impacts the other. Thus, program fidelity to a model, or a set of standards, is essential.

Along these lines of looking at service-learning as more of a philosophy rather than pedagogy, a second criterion is the importance of grounding practice in theory. Teachers need to understand why they are using certain techniques and strategies and not just merely know how to implement them. For the most part, service-learning in schools is perceived as a hands-on project to apply learning in an authentic setting without any real understanding of the underlying theories of why this type of learning is so effective and powerful, especially with disaffected youth. This study contributes to the research in positing a theory of how service-learning increases motivation in disaffected youth and thereby affects learning. The end result could be the development of lesson plans where, as part of the teaching and learning transaction, teachers purposefully include ideas on ways to motivate students as a means to connect with students' self-system and enhance learning. Teachers need to understand learning theory as a basis for grounding their practice and building service-learning experiences.

Given what we know about the role of the self-system in learning theory, as the center that controls motivation and engagement, and its connection to the metacognitive and cognitive systems and the knowledge domains, another answer involves structuring purposeful and methodical pre-reflection and reflection activities in conjunction with the experiential component of service-learning. This will enhance and assist students' knowledge and connection to service-learning goals and larger outcomes.

Given cultural reproduction theory, it is critical to structure service-learning in ways that disaffected students come to realize their participation in their own oppression and see service-learning as an empowerment strategy to transcend this oppression and transform their lives. To prepare young adults for an opportunity to participate positively within the community, adults need to help them develop a sense of values that reinforce their positive behavior. It is only when students experience success in the community that they will change their attitudes toward it. Service-learning with disaffected youth takes advantage of methods grounded in psychotherapeutic techniques to enable significant gains in academic achievement.

REFERENCES

Ajzen, I. (1985). From intentions to actions: A theory of planned behavior, in J. Kuhl, & J. Beckman (Eds.), *Action-control: From cognition to behavior* (pp. 11–39.) Heidelberg, Germany: Springer.

Ajzen, I., & Madden, T. J. (1986). Prediction of goal-directed behavior: Attitudes, intentions, and perceived behavioral control. *Journal of Experimental Social Psychology*, (22), 453–474.

Anderson, J. R. (1995). *Learning and memory: An integrated approach.* New York: Wiley & Sons.

Anderson, J. (1998). Service-learning and teacher education. (ERIC Document Reproduction Service, No. ED 421 481).

Benard, B. (1991). *Fostering resiliency in kids: Protective factors in the family, school, and community.* Portland, OR: Western Center for Drug-Free Schools and Communities.

Blueprints. (2001). *The importance of implementation fidelity*, 2(91). Boulder, CO: Center of the Study & Prevention of Violence, University of Colorado.

Bourdieu, P., & Passeron, J. C. (1977). *Reproduction in education, society, culture.* Beverly Hills, CA: Sage.

Delpit, L (1996). The politics of teaching literate discourse. In L. Delpit (Ed.), *Other people's children: Cultural conflict in the classroom* (pp. 152–166). New York: New Press.

Denzin, N., & Lincoln, Y. (1994). Introduction: Entering the field of qualitative research, in N. Denzin, N. & Y. Lincoln (Eds.), *Handbook of qualitative research* (pp. 1–17). Thousand Oaks, CA: Sage.

Foucault, M. (1980). *Power/knowledge: Selected interviews and other writings, 1972–1977.* (C. Gordon, L. Marshall, J. Mepham, & K. Soper, Trans.). NY: Pantheon. (Original work published in 1972)

Gergen, J. (1996). Beyond life narratives in the therapeutic encounter. In J. Birrens, G. M. Kenyon, J. Ruth, J. Schroots, & T. Svenson (Eds.), *Aging and biography: Explorations in adult development* (pp. 205–223). New York: Springer.

Giles, D., Jr., & Eyler, J. (1994). The theoretical roots of service-learning in John Dewey: Toward a theory of service-learning. *Michigan Journal of Community Service Learning, 1*(1), 77–85.

Goodman, G. S. (1999). *Alternatives in education: Critical pedagogy for disaffected youth.* New York: Peter Lang.

Higgins, G. (1994). *Resilient adults: Overcoming a cruel past.* San Francisco: Jossey-Bass.

Kraft, N. P., & Billig, S. H. (1997). *Linking Title I and service-learning: A model to promote authentic teaching.* Paper presented at the American Education Research Association annual meeting, Chicago, IL.

Lareau, A. (1989). *Home advantage: Social class and parental intervention in elementary education.* New York: Falmer Press.

Lindsay, P. H., & Norman, D. A. (1977). *Human information processing.* New York: Academic Press.

Maeroff, G. I. (1998). *Altered destinies: Making life better for school children in need.* New York: St. Martin's Press.

Markus, H., & Ruvulo, A. (1990). Possible selves. Personalized representations of goals. In L. Pervin (Ed.), *Goal concepts in psychology* (pp. 211–241). Hillsdale, NJ: Lawrence Erlbaum Associates.

Marzano, R. J. (1998). *A theory-based meta-analysis of research on instruction.* Aurora, CO: Mid-continent Regional Educational Laboratory.

McFarlane, A. H., Bellissimo, A., Norman, G. R., & Lange, P. (1994). Adolescent depression in a school-based community sample: Preliminary findings on contributing social factors. *Journal of Youth and Adolescence, 23*(6), 601–620.

Meier, D. (1995). *The power of their ideas: Lessons for America from a small school in Harlem.* Boston: Beacon Press.

National Service-Learning Cooperative. (1998). *Essential elements of service-learning.* Minneapolis, MN: National Youth Leadership Council.

Newmann, F., & Wehlage, G. (1995). *Successful school restructuring: A report to the public and educators.* Madison, WI: University of Wisconsin, The Center on Organization and Restructuring of Schools.

Olson, L. (2000, September). Children of change: High poverty among young makes schools' job harder, *Education Week, XX*(4), 40–41.

Payne, R. (1998). *A framework for understanding poverty.* Baytown, TX: RFT Publishing.

Pinto, A., & Francis, G. (1993). Cognitive correlates of depressive symptoms in hospitalized adolescents. *Adolescence, 28*(111), 661–672.

Pombeni, M. L., Kirchler, E., & Palmonari, A. (1990). Identification with peers as a strategy to muddle through the troubles of the adolescent years. *Journal of Adolescence, 13,* 351–369.

Poplin, M., & Weeres, J. (1992). *Voices from the inside: A report on schooling from inside the classroom.* Claremont, CA: Institute for Education in Transformation at the Claremont Graduate School.

Simon, T. R., Dent, C. W., & Sussman, S. (1997). Vulnerability to victimization, concurrent problem behaviors, and peer influence as predictors of in-school weapon carrying among high school students. *Violence and Victims, 12,* 277–289.

Sullivan, W. O., & Engin, A. (1986). Adolescent depression: Its prevalence in high school students. *Journal of School Psychology, 24*(2), 103–109.

Viet, C. Y., & Ware, J. E., Jr. (1983). The structure of psychological distress and well-being in general populations. *Journal of Consulting and Clinical Psychology, 51,* 730–742.

Unger, M., & Teram, E. (2000). Drifting toward mental health: High-risk adolescents and the process of empowerment. *Youth and Society, 32*(2), 228–252.

Willis, P. (1977). *Learning to labour: How working class kids get working class jobs.* Westmead, England: Saxon House.

PART VI

INTERNATIONAL PERSPECTIVES

CHAPTER 11

SERVICE-LEARNING INTERNATIONALLY
Developing a Global Civil Society

John Annette

The way in which service-learning is developing internationally is striking. This essay considers three things: the development of both community service and service-learning internationally with special attention to reviewing developments in the United Kingdom; ways to research service-learning in comparative higher education and some of the key issues that should taken into account in conducting this research, including the challenge of analyzing distinction between community service and service-learning in an international context; and how service-learning in higher education, through study abroad and exchange programs, can contribute to the development of a global civil society.

Service-learning in higher education can now be found, for example, in the Philippines, Singapore, Mexico, Brazil, Japan, the United Kingdom, and Eastern and Central Europe. In Australia, Muirhead has established the Community Service and Research Centre at the University of

Deconstructing Service-Learning: Research Exploring Context, Participation, and Impacts
A Volume in: Advances in Service-Learning Research, pages 241–249.
Copyright © 2003 by Information Age Publishing, Inc.
All rights of reproduction in any form reserved.
ISBN: 1-59311-071-5 (hardcover), 1-59311-070-7 (pbk.)

Queensland's Ipswich Campus, where a model of action research based on community partnerships has been developed. In South Africa, the Community Higher Education Service Partnership project (CHESP), under Lazens, is managed by the Joint Education Trust (JET) and supported by the Ford Foundation. CHESP involves five South African universities with pilot community partnership and service-learning programs. The aim of the CHESP project is "the reconstruction and development of South African civil society through the development of socially accountable models of higher education, research, community service and development." (JET, p. 2, 1999, cf. MacMillan & Saddington, 2000; Subotzky, 1999). Recently a community service program at the University of Jordan in Amman has been developed with the support of the British Council. This program is linked to the Muslim faith and the development of civil society.

In the United Kingdom, in 1997, a major Royal Commission headed by Lord Dearing was established to examine the future of British higher education. One of the main aims of higher education, according to the Dearing Report on "United Kingdom Higher Education in the Learning Society" (Niche, 1997), is to contribute to a democratic, civilized, and inclusive society. The emphasis on civic engagement highlights the need for the curriculum in higher education to prepare graduates to become active citizens and to participate in formal politics and play a leadership role in civil society.

In the United Kingdom this is particularly a challenge for higher education as the new citizenship curriculum in schools, following on from the "Crick Report on Education for Citizenship and the Teaching of Democracy in Schools" in 1998, resulted in the establishment of service-learning programs in secondary or high schools (Annette, 2000; QCA, 1999; Potter, 2002). An important research need resulting from these developments is to determine the necessary elements of a service-learning program, which can build not only social capital but also active citizenship (Annette, in press; Barber, 1998a, 1998b; Campbell, 2000; Ehrlich, 2003; Kahne, Westheimer, & Rogers, 2000).

The Dearing Report (NICHE, 1997) follows on from an increasing range of work done since the 1970s that has emphasized the importance in higher education of the development of what has been termed transferable, personal, core, or key skills (Drew, 1998). The challenge for higher education, according to the report, is how higher education can provide an academic framework based on the acquisition of critical knowledge that is mostly structured upon the present framework established by the academic disciplines and can also provide students with the opportunity to develop essential key skills and capabilities (cf. CVCP/DfEE, 1999). This emphasis on learning not only for academic knowledge but also for key skills and capabilities, including student leadership, can also be found in the United States in the work of Boyer and the Carnegie Foundation and more recently in the writings of Ehrlich (Boyer, 1994, 1996; Ehrlich, 2000, 2003). It is increasingly recognized that an important way in which students can develop key skills through work experience and also experience an education for citizenship is through service-learning or community-based learning.

In the United Kingdom the CSV/Council for Citizenship and Learning in the Community (CSV/CCLC) has been promoting and facilitating education for citizenship and service-learning in higher education by working in partnerships with over 200 programs in higher education institutions. The aim of this national, multidisciplinary, and community linked network is to promote service-learning through university/community partnerships that are accredited or certified and that develop students' skills and citizenship and meet community needs (Annette, 2000; Annette & Buckingham-Hatfield, 1999). In 2002, the UK government established the new Higher Education Active Community Fund, which has provided funding for the establishment of community service programs based on effective community partnerships in all English universities but not necessarily establishing service-learning programs. This fund, however, raises the possibility that citizenship education and service-learning could become an important feature of higher education in Britain by providing funding for the development of university/community partnerships.

The United Kingdom Department for Education and Skills has supported research into work experience (Brennan & Little, 1996; Little, 1998). The department only recently began to support research into service-learning, e.g., Fund for the Development and Teaching' (FDTL) projects, such as the Community-Based Learning and Teaching Project, based at the Universities of Birmingham and Liverpool and the forthcoming research work of Hall and Annette on the learning outcomes of service-learning.

It is interesting to note that the United Kingdom organization of university and college presidents' report on "Universities and Communities" (CVCP, 1994), highlighted the role of universities in local and regional development, but it did not consider how university and community partnerships would impact upon the curriculum of higher education, except for the appendix by Mohan (Annette, 2000; CVCP, 1994; for criticisms cf. Watson & Taylor, 1998). Internationally there are many examples of universities recognizing the challenge of establishing partnerships with local and regional communities. Evidence of the development of community service and service-learning programs as a response to this challenge is increasing. In some higher education systems, however, community partnerships are seen primarily in terms of economic development, cultural formation, and technology transfer and not in terms of the curriculum of higher education itself. In the United States there is an increasing emphasis on the need for service-learning programs to meet the needs of local community partners (Cruz & Giles, 2000; Enos & Morton, 2003). In an international context, it is even more challenging to research the out-comes for both students and the local communities.

RESEARCHING INTERNATIONAL SERVICE-LEARNING

With the support of the Ford Foundation in 1998, Berry and Chiholm (1999) began to investigate the extent to which what might be the equiva-lent of "service-learning" can be found in higher education institutions around the world. This is the first survey of its kind, and it discovered a remarkable range of universities and colleges that offer "service-learning" internationally. The study is already out of date, as the number of universi-ties around the world that are developing service-learning is growing rap-idly (cf. Berry, 1990a, Berry, 1990b; Berry & Chiholm, 1999). The research by Berry and Chisholm was informed by the outcomes of an international meeting in May 1998 at the Wingspread Conference Center, which was supported by the Ford Foundation and the Johnson Foundation. Approxi-mately 42 service-learning educators from 16 nations attended the event to report on service-learning in their countries and to consider ways to fur-ther develop it internationally. The Wingspread Resolutions are printed as an appendix to the report and provide fine principles for the promotion of international service-learning. The research for the report was based on a questionnaire that was sent to institutions around the world (no informa-tion is provided in the report as to the number of institutions or to their geographical spread). Sixty-four institutions of higher education in 23 nations responded, and the details from 23 additional service-learning pro-grams were also included. Finally, the opinions of higher education experts from other parts of the world, who are listed in the appendix of the report, were used in the analyses. The findings are presented in a thematic framework. While the report strives very hard to address the issue of cross-cultural understanding by largely utilizing the terms provided by the responses, this unfortunately sometimes leads to some conceptual confu-sion.

There does not seem to be a clear distinction between programs of national and community service as distinct from service-learning. There is also no clear discussion of how this service is based on effective community partnerships, how it promotes active citizenship, and what principles of ser-vice-learning are used to identify service-learning programs. These are important issues facing service-learning not only in the United States, but also internationally.

A particular problem for analyzing international service-learning will be the challenge of inter-cultural and cross-cultural understanding of key terms. A recent study by Coggan and Derricott (2000) on citizenship edu-cation involved 182 educators and 'expert' participants from England, The

Netherlands, Canada, the United States, Japan, Taiwan, Hong Kong, PR China, Thailand, and Singapore. The methodology used in the study was a cross-cultural adaptation of an Ethnographic Delphi Futures Research Method based on the Delphi Method (Linstone & Turoff, 1975). This research method provides a framework for arriving at a consensus as to the meaning of key terms, which can then be used for comparative analysis. Combined with national case studies, these studies can help develop a clearer understanding of the nature and extent of service-learning in international higher education. Involvement in service-learning in another culture encourages the student to become 'engaged' in their own society and gain a deeper level of cross-cultural learning than they would be able to achieve then through formal academic learning. An important aspect of research into international service-learning/study abroad programs is therefore the problem of cultural difference and inter-cultural or cross-cultural understanding.

An important, largely unexamined research question is what are the necessary elements of service-learning programs internationally that can build not only social capital but also active citizenship (Annette, in press; Battistoni, 2002; Campbell, 2000; Kahne et al., 2000; Putnam, 2002). A recent Ford Foundation workshop on "Youth Involvement" considered the development of youth civic engagement including the activities of higher education students. While there are many impressive examples of national civic service programs involving higher education students, few of these involve service-learning. For example, in Mexico the 'Servicio Social' requires higher education students to render civic service, and in 1999, some 299,000 students rendered civic service. A recent report on the 'Servicio Social' indicated that one of its key problems is that it needs to be integrated more fully with the curriculum of the students. The report, however, went on to indicate that some 60 percent of higher education institutions now recognize service-learning in some way as part of the curriculum (Ford Foundation, 2000). Underlying the report is an assumption that activities that increase social capital, including bridging social capital, will lead to an increase in active citizenship. As the research of Eyler and Giles (1999) shows, there is a need for a more analytical framework for understanding how service-learning can lead to an increase in active citizenship (cf. Ehrlich, 2003).

SERVICE-LEARNING AND GLOBAL CIVIL SOCIETY

The development of service-learning internationally provides key opportunities for universities in these countries to work in partnership with non-governmental organizations (NGOs) and community organizations for sustainable community development. (Edwards & Gaventa, 2001;

Gaventa, 1998). One of the key issues facing those who work in the area of international community development is how to get beyond the hype about what constitutes civil society in diverse societies. Do northern hemisphere NGOs represent the interests of local based NGOs or local community organizations? Two major participatory action research programs, which have attempted to include the 'voices' of the citizens of local communities across diverse global societies, are the surprisingly radical World Bank Survey of Poor Peoples (2000) and the Commonwealth Foundation study of civic participation involving 10,000 citizens in 47 countries (Knight et al., 2002). At the Institute of Development Studies, University of Sussex, United Kingdom, Gaventa and Valderrama (1999) are helping to develop participatory action research networks across global communities. The challenge of measuring either community outcomes or the promotion of assets for university/community partners in international service-learning programs is made more difficult by the increased range of variables that would be involved in such an international analysis. Nevertheless any analysis of international service-learning will need to consider the outcomes of the university/community partnerships involved.

The development of service-learning in international higher education provides opportunities for students from these countries to engage in student exchanges involving service-learning with students from different global cultures and social, political, and economic contexts. Universities can also play a key role in developing networks for a global civil society and global citizen action (Annette, 2001). This will enable students to develop both an understanding of globalization and an intercultural understanding of community development across national and regional boundaries. Therefore, international service-learning can, through experiential engagement and reflective learning activities, enable students to recognize 'difference' while developing a sense of shared global citizenship. Many of the ethical issues raised in the recent DEA/AUT publication, *Globalization and Higher Education* (1999), such as international partnerships, human rights, and sustainable development, can be addressed by students engaged in global service-learning through international partnerships between universities. Middlesex University, for example, has established an 'International Service-learning Program' that provides learning opportunities for international students, exchange students, and study abroad students to learn about citizenship and community development in a global context. According to Barber (2000), "These civic efforts-the work of citizens rather than governments, or the work of governments reacting to citizens (and not just their own) embody a global public opinion in the making, a global civic engagement that can alone give the abstraction of international politics weight."

To what extent, then, can higher education institutions contribute to the development of a global civil society and assist local communities in having a democratic voice concerning the process of globalization? To what extent do they provide for their students the opportunities to develop the key skills and capabilities to understand the process of globalization, which is shaping their lives so rapidly, and enable them to develop as global citizens? Service-learning is an important new way of learning in U.S. and UK higher education and increasingly in universities internationally. The nature and extent of service-learning in international education now needs to be analyzed, and this chapter has raised some points about how this might be done. It is also a means to provide just such an education for global citizenship in international higher education. The challenge for international service-learning will be to provide the basis for the development of a global network of university/community partnerships, which can provide an education for global citizenship for its students and the opportunity to engage in global civic engagement.

REFERENCES

Annette, J. (2000). Citizenship and service-learning in higher education. In D. Lawton, R. Gardner, & J. Cairns (Eds.), *Education for Values: Morals, Ethics and Citizenship in Contemporary Teaching.* London: Kogan Page.

Annette, J. (2001a). Citizenship education and experiential and service-learning in schools. In D. Lawton, J. Cairns, & R. Gardner (Eds.), *Education for Citizenship.* London: Continuum.

Annette, J. (2001b). Global citizenship and learning in communities. *The Development Education Journal, 8*(1).

Annette, J. (in press). Community, social capital, and education for citizenship. In A. Lockyer, B. Crick, & J. Annette (Eds.), *Education for Citizenship.* London: Ashgate.

Annette, J., & Buckingham-Hatfield, S. (1999). *Student-community partnerships in higher education.* London: CSV Publications.

Barber, B. (1998a). *A place for us: How to make society civil and democracy strong* New York: Hill and Wang.

Barber, B. (1998b). *A passion for democracy.* Princeton, NJ: Princeton University Press.

Barber, B. (2000). Globalizing democracy. *American Prospect, 11*(20). Retrieved online July 3, 2003, from http://www.prospect.org/print/V11/20/barber-b.html

Battistoni, R. (2002). *Civic engagement across the curriculum.* Providence, RI: Campus Compact.

Berry, H. (1990a). Service-learning in international and intercultural settings. In J. Kendall, *Combining service and learning, Vol.1: A resource book for community and public service* (pp. 311–314). Springfield, VA: National Society for Internships and Experiential Education.

Berry, H. (1990b). Experiential education: The neglected dimension of international/intercultural education. In J. Kendall, *Combining service and learning,*

Vol.1: A resource book for community and public service (pp. 324–335). Springfield, VA: National Society for Internships and Experiential Education.

Berry, H., & Chiholm, L. (1999). Service-learning in higher education around the world: An initial look. New York: International Partnership for Service-Learning.

Boyer, E. (1994, March). Creating the new American college. *The Chronicle of Higher Education.*

Boyer, E. (1996). The scholarship of engagement. *The Journal of Public Service and Outreach, 1*(1).

Brennan, J., & Little, B. (1996). A review of work based learning in higher education. London: DfEE.

Campbell, D. (2000). Social capital and service-learning. *Political Science and Politics, 33*(4).

Coggan, J. & Derricott, R. (2000). Citizenship for the 21st century: An international perspective on education (revised). London: Kogan Page.

Cruz, N., & Giles, D., Jr. (2000, Fall). Where's the community in service-learning research? *Michigan Journal of Community Service Learning,* Special Issue. Retrieved online July 3, 2003, from http://www.umich.edu/~mjcsl/

CVCP. (1994). *Universities and their communities.* London: Author.

CVCP/DfEE. (1999). *Skills development in higher education.*

DEA/AUT. (1999). *Globalization and higher education.* London: Association of University Teachers and Development Education Association.

Drew, S. (1998). *Key skills in higher education: background and rationale.* London: SEDA.

Edwards, M., & Gaventa, J. (Eds.). (2001). *Global citizen action.* London: Earthscan.

Ehrlich, T. (Ed.). (2000). *Civic responsibility and higher education.* Washington, DC: Oryx Press.

Ehrlich, T. (2003). *Educating citizens.* San Francisco: Jossey-Bass.

Enos, S., & Morton, K. (2003). Developing a theory and practice of campus-community partnerships. In B. Jacoby (Ed.), *Building partnerships for service-learning.* San Francisco: Jossey-Bass.

Eyler, J., & Giles, D., Jr. (1999). *Where's the learning in service-learning?* San Francisco: Jossey-Bass.

Ford Foundation. (2000, December). *Youth service report: Worldwide workshop on youth involvement as a strategy for social, economic, and democratic development.* Detroit, MI: Author. Retrieved online August 5, 2003, from
http://www.fordfound.org/publications/recent_articles/docs/youth.pdf

Gaventa, J. (1998). Crossing the Great divide: Building links between NGOs and community-based organizations in north and south. In D. Lewis (Ed.), *International perspectives on the third sector.* London: Earthscan.

Gaventa, J., & Valderrama, C. (1999, June). *Participation, citizenship, and local governance.* Background paper prepared for Strengthening Participation in Local Governance workshop. Retrieved online August 5, 2003, from
http://www.ids.ac.uk/ids/particip/research/localgov.html

JET Bulletin No.10, September 1999, p. 2.

Kahne, J., Westheimer, J., & Rogers, B. (2000, Fall). Service-learning and citizenship: Directions for research. *Michigan Journal of Community Service Learning.* Retrieved online July 3, 2003, from http://www.umich.edu/~mjcsl/

Linstone, H., & Turoff, M. (1975). *The Delphi Method: Techniques and applications.* Boston: Addison and Wesley.

Little, B. (1998). *Developing key skills through work placement.* London: CIHE.

MacMillan, J., & Saddington, T. (2000). *Service-learning partnerships as a catalyst for higher education transformation: Reflections on a South African initiative.* NSEE Conference paper.

National Committee of Inquiry into Higher Education (NICHE). (1997). *Higher education in the learning society.* The Dearing Report retrieved online August 6, 2003, from http://www.leeds.ac.uk/educol/ncihe/

Potter, J. (2002). *Active citizenship in schools.* London: Kogan Page.

Putnam, R. D. (Ed.). (2002). *Democracies in flux.* London: Oxford University Press.

Qualifications and Curriculum Authority (QCA). (1999). *Education for citizenship and the teaching of democracy in schools.* London: Author.

Subotzky, G. (1999). Alternatives to the entrepreneurial university: New modes of knowledge production in community service programs. *Higher Education, 38*(4).

Tandon, R., Knight, B., & Chigudu, H. (2002). *Reviving democracy: Citizens at the heart of governance.* London: Earthscan.

Watson, D., & Taylor, R. (1998). *Lifelong learning and the university.* London: Falmer Press.

World Bank Survey of Poor Peoples. (2000). http://www.worldbank.org/poverty.

PART VII

THE STATE OF THE FIELD

.

CHAPTER 12

THE STATE OF SERVICE-LEARNING AND SERVICE-LEARNING RESEARCH

Shelley H. Billig and Janet Eyler

Service-learning has become more popular among practitioners and researchers at both the K–12 and higher education levels. Is service-learning distinct enough to be a "field?" Are service-learning practitioners and researchers engaged in the types of activities that are associated with field-building? This chapter addresses the state of service-learning as a field, contextual factors that may be associated with its health and prospects, and the state of service-learning research in terms of progress made toward actualizing the research agendas and building a strong foundational base for practice.

In the year 2003, service-learning as a teaching and learning practice is faring well. While the most recent survey of prevalence of service-learning occurred in 1999 (NCES, 1999), it is clear from the number of articles being written, the media attention, conference attendance, and word-of-mouth that service-learning is becoming more entrenched in both

Deconstructing Service-Learning: Research Exploring Context, Participation, and Impacts
A Volume in: Advances in Service-Learning Research, pages 253–264.
Copyright © 2003 by Information Age Publishing, Inc.
All rights of reproduction in any form reserved.
ISBN: 1-59311-071-5 (hardcover), 1-59311-070-7 (pbk.)

institutions of higher education and K-12 schools. In addition, while there is no major funding stream for service-learning research, this book series and the number of other publications in educational journals shows that there is great amount of activity among researchers interested in service-learning. As the chapters in this book demonstrate, the practice of service-learning and the conduct of service-learning research is expanding, deepening, and becoming anchored in educational institutions in the United States and abroad.

This final chapter of the third volume in the series in *Advances in Service-Learning Research* discusses the state of service-learning as a field and the progress made on the research agendas formulated for the field. Using a field-building framework developed by Fine (2001), the field of service-learning is analyzed, areas of progress and challenge are noted, and an appraisal of the research progress and needs is presented. The chapter concludes with suggestions for next steps for field-building and research.

SERVICE-LEARNING AS A FIELD

Fine (1999), in her review of the literature, found that "fields" have the following characteristics:

1. *Distinct Identity:* Specification of clear, differentiated, and recognized activities that can be described;
2. *Standard Practice:* Creation of criteria for quality practice known to be linked with the achievement of desired outcomes and the contextual, developmental, and cultural conditions that foster the outcomes;
3. *Knowledge Base:* Establishment of a cumulative foundation of research and practice that identifies results connected to activities and the conditions necessary to achieve desired outcomes;
4. *Leadership and Membership:* Identification of practitioners who are prepared and are supported by organizational structures, including those that offer professional development, to advance the quality of practice and to credential practitioners;
5. *Information Exchange:* Formation of communication avenues for disseminating knowledge;
6. *Resources:* Development of structures and organizations that facilitate collaboration between and among practitioners and allies; and
7. *Committed Stakeholders and Advocates:* Presence of individual and collective support from practitioners, researchers, administrators, policymakers, clients, influential leaders, and others to sustain activities and ensure continued support of key stakeholders.

The theory underlying the review posits that the extent to which each of these is present will determine the institutionalization of the field. An exploration of each factor yields the answer to the question: Is service-learning a field?

Distinct Identity

Service-learning has its roots in experiential education, internships, volunteerism, and project-based learning (Stanton, Giles, & Cruz, 1999). What is different about service-learning is the unique way in which service and learning have been combined (Furco, 1996; Sigmon, 1994) and the ways in which service-learning are currently being discussed as a pedagogy in K–12 schools and higher education institutions. A review of the research shows that the most prevalent definition of service-learning that is cited is that developed by the Alliance for Service-Learning in Education Reform in 1995. This definition specifies:

> service-learning is a method under which students learn and develop through active participation in thoughtfully organized service experiences that meet actual community needs and are coordinated in collaboration with the school and community; that is integrated into students' academic curriculum and provides structured time for a student to think, talk, or write about what they did and saw during the actual service activity; that provides students with opportunities to use newly acquired skills and knowledge in real-life situations in their own communities; and that enhances what is taught in school by extending student learning beyond the classroom into the community, thereby helping to foster the development of a sense of caring for others. (p. 1)

This definition has variations in the literature, but most extant definitions, at a minimum, include the connection between community service and learning and the process of planning, action, reflection, and celebration.

Within the community of service-learning practitioners and researchers, there appears to be definitional agreement. Outside of the field, however, there is widespread misunderstanding, and particularly confusion around the differences between community service and service-learning. Practitioners of place-based learning also often implement service-learning without knowing they are doing so. This may be a marketing problem rather than a definitional one, but is a problem nonetheless.

Standard Practice

Early leaders in the nascent field of service-learning were instrumental in the formulation, dissemination, and promotion of K–12 standard practice in service-learning through the development of quality indicators and Essential Elements (NSLC, 1998); model programs; development of curricula; creation of job aids; and other tools for planning and reflection. Also included was development of a system of training and technical assistance to help individuals, schools, and programs to initiate, develop, and refine service-learning practice.

Many leaders received funding from the W. K. Kellogg Foundation (WKKF) and that funding, along with facilitation by key personnel at WKKF, led to the creation of the Alliance for Service-Learning and Education Reform (ASLER), a group that defined an initial set of quality indicators, which are called the ASLER standards by many service-learning practitioners. Experimentation with the ASLER standards among the grantees and others eventually led to the development of the Essential Elements of service-learning, a group of standards widely used to define quality practice in the field, developed by leaders in the field during the 1990s and funded with WKKF assistance. In K–12 education, *model programs* to encourage standard practice were also developed by many organizations, including the National Youth Leadership Council (Generator Schools) and the National Indian Youth Leadership Program (Turtle Island Project). *Service-learning curricula* were developed by WKKF grantees, including curricula on ethics by The Giraffe Project, on environmental service-learning projects by the YMCA of Greater Seattle, and on more general service-learning projects by Quest International. Most of the projects, through intentional evaluation efforts, discovered the contextual, cultural, and developmental conditions necessary to maximize success.

Efforts at the higher education level, though less well defined, also became somewhat standardized, using an approach that looked more like individual or group apprenticeship and internships. Practice also became more standardized through information dissemination at national conferences and through publications in journals such as *The Michigan Journal of Service-Learning*. Curricula in many content areas were shared, though the individualization and independence of faculty members expected at institutions of higher education was respected. The culture of higher education served as a strong facilitator for the practice of service-learning since young people attending these institutions were already being inspired to explore their identities and career paths, and were also strongly encouraged to learn independently and through experiences that complemented what they learned in their courses.

Knowledge Base

Accumulating a knowledge base for the field has been a natural outgrowth for higher education of the context in which the practice occurs.

Since faculty are encouraged to conduct research and to publish, many have turned to their own students as respondents for their service-learning studies. Many faculty have addressed impacts of service-learning on students in their courses, both in this volume and in many other studies. Others have conducted research in nearby schools and communities. The result for higher education has been a growing body of evaluation and research studies that have converged on a number of themes (Eyler, Giles, Stenson, & Gray, 2001). In the K–12 arena, there have been a few compilations of research (e.g., Billig, 2000; Conrad & Hedin, 1990), also identifying converging themes. Impacts on students have been identified for both higher education and K–12 service-learning participants in the areas of personal/social development, academic achievement, civic responsibility and citizenship, and career exploration. There is less research on the impacts on participating community members, participating faculty, and institutions in which the service-learning occurs, though there are some notable evaluations (see Billig, 2002; Eyler, Giles, Stenson, & Gray, 2001, for example, for a review).

Leadership and Membership

There are many organizations that offer professional development to teach service-learning methodologies for both faculty in higher education institutions and teachers in K–12 schools. While there are no specific credentials needed to implement service-learning as a teaching and learning approach, there is a growing awareness of being either a subscriber or one who does not utilize the method. In addition, membership groups are just starting to blossom. The National Service-Learning Partnership (http://www.service-learningpartnership.org/), for example, is a no-cost membership organization with thousands of members who are associated in some way with K–12 service-learning. Campus Compact (http://www.compact.org/) is an organization of member campuses whose presidents support service-learning. The American Association of Colleges for Teacher Education (AACTE) has a service-learning partnership, and many organizations, such as the American Educational Research Association (AERA), have special interest groups on service-learning. A new National Center for Teacher Education has been created at Clemson University, and many local universities have offices or centers dedicated to service-learning. The field also has several clearly recognized leaders and champions. However, while leadership and membership is growing, the field is still not organized well and has a hard time mobilizing itself in time of need.

Information Exchange

Individuals can access information on service-learning from the National Service-Learning Clearinghouse Website (http://www.service-learning.org) and from a myriad of listservs. Learn and Serve grantees of the Corporation of National and Community Service have annual meetings where information is shared, and other networks such as SEANet, a group for state Learn and Serve coordinators, and the Compact for Learning and Citizenship, developed by the Education Commission of the States, have been formed as strong, ongoing collaboratives over the past several years. The technical assistance exchange operated by National Youth Leadership Council (http://www.nylc.org/) is a robust network of experts who provide consultation and expertise to local sites. These organizations and networks are all active, and information about service-learning is relatively easy to find, thanks especially to the Internet. Newsletters, websites, and other information exchange vehicles abound.

Resources

Service-learning is not an expensive undertaking (Melchior, 2000), but resources are still needed to conduct service-learning, particularly at the K–12 level where transportation is more of an issue. Many service-learning projects are funded through local budgets, such as a school, district budget, or a college departmental budget. Many others receive funding through grants made by the Corporation for National and Community Service. A few foundations, notably the W.K. Kellogg Foundation, Surdna Foundation, the Pew Charitable Trusts, the Ewing Marion Kauffman Foundation, and the Carnegie Foundation of New York, have funded projects related to service-learning or service-learning research. However, funding is not plentiful and none of the external sources make long-term commitments to large-scale initiatives with the exception of WKKF.

Committed Stakeholders and Advocates

Many researchers and practitioners alike have noted the passion that tends to be associated with service-learning (see, for example, Billig, 2002). Stated simply, instructors who try service-learning usually like it. However, the educational context in which stakeholders operate is starting to erode some of the commitment, and the political loading of the term is beginning to undermine its support. These issues will be articulated in deatil in the next section.

This brief analysis of service-learning in the context of field building shows that service-learning does indeed appear to satisfy most, if not all, of the criteria for being a "field." However, the status of service-learning within many of the categories is precarious in some ways, and there is no specific widely held vision for the future nor agreement around a strategic plan driving the field to institutionalization and sustainability.

THEORETICAL FOUNDATIONS OF SERVICE-LEARNING

As demonstrated in this book, service-learning is beginning to establish a strong theoretical base. The nature of service-learning appears to dictate that no single specific theory is appropriate. Rather, service-learning can be rooted in theories related to experiential learning, contextual learning, place-based learning, problem-based learning, constructivism, environmental and ecological education, democratic education, cognitive psychology, and numerous other theories connected to learning. Service-learning draws from multiple theories because it is centered on individuals, relationships between individuals, and relationships between individuals and structures. It is inherently multidisciplinary, attached to both academic and civic institutions, and linked to personal development in one form or another.

Conundrums Associated With Versatility

The versatility of service-learning is both a strength and a challenge. The versatility allows young people and instructors to customize learning opportunities, seize teachable moments, and provide social emotional and academic learning experiences that vary from one individual to another. The versatility, though, also often leads to implementation that does not maximize learning since the learning theory behind service-learning is often not well articulated or understood by service-learning practitioners. The result of this lack of articulation is an experience that sometimes lacks depth and/or academic quality. Students may enjoy the experience, but they may know nothing more about the academic subject matter than before they engaged in service.

This possibility—learning no academic content but enjoying the experience—itself is a conundrum, because the experience still yields value. Research (e.g. Billig, 2002; Eyler, Giles, Stenson, & Gray, 2001) repeatedly indicates that the service-learning experience in and of itself typically leads to at least some sort of personal and social development outcomes, such as a sense of efficacy or valuing diversity, and some connection to civic life, that would not have occurred in the absence of service-learning. Thus for some students, learning about themselves, others, and the community *is* the learning in service-learning. But is this phenomenon service-learning?

Must service-learning, by definition, include acquisition of *academic* knowledge and skills?

There is disagreement among scholars about the answer to these questions. In higher education, the answer appears to be "maybe," but in K–12 education, the answer is clearly "no."

Context Counts

In higher education, there is more latitude than in K–12 education for the student to explore his/her place in society, to understand the way society, a profession, an agency, a community, or even a task works. Instructional objectives for many courses can be achieved through individual reflection on experience or effort to tie the experience to specific learning objectives through assigned readings or classroom discourse. There is often encouragement for inductive and deductive learning and the ability to construct multiple meanings from experience. Scaffolding the learning is also encouraged through discussion of previous experiences and knowledge that the service-learning participant has. The individual student in higher education has much more responsibility and accountability for his/her own learning than students in K–12 settings where accountability is more likely to rest on teachers.

This accountability phenomenon is one factor that begins to explain the differences in the state of service-learning in higher education and K–12 schools. Accountability in K–12 also plays out in the greater prescriptiveness of classroom content, typically in the form of standards; that is, specific definitions of what students should know and be able to do (content standards) and at what level (performance standards). Teachers in K–12 settings can apply favorite pedagogies to their efforts to teach to the standards, though even the notion of choice of instructional techniques is starting to narrow. An example of this is the way teachers currently facilitate acquisition of literacy skills, currently narrowing into conformity with the U.S. Department of Education's interpretation of the National Reading Council's recommendations focused on phonemic awareness, phonics, oral fluency, vocabulary development, and comprehension. While this narrowing phenomenon has not yet widely occurred in other content areas and grade levels, there are signs that it could occur in secondary school mathematics around algebraic thinking. The standards movement seeks to provide greater clarity of instructional targets and equity in results in its high expectations and performance targets for all children. However, at least at the present time, standards still allow for differentiated instruction and local control of many school and district policies and practices.

The movement in K–12 toward adoption of "best practice" based on "scientifically based research" also plays a dual role in the K–12 arena that has important implications for the practice of service-learning. The current stress on effective practice grows from the focus on performance and results. According to the prevailing logic, teachers should adopt those instructional strategies that have a proven track record of success.

The good news is that this thinking elevates the need for and status of high quality research. The bad news is that only a limited amount of new research is being conducted, so that those implementing this policy are relying on research that has already been completed. Relatively new pedagogies like service-learning have a record of research that is somewhat sparse, reliant on evaluations rather than applied research, and heavily dependent on qualitative methods that explore the richness of the pedagogy and its impacts without specifically applying the scientific methods that are currently valued. There is a preponderance of evidence of the effectiveness of service-learning at both the K–12 and higher education levels, but the body of research does not meet the expectations for a "scientific research" base as defined by the U.S. Department of Education.

Some studies that fit the definition of scientifically-based, that is, that use experimental or quasi-experimental designs, are already in place. For example, a study of the academic impacts of service-learning on K–12 students in Michigan (Klute & Billig, 2003) used a quasi-experimental design with matched classrooms of students in "treatment" and "comparison" conditions, using hierarchical linear modeling analysis techniques to demonstrate statistically significant differences in outcomes in specific content areas as measured by the state assessment. Service-learning students outperformed their peers at 5th grade and middle/secondary school in several content areas. This study also examined affective, behavioral, and cognitive engagement, and in some areas and grade levels, produced statistically significant differences in favor of service-learning. The national study of Learn and Serve grantees (Melchior, 1999) used a pre-/post-design with comparison groups and also yielded statistically significant differences in some subject matters. Eyler and Giles (1999) used a similar quasi-experimental design in a national study of college students that showed significant results in favor of service-learning, although the academic measures were not subject matter specific. The reviews of the literature cited previously provide about a dozen more examples of studies that may qualify as "scientific research." However, the total number that would be acceptable by federal definitions is very limited.

THE STATE OF SERVICE-LEARNING RESEARCH

As discussed previously, there are many studies showing the impact of service-learning. Many are case studies and many more are evaluations of programs. There are some, but too few, that use a quasi-experimental design and almost none that employ a "pure" experimental design with random assignments. The bulk of the studies still focus on personal and social outcomes for young people, though there are increasing numbers that are beginning to focus on other impacts, primarily academic and civic. There are still too few studies that build upon each other or that use common instruments. There are few studies that clearly specify the actual experiences defined as service-learning. Too few studies ground their hypotheses in theory or even test particular hypotheses.

While the preponderance of evidence would likely place service-learning in the *promising* rather than *proven* practice category in terms of its ability to impact learning of particular academic content, service-learning still appears to be viewed favorably, particularly as a strategy for helping achieve the civic mission of education. The increased interest in the promotion of civic engagement and citizenship appears to be associated with the current political climate in which fewer young people are voting, working on political campaigns, or are even interested in politics (Carnegie Corporation & CIRCLE, 2003). Policymakers at the national and state levels have become concerned about the future of democracy given the current apparent political malaise of youth.

The trend of increased volunteerism (Putnam, 2000) stands at striking contrast to the lack of traditional political engagement. Several efforts have been initiated to understand this situation and to stimulate greater youth engagement in civic life. In this context, service-learning has also emerged as a promising practice. Once again, though, too little research is available to elevate the status of service-learning from *promising* to *best* practice. While there appears to be quite a bit of new research underway to examine the role of service-learning in engaging students in civic life, it will take some time before the research is completed, published, and constitutes a body of high quality evidence with reliable results.

The state of service-learning research, then, appears to best be described as "promising." There remains a great need to move beyond surveys in which neither the service-learning intervention nor the outcomes are clearly specified. There is a need for a series of carefully designed coordinated studies for both K–12 and higher education, that use multiple methods to explore the impacts of service-learning on its participants. There is still a woeful lack of research on the impact of service-learning on communities. The K–12 research agenda published in this book series in 2002 (Billig & Furco, 2002) has barely been addressed, and the higher education research agenda published by Eyler and Giles (2000) has not fared much better.

SIGNS OF HOPE

The signs for the future are good; however, relative to a few years ago, there is more interest in research, more funding available, more researchers who are interested in conducting studies of service-learning, and more venues for publication. There are yet lessons to be learned to scale up and institutionalize service-learning, drawing on the analysis of field-building in this chapter, but signs are that this type of information is being widely shared through the annual International K–H Service-Learning Research Conference and elsewhere. In short, visibility and credibility are on the rise.

Researchers and practitioners must focus on improving practice and continue to explore the parameters of service-learning and those qualities that are most likely to lead to robust outcomes. Research should explore both impacts of participation and the context in which those impacts are maximized. More research is needed on a range of constructs associated with citizenship, civic responsibility, and political engagement. Best practice in each of the outcome areas should be established through the conduct of rich qualitative studies and robust quantitative studies.

Researchers should build upon one another's work. The research agendas that have been published for K–12 and higher education provide information on what has been done and what is needed. The chapters in this and other books in the *Advances in Service-Learning Research* series can stand as grist for replication, theory and hypothesis testing, and further exploration. Theories that help explain the impacts of service-learning should be advanced and tested. Moderating variables should be identified and explored.

Funders should take heed. There are a growing number of researchers who wish to perform this research, a growing number of practitioners who intend to use research to inform practice, and a growing number of policy-makers who demand results before they will allow practices in educational institutions to continue. The will is there but resources are needed.

Service-learning has indeed become a field, but its future relies on building the knowledge base as much as on standard practice, leadership, and membership, and the other factors associated with field building. There is much promise, both in the field and the individuals who are endeavoring as researchers and practitioners within it. However, the field will still need research-based "proof" to thrive and be sustained.

REFERENCES

Alliance for Service-Learning in Educational Reform. (1995). *Standards for school-based and community-based service-learning programs.* Alexandria, VA: The Close Up Foundation.

Billig, S. H. (2000, May). Research on K–12 school-based service-learning: The evidence builds. *Phi Delta Kappan, 81*(9), 184–189.

Billig, S. H. (2002, Summer). Support for K–12 service-learning practice: A brief review of the research. *Educational Horizons, 80*(4), 184–189.

Billig, S. H., & Furco, A. (2002). Research agenda for K-12 service-learning: A proposal to the field. In A. Furco & S. H. Billig (Eds.), *Advances in service-learning research: Vol.1. Service-learning: The essence of the pedagogy* (pp. 271-279). Greenwich, CT: Information Age Publishing.

Carnegie Corporation & CIRCLE. (2003). *The civic mission of schools.* New York: Carnegie Corporation of New York.

Conrad, D., & Hedin, D. (1991, June). School-based community service: What we know from research and theory, *Phi Delta Kappan*, 743–749.

Eyler, J., & Giles, D. (1999). *Where's the learning in service-learning.* San Francisco: Jossey-Bass.

Eyler, J. S., Giles, D. E., Jr., Stenson, C. M., & Gray, C. J. (2001). *At a glance: What we know about the effects of service-learning on college students, faculty, institutions, and communities, 1993–2000* (3rd ed.). Washington, DC: Corporation for National Service, Learn and Serve America; Scotts Valley, CA: National Service-Learning Clearinghouse.

Fine, M. (1999). *Field-building components.* New York: Academy for Educational Development.

Fine, M. (2001). *What does field-building mean?* New York: Academy for Educational Development.

Furco, A. (1996). Service-learning: A balanced approach to experiential education. In B. Taylor (Ed.), *Expanding boundaries: Service and learning* (pp. 2-6). Washington, DC: Corporation for National Service.

Giles, D. E., Jr., & Eyler, J. (1998). A service-learning research agenda for the next five years. In R. Rhoads & J. Howard (Eds), *Academic service-learning: A pedagogy of action and reflection: New Directions for Teaching and Learning, #73.* San Francisco: Jossey-Bass.

Klute, M. M., & Billig, S. H. (2003). *The impact of service-learning on MEAP: A large-scale study of Michigan Learn and Serve grantees.* Denver, CO: RMC Research Corporation.

Levine, P., & Lopez, M. H. (2002, September). *Youth voter turnout has declined, by any measure.* Report from The Center for Information & Research on Civic Learning & Engagement (CIRCLE), College Park, MD.

Melchior, A. (1999). *Summary report: National evaluation of learn and serve America.* Waltham, MA: Center for Human Resources, Brandeis University.

Melchior, A. (2000, August). Costs and benefits of service-learning. *The School Administrator* (Web edition). Retrieved online July 2, 2003, from http://www.aasa.org/publications/sa/2000_08/contents.htm

National Center for Education Statistics. (1999). *Service-learning and community service in K–12 public schools.* Report Number NCES-1999-043, Washington, DC: Author.

National Service-Learning Cooperative. (1998). *Essential elements of service-learning.* Minneapolis, MN: National Youth Leadership Council.

Putnam, R. D. (2000). *Bowling alone: The collapse and revival of American community.* New York: Simon & Schuster.

Sigmon, R. (1994). Serving to learn, learning to serve in promoting school success. *Linking Service With Learning.* Council of Independent Colleges monograph. Retrieved online July 2, 2003, from http://www.cic.org/publications/books_reports/pubs_online.asp#lin king

Stanton, T. K., Giles, D. E., Jr., & Cruz, N. I. (1999). *Service-learning: A movement's pioneers reflect on its origins, practice, and future.* San Francisco: Jossey-Bass.

ABOUT THE AUTHORS

Professor John Annette is the Director of the University Institute for Community Development and Learning (ICDL) at Middlesex University, London, United Kingdom, and is also the university coordinator of the Community Service-Learning Programme. Working with international colleagues, he has developed a new 'International Service-Learning Programme,' which provides opportunities for international students along with UK students to study abroad and perform service-learning. He has published on citizenship and service-learning in schools, higher education, and lifelong learning and he is currently working on a study of citizenship and community leadership in the UK. He is the chair of the CSV/Council for Citizenship and Learning in the Community (CSV/CCLC), the main UK network for service-learning programs and has worked with the British Council to advise international universities on establishing service-learning programs. He is also an advisor to the UK Department for Education and Skills on citizenship education and service-learning both in schools and in higher education.

Shelley H. Billig, Ph.D., is Vice President of RMC Research Corporation in Denver, Colorado. She directs the Research Network for the W. K. Kellogg *Learning In Deed* initiative that seeks to give every K–12 student an opportu-

Deconstructing Service-Learning: Research Exploring Context, Participation, and Impacts
A Volume in: Advances in Service-Learning Research, pages 265–269.
Copyright © 2003 by Information Age Publishing, Inc.
ISBN: 1-59311-071-5 (hardcover), 1-59311-070-7 (pbk.)

nity to engage in school-based service-learning. She is series editor of the volumes entitled *Advances in Service-Learning* and co-edited *Service-Learning: The Essence of the Pedagogy, Service-Learning Through a Multidisciplinary Lens* with Andrew Furco, and *Studying Service-Learning* with Alan Waterman. She directs multiple service-learning research and educational reform projects at the national, state, and local levels and directs several K–12 educational reform projects.

Robert G. Bringle is Chancellor's Professor of Psychology and Philanthropic Studies and Director of the Center for Service and Learning at Indiana University-Purdue University Indianapolis (IUPUI). His programmatic and research interests include developing ways to implement and institutionalize service-learning and civic engagement. His research interests for service-learning and community service include student and faculty attitudes, educational outcomes, and institutionalizing service-learning. At IUPUI, his work as Director of the Center for Service and Learning has resulted in an expansion of the number of service-learning courses, a curriculum for faculty development, a Community Service Scholars program, and an America Reads tutoring program. Dr. Bringle received his Ph.D. from the University of Massachusetts.

Jane Callahan, Ph.D., is an Associate Professor in the Education Department at Providence College. In 1994, she was a member of the faculty research team that developed the Feinstein Institute for Public Service and the first major in Public and Community Service in the country. She currently divides her professional responsibilities between the Education Department and the Public and Community Service Program.. Her research is in the areas of service-learning and teacher education and the institutionalization process necessary for the integration of service-learning into schools and teacher education programs. She has authored a number of articles and chapters on service-learning and presented at numerous conferences on service-learning pedagogy and the effects of service-learning on preservice and inservice teachers. She is a founding member of the International Center for Service-Learning in Teacher Education at Clemson University.

Dr. Melinda M. Clarke is Director of the Ed.D. degree in Higher Education Program and Assistant Professor of Education at Union University, Jackson, Tennessee. Dr. Clarke's research interests include service-learning in higher education and her research has focused more specifically on the community impact of service initiatives. She received her B.A. degree from Lambuth University and her M.Ed. and Ed.D. degrees from Peabody College of Vanderbilt University.

Janet Eyler is a Professor of the Practice of Education at Vanderbilt University, where she is Director of Undergraduate Education and directs three masters degree programs in the department of Leadership Policy and Organizations. She has taught service-learning courses at both the undergraduate and graduate level and facilitates a faculty seminar for colleagues implementing service-learning in their courses. She chaired the Second Annual International Conference on Service-Learning Research in October 2002 and has been active in national groups of service-learning practitioners and researchers. She is the co-recipient, with Dwight Giles, of Campus Compact's 2003 Thomas Ehrlich Service-Learning Award. Her work has focused on various forms of experiential learning including a number of publications on internships and service-learning.

Dr. Peggy Fitch is an Associate Professor of Psychology at Central College in Pella, Iowa, whose research interests include service-learning, student intellectual development, and cultural awareness. She uses service-learning in her developmental psychology courses and currently serves as the Chair of Central's Diversity Task Force.

Dwight E. Giles, Jr., is a Professor of Higher Education Administration and Senior Associate at the New England Resource Center for Higher Education (NERCHE) in the Graduate College of Education, University of Massachusetts, Boston. He has co-authored numerous books and articles on service-learning research and is coauthoring a faculty handbook called "Designing Effective Service-Learning." He is co-chair of the Service-Learning Advisory Committee at U Mass, Boston, and a member of the National Peer Review Board for the Scholarship of Engagement. Dr. Giles has been a faculty member and director of several experiential education programs at Cornell and Vanderbilt Universities and was active on both campuses in establishing campuswide public service and service-learning. He holds a Ph.D. in Community Development from Penn State University. He is the co-recipient, with Janet Eyler, of Campus Compt's 2003 Thomas Ehrlich Service-Learning Award.

Deborah Hecht, Ph.D., is an educational psychologist and researcher who specializes in service-learning, character education, and applied learning. She has been involved in research and evaluation of service-learning for over 10 years. Dr. Hecht is a Project Director at the Center for Advanced Study in Education, at the Graduate Center of the City University of New York. She is a member of the National Service-Learning Partnership Research and Practice Committee and works closely with schools in New York and New Jersey as they implement and evaluate their service-learning and character education initiatives. She has led several research studies of service-learning and has consulted on numerous projects.

Katherine M. Kapustka, Ed.D, is an Assistant Professor of Elementary Education at the Naperville, Illinois, campus of DePaul University. She received her Ph.D. from Teachers College, Columbia University, and holds a B.A. in humanities and history and a M.A. in teaching from Trinity University in San Antonio, Texas. Her research interests include the experiences of K–12 service-learning teachers and the use of dilemma theory to understand service-learning implementation.

Nancy Kraft, Ph.D., has been involved in developing, facilitating, writing about, and researching service-learning for eight years. She co-directed a national service-learning project and co-authored a book linking service-learning to federal programs. While teaching at the University of Kansas, she incorporated service-learning as authentic pedagogy into curriculum and methods classes. Dr. Kraft is currently the Director of the Kansas Parent Information Resource Center and has included service-learning as one strategy to enable teacher education candidates to learn to work more effectively with diverse families.

Jenell Williams Paris is Associate Professor of Anthropology at Bethel College in St. Paul, Minnesota. She has used service-learning in teaching qualitative research methods, focusing on antiracism and community history in a St. Paul neighborhood.

Bruce Pontbriand received his doctorate from Boston College in Educational Administration and has been a service-learning practitioner in both public and private settings for over 17 years. His research interests focus on the sustainability and institutionalization of educational innovation. He currently serves as the Vice Principal for Mission and Identity of Boston College High School.

Dr. Susan Root is a Research Associate at RMC Research Corporation. For the past six years, Dr. Root was one of seven regional directors of the AACTE/National Service-Learning in Teacher Education Partnership, a training and technical assistance project to aid teacher education faculty to integrate service-learning in their courses. Dr. Root is the author of several publications on service-learning in teacher education, including *Service-Learning in Teacher Education: A Handbook* and *Teacher Research in Service-Learning,* a chapter in *Studying Service-Learning: Innovations in Education Research Methodology.* Dr. Root recently received Michigan Campus Compact's Lifetime Achievement Award in service-learning.

Marjorie A. Schaffer is a Professor in Nursing at Bethel College in St. Paul, Minnesota. Her Ph.D. is in Family Social Science, and she has an M.S. in Community Health Nursing. Her areas of interest are service-learning in nursing education, ethics of teaching, and ethical professional practice.

She has facilitated service-learning projects in health care services with undergraduate and graduate students.

Pamela Steinke, Ph.D., is a Professor of Psychology at Lincoln Land Community College in Springfield, Illinois. At the time of this research project she was an Associate Professor of Psychology at Central College in Pella, Iowa, where she previously coordinated the program responsible for the experiential component of Central's core curriculum. Her research focuses on cognitive outcomes of service-learning and she uses service-learning in all of her classes.

Christine Stenson received her B.A. in Psychology from Northwestern University. She earned her M.A. in Anthropology from the University of Illinois at Chicago and is currently a candidate for a Ph.D. in Education and Human Development at Peabody College of Vanderbilt University. Her dissertation research centers on civic education across the curriculum at a predominantly white middle-class suburban high school. She lives and works in Nashville, Tennessee.

Kristin Vogel is a senior student in sociocultural studies, who has participated in course-related service-learning activities. For two years, she assisted the Bethel College coordinator of a community-campus partnership program with the coordination of service-learning projects.

Jim Wheeler, Ph.D., is the Executive Director of the Northeast Kansas Education Service Center. In this capacity he oversees a regional charter high school, for which he wrote the charter, that incorporates service-learning as the core and mission of the school. At the charter high school, Dr. Wheeler actively supports faculty development in service-learning and promotes authentic pedagogy grounded in service-learning philosophy

SUBJECT INDEX

3-"I" model, 125-145
  change evaluation, 128-132
  dimensions of, 128
  evaluation response of, 127-128
  good practices in, 133
  pilot test of, 132
3-"I" model research,
    community involvement, 144
  conclusions, 144
  data analysis of, 137-138
  data collection in, 137
  framework, 132
  impact, 135, 141-143
  indicators, 134-135
  initiative, 134-135, 139-141
  initiative effectiveness, 139
  initiator, 134, 139
  initiator insights, 139-140
  mean values, 143
  measurements, 134-135
  sample, 136
  service activities, 136

  site, 136
  statistical data from, 138
  survey results, 139-143
  unit of analysis in, 136
  variables, 134-135
  utilization focused evaluation of,
    130-132

AACTE, (*see* American Association of
    Colleges for Teacher Education)
AERA, (*see* American Education
    Research Association)
Alliance for Service-Learning and
    Education Reform (ASLER), 255,
    256
American Association of Colleges for
    Teacher Education (AACTE), 257
American Education Research
    Association (AERA), 257
Analysis matrix, 138
ANOVA analysis, 53
Approximation model, 43-44

Deconstructing Service-Learning: Research Exploring Context, Participation, and Impacts
A Volume in: Advances in Service-Learning Research, pages 271–276.
Copyright © 2003 by Information Age Publishing, Inc.
All rights of reproduction in any form reserved.
ISBN: 1-59311-071-5 (hardcover), 1-59311-070-7 (pbk.)

Printed in the United States
1379300004B/52-357